french with ease

Day by day method

french with ease

by

Anthony BULGER

with the editorial assistance of

Jean-Loup CHEREL

Illustrations by J.L. BELIN

(VITAMINE)

ASSIMIL S.A.

B.P. 25, 13, rue Gay-Lussac

94430 CHENNEVIERES S/MARNE

FRANCE

"ASSIMIL" METHOD BOOKS

Bound books, lavishly illustrated, containing lessons recorded on cassettes

* * * * *

French with ease
German with ease
Spanish with ease
Italian with ease
Dutch with ease
Arabic with ease
Using French

* * * * *

 N° ISBN : 2-7005-0095-4

INTRODUCTION

This method is not complete– it requires one vital element : your intuitive gift of assimilation. You will learn French in much the same way as you learned English : by listening, repeating and drawing conclusions. And finally by speaking for yourself.

There is no miracle nor mystery. The first part of the course requires little effort : it is passive. You listen, repeat and understand. The 'second wave' will draw upon the knowledge you have acquired to form new sentences and to express your ideas.
We have cheated a little bit by choosing a progression which introduces the particularities of the language little by little, instead of all mixed together as would be the case if you 'picked up' French with native speakers (and was the case when you learned English). But even so, we aim not to impair your natural gift of assimilation by explaining everything at once and in a wealth of detail that can only lead to confusion and inefficiency.

You will often meet and use a construction or a tense a couple of times in a natural context before reading the 'explanation'. In this way, you order your knowledge after acquiring it rather than trying to learn through sets of rules.

If you approach this course in a relaxed fashion, if you accept rather than analyse (the problem of most adult learners), if you appreciate the pleasure of comprehension, you will follow the 'line of least resistance' and assimilate the language in a natural way and in a relatively short space of time.

What kind of French ?

May the purists forgive us ! We have deliberately ignored in this volume the more literary aspects of the language. The conversations right from the beginning are written 'with the ear' and are as natural as any language-method can make them. They use everyday speech, colloquialisms and vocabulary which the visitor to France will hear all the time. **They aim, at the end of about four months part-time study, to make you able to understand normal, non-technical conversations and to express yourself in usual situations, both formal and informal.**

We do not attempt to cover all the grammar, but we concentrate on those elements which allow us to achieve our aim as efficiently as possible. This is for two very good reasons. Firstly, what deters Anglo-Saxons from learning a Romance language is often the seeming over-emphasis on grammatical exactitude to the detriment of expression (an emphasis not shared, moreover, by the type of French person you will encounter in this volume. If the 'Académie Française' exists it is to lay down the law for French people rather than for foreigners.) We believe, as the French writer Rivarol said, that 'grammar is the art of lifting the difficulties out of a language ; the lever must not become heavier than the burden.'

The second reason, as we have explained, is one of expediency. This book will provide you with the tools to continue in your exploration of the language, both in France and by using our second volume.

How ?

Our first and foremost rule is : do a little every day. It is only through constant contact that one's natural powers of learning are exploited to the full. Even if you only devote ten minutes to the course, do so **every day,** and when you are relaxed.

The 'first wave' (Lesson 1-50) demands no more than listening, comparing the translation and notes and repeating **aloud.** From Lesson 50 onwards - the 'second wave' - for each new lesson, you will go back to another one, starting from Lesson 1, and translate from English into French.

At both stages, the exercises will help to consolidate your knowledge.

The more complex points of grammar are examined in every seventh lesson ('Révision et Notes'). In the texts such points are indicated by [N-] and a number. Each time you come to one, read the relevant Note but **no more**. In this way, when you reach the 'Révision et Notes' lesson, it will be a real revision.

Do not try to do too much at once. We have made things as simple as possible but we believe, like Einstein (and what better reference !) that 'things should be as simple as possible, but no simpler.'

Pronunciation

Obviously, the only way to acquire a correct pronunciation is to listen to the recordings. However, to make things easier, we have reproduced French pronunciation using, not a phonetic alphabet nor a contrived one, but the nearest equivalent English phoneme. These are unfortunately imperfect, so remember the following points :

1. Vowel-sounds in French are constant (except in regional accents) and are half-way between an English 'short vowel' and a 'long one'. For example [i] in French is neither the [i] of ship nor the long sound of 'sheep' but somewhere in between.

2. Nasal vowels. These do not exist in English (some Americans produce them naturally - or you can always hold your nose !) These occur at the end of a syllable and are **-en -in -on -an and -un.** We have reproduced them by placing an 'h' before the consonant to soften it, but this is not the real pronunciation. If you let your breath out through your nose rather than through your lips you will find that, in fact, the consonant is not pronounced.

3. Word-endings. Since French is more of a written language than a spoken one, a lot of the grammatical nuances can only be seen in print. Except for some exceptions (usually foreign words) the final 's' is never pronounced ; the endings of the pronoun and the verb are pronounced the same in the third persons singular and plural in all verbs (the majority) ending in **-er**. However, these details will lose their ominousness after two weeks' practice.

4. Stress. This is perhaps the biggest problem for an English-speaking learner. Our tendency is to stress one syllable of a word, to the detriment of all the others in the word (for example : 'comfortable' or 'fireman-firemen' where, in this pair, it is impossible to hear whether one is singular or plural.)
In French, syllables are pronounced fully and in a even tone (but pay special attention to verb-endings) If there is a tendency to stress, it is less pronounced than English and falls regularly on the last syllable of a word.

Let these indications suffice for the time being. Remember that no-one speaks a language without making mistakes, especially a new learner.

Vous êtes prêt ? Allez ! En avant !
(*You are ready ? Let's go ! Forward !*)

PREMIERE (1ère) LEÇON

A Paris

1 — Pardon, monsieur **(1)**. Où est le métro **(2)** St. Michel ?
2 — Le métro St Michel ? Attendez une minute. . .
3 — Nous sommes au Boulevard St. Michel. La fontaine est là-bas.
4 — Oui, d'accord. Mais où est le métro s'il vous plaît **(3)** ?
5 — Mais bien sûr ! Voilà la Seine, et voici le pont **(4)**.
6 — C'est joli ; mais s'il vous plaît. . .
7 — Ce n'est pas‿à gauche, alors c'est‿à droite **(5)**.

PRONONCIATION

A paree
1 pardohn mesyeu. Oo ay le metro sah meeshel ?
2 . . . attenday oon minyoot.
3 Noo somm oh boolevar sah meeshel. . la fonten ay la-ba.
4 Wee, daccor. May oo ay le metro seel voo play ?
5 May biehn syoor. Vwala la senn ay vwassi le pohn
6 Say zholi. . .
7 Se nay paza gohsh alor seta drwat.

FIRST LESSON

In Paris

1 – Excuse me (pardon) sir. Where is the metro [station] St. Michel ?
2 – The metro [station] St. Michel ? Wait a minute. . .
3 – We are at [the] boulevard St. Michel. The fountain is over there.
4 – Yes, o.k. But where is the metro [station] please ?
5 – But of course ! There [is] the Seine and here [is] the bridge.
6 – It's pretty ; but please. . .
7 – It's not on (to) [the] left, so it's on (to) [the] right.

NOTES

(1) French is quite a formal language in many ways, and the use of *monsieur* and *madame* when addressing strangers of almost any age is the general rule.
– Notice that in this lesson there are several words which are similar in spelling and meaning to English words. **Pay close attention to their pronunciation ! -**

(2) *Le métro* (short for *métropolitain)* is the Parisian underground railway system. It is similar to the London Underground and the New York Subway. The word is also used to mean "the metro **station**".– *Le métro République :* The République station.

(3) *S'il vous plaît* (literally "if it pleases you") is the usual way of saying "please". Don't look for reasons, just memorise it ! (On formal invitations in both English and French, we use the abbreviation "RSVP" which stands for *Répondez s'il vous plaît* : Please reply).

(4) *Voici* is equivalent to Here is/are and *Voilà* to There is/are. In line 8 we see an idiomatic use of *Voilà* : There we are... I've found it !

(5) Prepositions are less numerous in French and often serve several functions. "A" in the title translates as "in". In sentence seven, it translates as "on". Just memorise each individual use. It will soon become a reflex.

* * *

Note : *c'est* : it is, *ce n'est pas :* it is not.

8 — Voilà. Le métro est‿à droite !
9 — Mais vous‿êtes sûr ?
10 — Non. Je suis touriste aussi !

PRONONCIATION

8 . . . le metro eta drwat.
9 May voozet syoor ?
10 Noh. Zhe swee tooreest ohsee

EXERCICES

1. Je suis à Paris ; nous sommes à Paris. – **2.** Vous êtes sûr ? – **3.** Attendez une minute, s'il vous plaît. – **4.** Voilà la fontaine et voici le métro. – **5.** Mais bien sûr !

Fill in the blanks with the correct word(s). Each dash represents a letter.

1 Vous .... à Paris.

2 Nous ...... au Boulevard St. Michel.

3 Oui, .'...... mais où est le métro, s'il vous ..... ?

4 La fontaine est . gauche.

5 .. est le métro, s'il vous ..... ?

8 — There we are. The metro [station] is (on) [to the] right !
9 — But you are sure ?
10 — No. I'm a tourist, too !

EXERCISES

1. I am in Paris ; we are in Paris. — **2.** You are sure ? — **3.** Wait a minute please. — **4.** There is the fountain and here is the metro. — **5.** But of course !

Fill in the blanks

1 êtes — **2** sommes — **3** d'accord - plaît — **4** à — **5** ou - plaît.

Please remember *that for the time being, all you are required to do is to* **understand** *the French text and to repeat each paragraph immediately after you have heard it. Don't worry about little differences in construction or a word that isn't explained immediately ; we want you to assimilate them before learning a "rule".*

The liaison *is the name given to the sound produced by carrying over the last consonant of one word to the first vowel of the next, rather like "an apple" or like "nous allons" which we pronounce "noozallon". There is no written indication of this so we point it out in our text with the symbol* ‿

DEUXIEME (2ème) LEÇON

Au magasin

1 — S'il vous plaît, madame, est-ce qu'il **(1)** est cher, ce chapeau ?
2 — Non, il n'est pas cher. Il coûte quarante francs (40 F.).
3 — Bon. Et. . . Où sont les gants ?
4 — Les gants sont là-bas. Vous voyez **(2)** ?
5 — Ah, merci . . . Mais, est-ce qu'ils **(3)** sont‿en laine ?
6 — Non, ils ne sont pas‿en laine, ils sont‿en nylon.
7 — Bon. Euh . . . est-ce qu'il est cinq heures?
8 — Comment ? Ah ! Est-ce-que vous‿attendez votre mari, par hasard ?
9 — Oui, c'est ça **(4)** . . . et . . . il pleut dehors . . .
10 — Alors, non, madame . . . Il n'est **(5)** pas cinq heures !
11 — Est-ce que. . ? Est-ce qu'il. . ? Est-ce-qu'il est cinq heures ?

PRONONCIATION

1 . . . eskeel ay shair, se shapoh ?
2 . . . . . eel koot karont frohn
3 bohn . . oon sohn lay gohn
4 . . . voo vwayay
5 . . . merssee . . . may eskeel sontohn len.
6 . . . ohn neelohn . .
7 Bohn . . . eu. . . sank eur
8 Kommohn . . eske vooz attohnday vot maree, pahazar ?
9 . . eel pleu deor
10 Alor. . .
11 eske . . ? eskeel . . ?

2nd LESSON

In the shop

1 — (If you) please madam, is it dear, this hat ?
2 — No, it's not dear. It costs 40 francs.
3 — Good. And. . . where are the gloves ?
4 — The gloves are over there. (Do) you see ?
5 — Ah thank you . . . . But, are they in wool ?
6 — No they are not in wool, they are in nylon.
7 — Good. Um . . . is it 5 o'clock (hours) ?
8 — What ? (How ?) Ah ! Are you waiting [for] your husband, by [any] chance ?
9 — Yes, that's right (it is that) . . . and . . . it [is] raining outside
10 — So, no, madame, it's not 5 o'clock (hours) !
11 — No translation : Est-ce-que introduces a question : equivalent of is/are . . . ? or do/does. . .? Is it 5 o'clock (hours) ?

NOTES

(1) We are seeing one way of asking questions, and perhaps the simplest and most common. *Est-ce que* (eskë) (literally : "Is it that ? " is placed before the phrase you wish to make interrogative. . . and *voilà*, you have your question. The final "e" of "que" is elided before a vowel, so we find *Est-ce qu'il est cinq heures ?* or *Est-ce qu'elle est jeune ?* (Is she young ?). We will see other ways of asking questions later on.

(2) Another simple way of asking questions, which is the same as in English. The affirmative statement *Vous voyez* (you see) is pronounced with a rising, interrogative intonation, just like "You see ? ". Listen carefully to the tape recording. Both **(1)** and (2) are conversational, rather informal ways of asking questions and even grammatically incorrect though used all the time.

(3) Notice that we cannot hear the plural "s". The sound is exactly the same as in the first sentence.

(4) A very useful idiom, literally "it is that". It expresses agreement, and can be translated as 'That's it" or "Yes, you're right" or "That's right".

(5) *Ils ne sont pas* : they are not ; — *il n'est pas :* it is not. We "elide" (i. e. remove) the "e" of "ne" before a word beginning with a vowel to make pronunciation easier.

EXERCICES

1. Est-ce que vous êtes sûr ? – **2.** Est-ce qu'il est cher, ce chapeau ? – **3.** Est-ce que vous voyez la fontaine ? – **4.** Il n'est pas cinq heures – **5.** Est-ce qu'il coûte quarante francs ?

Fill in the blanks :

1 Est-ce qu' .. ... cinq heures ?

2 Vous attendez ..... mari ?

TROISIEME (3ème) LEÇON

Au café

1 – Messieurs (1) vous désirez (2) ?

PRONONCIATION

1 Messyeu. Voo deziray

EXERCISES

1. Are you sure ? – 2. Is it expensive, this hat ? 3. Do you see the fountain ? – 4. It is not 5.00. – 5. Does it cost 40 francs ?

3 Est-ce-qu' ... . en laine ?

4 Vous attendez Monsieur Legrand ? Oui, c ... .. .

5 Le métro St. Michel est là- ... .

Fill in the blanks

1 il est – **2** votre – **3** ils sont – **4** 'est ça – **5** - bas.

Remember *that French isn't stressed as heavily as English. Put a slight emphasis on the ends of the words, but not too much. The lack of heavy intonation is somewhat similar to a Liverpool accent. Pronounce each vowel fully and correctly.*

THIRD LESSON

In the café

1 – Sirs (Gentlemen) what do you want ? (you desire ?)

NOTES

(1) *Messieurs* is the plural of *monsieur* ; *mesdames* is the plural of *madame*. In both cases, the plural "s" is silent.
(2) See Leçon 2 (2) : *désirer* is a formal way of saying "to want" and is used by salespeople, waiters, etc. . .

2 – Deux cafés, s'il vous plaît, et deux croissants chauds **(3)**.
3 – Alors, vous‿êtes anglais ? – Oui, je suis de London, pardon, Londres **(4)**.
4 – Mais vous parlez bien le français. – Merci, vous‿êtes gentil.
5 – Nous, Français, nous sommes tous gentils **(3)** !

(Le garçon à une autre table :)

6 – Pardon messieurs, voici les cafés et les tartines beurrées **(5)**.
7 – Et alors ! Où sont les croissants ?
8 – Excusez-moi messieurs. . . – Et dépêchez-vous ! **(6)**

(A notre table :)

9 – Alors, vous‿êtes sûr qu'ils sont toujours gentils ?

PRONONCIATION

2 Deu kaffay. . krwassohn show
3 .. voozet onglay. . zhe swee . . pardohn londr
4 May voo parlay . . voozet zhentee.
5 . . . noo somm tooss. . le garssohn. . oon ohtr tahbl. . . lay tarteen beuray.
8 . . . . daypeshay-voo. not tahbl. . toozhoor

2 – 2 coffees, please, and 2 hot "croissants".
3 – So, you are English ? – Yes, I' m from London, excuse me (pardon) Londres.
4 – But you speak French well (well the French). – Thank you, you are kind.
5 – We French [people] we are all kind, (The waiter at another table).
6 – Excuse me gentlemen (pardon, sirs) here are the coffees and the buttered slices [of bread].
7 – So what ? (and so ?) Where are the "croissants" ?
8 – Excuse me, gentlemen – And hurry up (you) ! (At our table)
9 – So, you are always kind ?

NOTES (suite)

(3) First, notice the silent plural "s". Adjectives usually come after the noun in French and "agree" in number, which means that if the nouns they qualify are plural, the adjectives must take a (silent) "s" also. E.g. : *Un livre rouge* (a red book) – *deux livres rouges* (two red books).
A *croissant* is a delicious pastry eaten for breakfast in France.

(4) The French have two cities in Gallic form, the other being *Douvres* (Dover). No such alteration occurs for American cities.

(5) Nouns in French have a "gender"; they are either masculine or feminine. A masculine noun is preceded by the indefinite article *un* or the definite article *le*, feminine nouns are preceded by the indefinite article *une* or the definite article *la*. The plural definite article is *les* for masculine and feminine.
Adjectives must agree not only with the number (see **(1)**) but also with the gender of the noun they qualify. This usually means adding "e" to the masculine form. E.g. : *beurré* is the masculine form meaning buttered. To make it agree with a feminine singular noun, we add "e" : *une tartine beurrée.* To make it agree with a feminine plural noun, we add both "e" and "s". **These letters make no difference to the pronunciation.**

(6) This is the imperative form of our first class of verbs. The infinitive of this class ends in "er" *(excuser, dépêcher, parler).* The "you" form of the verb ends in "-ez" : *vous parlez.* Like in English, we can use this form to give an order or a command : "Hurry !", "Wait !", but in French we must also add the pronoun : *Dépêchez-vous !, Excusez-moi".*

11 onze (onz)

EXERCICES

1. Vous parlez bien le français. – **2.** Deux cafés, s'il vous plaît. – **3.** Voici les cafés et les croissants. – **4.** Ah, vous êtes anglais ? – Oui, c'est ça. – **5.** Est-ce-que vous êtes toujours gentil ?

Fill in the blanks :

1 Nous Français, nous ...... tous .... !

2 Où .... les croissants ?

3 Voici les tartines .... , messieurs.

QUATRIEME (4ème) LEÇON

Au café (II)

1 – Alors, commandons : (1)
2 – Deux tartines beurrées, s'il vous plaît, et deux cafés chauds !
3 – Trois bières (2) allemandes et un verre de vin blanc.

PRONUNCIATION

1 . . . . kommohndohn. . .
3 trwa beeair almohnd ay eun vair de van blohn

EXERCISES

1. You speak French well. – **2.** Two coffees, please. – **3.** Here are the coffees and the croissants. – **4.** Ah, you are English ? Yes, that's right (it is that) – **5.** Are you always kind ?

4 Vous ...... bien le français. Merci, vous .... gentil.

5 Je .... .. Londres

Fill in the blanks

1 sommes - gentils – **2** sont – **3** beurrées – **4** parlez - êtes – **5** suis de.

FOURTH LESSON

In the café (II)

1 – So, let's order :
2 – Two buttered slices [of bread], please, and 2 hot coffees !
3 – Three German beers and a glass of white wine.

NOTES

(1) We saw yesterday that *Excusez* was the imperative form (Leçon 3 **(6)**). There is another type of imperative which in English has the form "Let's. . ." (Let's go, etc. .). This is rendered in French by using the first person plural of the verb without the pronoun, so : *nous commandons* : we order – *commandons !* : Let's order !

(2) *La bière* (beer) is a feminine noun, so our adjective must take an "e" to "agree". So *un livre allemand* : a German book – *une bière allemande* : a German beer.
(Notice also that the adjective doesn't take a capital letter like in English).

Au tabac (3)

4 – Trois paquets de cigarettes brunes s'il vous plaît (4) et un cigare hollandais !
5 – C'est tout ?
6 – Non ; est-ce que vous‿avez un briquet rouge ?
7 – Non monsieur. Excusez-moi.

Dans la rue

8 – Pardon monsieur. Est-ce que vous‿avez du feu (5) s'il vous plaît ?
9 – Non, je ne fume pas.
10 – Alors moi non plus (6) !
11 – Je ne fume pas ; est-ce que vous fumez ?

PRONONCIATION

Oh taba
4 Trwa pakay. . . broon. . . seegah ollohnday
5 Say too ?
6 . . . . eun breekay roozh
8 . . . eske voozavay dyoo feu. .
10 . . mwa nohn plyoo

EXERCICES

1. Un paquet de cigarettes brunes s'il vous plaît. – **2.** Est-ce que vous avez du feu ? – **3.** Non, je ne fume pas. – **4.** Deux tartines beurrées et deux cafés chauds ! – **5.** Est-ce que vous avez un briquet rouge ?

In the tobacco - (shop)

4 — 3 packets of brown (tobacco) cigarettes please and a Dutch cigar.
5 — Is that (It is) all ?
6 — No.Do you have a red lighter ?
7 — No, sir. Excuse me.

In the street

8 — Excuse me (pardon) sir. Do you have a light (some fire) please ?
9 — No ; I don't smoke.
10 — So, me neither ! (me not more).
11 — I don't smoke ; do you smoke ?

NOTES (suite)

(3) *Un tabac* is a café which also has a cigarette counter. The sale of tobacco in France is a state monopoly and cigarettes can usually only be sold in specially-licensed places.A *'tabac'* also sells stamps, metro tickets and lottery tickets. Not every café is a *tabac.*
(If asking for a *'tabac'* in the street, always ask for *' un* **bureau** *de tabac')*

(4) *Une cigarette* is feminine. *Brun* (brown) refers to the dark tobacco popular in France (as opposed to Virginia tobacco). In order to agree with the feminine plural form *les cigarettes",* the word *"brun"* must add an "e" and an "s". So *"un cigare brun"* but *"une cigarette brune"* and *"deux cigarettes brunes".* **Remember** that the final "s" **is not pronounced.**

(5) *Est-ce que vous avez.. .* : Do you have. . .(We could also say- Leçon 2 **(2)** – *Vous avez. . . ?* with a rising intonation. This is an idiomatic phrase to ask for a light which literally translates as "Do you have some fire ?"

(6) *Alors* is one of these wonderful words that can be used almost anywhere. Its literal translation is "then", but it is used like "Well" as in "Well, I agree, etc. ." It can variously be translated as "Right !", "Well then. . .", "In that case. .", and many others. Watch out for it !

EXERCISES

1. A packet of brown (tobacco) cigarettes, please. – **2.** Do you have a light ? – **3.** No, I don't smoke. – **4.** Two buttered slices (of bread) and two hot coffees ! – **5.** Do you have a red lighter ?

2ème EXERCICE – Look at the following nouns and write down their genders :

1 une voiture. . . . .
2 un homme . . . .
3 une table . . . .
4 une route. . . . .
5 un arbre. . . . .

CINQUIEME (5ème) LEÇON

Une conversation

1 – Est-ce que Monsieur Legrand est là s'il vous plaît ?
2 – Non, il est‿absent pour le moment.
3 – Ah bon **(1)** ? Est-ce qu'il est là cet‿après midi **(2)** ?

PRONONCIATION

Oon konversasseeohn
1 . . messye legrohn. .
2 . . eelet absohn poor le momohn
3 . . . . setapray midi

Now, look at the following adjectives in the masculine singular form :
vert (green), rond (round), haut (high), court (short), intelligent.

Now, write the following pairs in French :

6 Two green cars . . . .
7 A round table . . . .
8 A short road. . . . .
9 Two high trees . . . .
10 Two intelligent men. . . . .

2nd EXERCISES

1.feminine (la) – **2.** masculine (le). – **3.** feminine (la). – **4.** feminine (la). – **5.** masculine (le). – **6.** Deux voitures vertes. – **7.** Une table ronde. – **8.** Une route courte. – **9.** Deux arbres hauts. **10.** Deux hommes intelligents.

FIFTH LESSON

A conversation

1 – Is Monsieur Legrand there please ?
2 – No he is out (absent) for the moment.
3 – Oh really (good) ? Is he in (here) this afternoon ?

NOTES

(1) Literally "oh good" this exclamation is used when receiving information and is best translated as "I see" or "Really ?".
(2) As in English, the French present tense can be used to express future time (e.g. : I'm flying to London tomorrow). Here, the secretary replies to the question in the present with a statement in the present - but both refer to the afternoon.

4 — Oui. Il arrive à trois‿heures (2).
5 — Merci beaucoup, mademoiselle. — De rien, monsieur (3).

et des proverbes...

6 — Les Français aiment les voitures rapides...
7 — mais les‿Anglais aiment les voitures confortables (4).
8 — Les bons comptes font les bons‿amis.
9 — Une hirondelle ne fait pas le printemps (5).
10 — Je ne suis pas ; vous n'êtes pas ; il n'est pas ; elle fait ; ils font.

PRONONCIATION

4 . . eel arreev a trwazeur.
5 merssee bowkoo, mamwazel. De ree-ehn
6 . . . emm lay vwatyoor rapeed
7 . . layzonglay emm. . .kohnfortabl
8 . . . bohn cohnt fohn lay bohnzamee
9 Oon eerondel ne fay pa le prahntohn

EXERCICES

1. Les voitures anglaises sont confortables. — **2.** Est-ce que Monsieur Legrand est là s'il vous plaît ? — **3.** Merci beaucoup, mademoiselle. — De rien, monsieur. — **4.** Est-ce qu'il arrive à trois heures ? — **5.** Les Français aiment les voitures rapides.

4 – Yes. He arrives at 3 o'clock (hours).
5 – Thank you [very] much, miss. – You're welcome (for nothing) sir.

and some proverbs . . .

6 – The French like (the) fast cars. .
7 – but the English like (the) comfortable cars.
8 – (The) good accounts make (the) good friends.
9 – One swallow does not make (the) spring.
10 – I'm not ; you're not ; he's not ; she does/makes; they do/make.

NOTES (suite)

(3) *De rien* is the polite answer to *Merci beaucoup* and is equivalent to the American usage of "You're welcome". It is a very common expression.

(4) A particularity of French is that it always uses an article before its nouns. Whereas an Englishman would say "Good accounts make good friends" (sentence 8), a Frenchman must use the article. This takes a little getting used to, but you quickly acquire the habit. Look at the examples in the lesson carefully.

(5) Here is our first irregular verb *faire*, which means "to do " or "to make". It is used extensively, so we want you to remember - *Il (or* **elle)** *fait* : (s)he does **or** makes. – *Ils (or* elles) *font* : they do **or** they make.

EXERCICES

1. English cars are comfortable. – **2.** Is Monsieur Legrand there please ? – **3.** Thank you very much, miss – You're welcome sir. – **4.** Is he arriving at 3 o'clock ? – **5.** The French like fast cars.

19 dix-neuf (deez-neuf)

Fill in the blanks :

1 ... bons comptes font ... . amis.

2 ... voitures .... sont rapides.

3 Une hirondelle ne .... pas .. printemps.

4 ... cigarettes françaises .... brunes.

5 Vous n' .... anglais, Monsieur Legrand ? Non,

je .... français.

SIXIEME (6ème) LEÇON

Les achats

1 — -Bonjour Monsieur Lefèvre. Comment ça va (1) ?

2 — -Bien, merci, et vous ? -Çà va, merci. -Qu'est-ce que vous voulez ?

3 — -Est-ce que vous‿avez (2) du beurre ? -Oui, bien sûr.

PRONONCIATION

Layzasha
1 Bohnzhoor. . . kohmohn sa va. .
2 . . . . . voolay
3 . . . beur . .bee-ehn syoor

Fill in the blanks

1 Les - les bons. — **2** Les - françaises. — **3** fait - le . — **4** Les - sont. — **5** êtes pas - suis.

Don't worry about what may appear "strange" constructions like est-ce que *or expressions like.* Eh bien. *Just let them sink into your memory. You will soon be able to use them naturally. Practise repeating them aloud !*

6th LESSON

(The) purchases

1 — -Good morning (good day), Monsieur Lefèvre. How's things ? (How it goes ?).
2 — -Well, thanks, and you ? -Fine (it goes), thanks. -What do you want ?
3 — -Do you have any butter ? -Yes, of course.

NOTES

(1) A familiar greeting very often used even with acquaintances. It literally means : "How goes it ? " and is the equivalent to an expression like : "How's life" or "How's by you ?". The "ritual" answer is *Bien merci, et vous ?.*

(2) To say "some" or "any" in statements or questions, we replace the article *(le* or *la)* by the words *du* (masculine) and *de la* (feminine). For the plural, we use *des* for both genders. So : *Vous avez des cigarettes brunes* (You have dark-tobacco cigarettes). —*Je veux de la bière* (I want some beer). — *Est-ce que vous avez du vin ?* (Do you have any wine ?).

4 — -Alors, une livre **(3)** de beurre. Est-ce que vous‿avez du fromage italien ?

5 — -Du parmesan ? Non, je n'ai pas de **(4)** fromage italien. -Dommage **(5)**!. . .

6 — -Eh bien, donnez-moi du fromage ordinaire.

7 — -Mais, Monsieur Lefèvre, nous n'avons pas de fromage ordinaire en France.

8 — Nous‿avons un fromage pour chaque jour de l'année !

9 — -Alors, donnez-moi le fromage d'aujourd'hui !

PRONONCIATION

4 . . .leevr. .fromahzh eetaleeahn
5 pahmayzohn. .dohmahzh. . .
7 . .ohn frohnss
8 noozavoh. .shak zhoor de lannay
9 . . .dohzhoordwee

EXERCICES

1. Qu'est-ce que vous voulez ? – **2.** Bonjour monsieur, comment ça va ? – **3.** Bien, merci, et vous ? – **4.** Donnez moi du fromage et de la bière. – **5.** Est-ce que vous avez des cigarettes anglaises ?

4 — -Well (so), one pound of butter. Do you have any Italian cheese ?
5 — -Any parmesan ? No, I don't have any Italian cheese. -Pity. . . !
6 — -(And) well, give me some ordinary cheese.
7 — -But, Monsieur Lefèvre, we don't have any ordinary cheese in France.
8 — We have a cheese for each day of the year !
9 — -So, give me today's cheese (cheese of today) !

NOTES (suite)

(3) *Une livre* — In France, the metric system is used, so food, etc. . ., is bought by the *kilo* (35 oz.) or the *demi-kilo* (17 oz) This latter "half-kilo" is also referred to as "a pound". *Une livre* is also used for the British currency. Notice the gender very carefully.
(4) (See also (2)) — *Du, de la, des* become simply *de* in the negative : — *Vous n'avez pas de fromage.* — *Vous n'avez pas de cigarettes,* etc. . . Simple, isn't it ?
(5) *Dommage* or *Quel dommage* means "What a pity" or "What a shame".

We have seen many things in this first week ; of course, we don't expect you to remember everything : all the important elements will be repeated and developed in later lessons. Just relax and listen to the French text and look at the English translation. We'll do the rest !

EXERCISES

1. What do you want ? — **2.** Good morning, sir. How are you ? — **3.** Well, thank you, and you ? — **4.** Give me some cheese and some beer. — **5.** Do you have (some) English cigarettes ?

Fill in the blanks :

1 Nous n' ..... pas .. fromage ordinaire en France.

2 Est-ce que vous voulez .. la bière ? Oui, bien ... !

3 Donnez-moi .. beurre, .. fromage et ... cigarettes, s'il vous plaît.

SEPTIEME (7ème) LEÇON

REVISION ET NOTES

(At the end of each week of six lessons, you will find a revision lesson which will review the most important points covered in the preceding week)

1 **Gender : This is perhaps** the major difficulty facing an English-speaking person : we have to accept the fact that nouns are either masculine or feminine. Each time you learn a new word, learn its gender at the same time. Remember the following words :

Le métro ; le pont ; le chapeau ; le croissant ; le briquet ; le fromage ; la bière ; la cigarette ; la voiture ; la tartine ; la fontaine.

un ; le for masculine – **une ; la** for feminine – **les,** plural for both genders.

2 **Adjectives :** Adjectives **usually** follow the noun they describe. If the noun is plural, the adjective takes a plural form, and if the noun is feminine, we put the feminine form, usually by adding an "e" or by doubling the final consonant and adding "e".

un briquet rouge ; deux bières blondes ; une tartine

4 Je n'ai pas .. cigarettes anglaises. - Eh .... donnez-moi .. cigare.

5 Est- .. ... vous avez ... fromages .... ?

Fill in the blanks

1 avons - de — **2** de - sûr — **3** du - du - des — **4** de - bien - un — **5** ce que des - italiens ?

7th LESSON

beurrée.
Remember : the final "s" is not pronounced.

3 Our verbs : We have seen the present tense of several verbs :

vous parlez — you speak ; **je parle** — I speak
vous fumez — you smoke ; **je fume** — I smoke
vous arrivez — you arrive ; **j'arrive** — I arrive

(We "elide" the "e" of "je" before another vowel so as not to say *je arrive.* We saw this with **il n'est pas** in Lesson 2).
The infinitive (our equivalent of "to speak") of these verbs is **parler ; fumer ; arriver.**
We also saw three very common irregular verbs : do you remember ?

Je suis de Londres — I am from London
Il est gentil — He is kind
Nous sommes touristes — We are tourists
Vous êtes français — You are French
Ils sont anglais — They are English

The infinitive of this verb is **être** — to be

We also saw :

Vous avez un briquet – you have a lighter
J'ai du fromage – I have some cheese

To have in French is **avoir**

and :

Il fait un exercice – he does an exercise
Ils font des bons amis – they make good friends

HUITIEME (8ème) LEÇON

Une visite

1 – -Bonjour mademoiselle, est-ce que votre père est à la maison ?
2 – -Non, monsieur ; il est au **(1)** bureau.
3 Vous voulez parler à ma mère ?
4 – -Non, ne la dérangez pas.
5 A quelle heure est-ce qu'il rentre normalement ?
6 – -Oh, pas avant **(2)** huit heures.
7 Vous voulez l'adresse de son bureau ?
8 – -S'il vous plaît. -Attendez, je la cherche **(3)**.

PRONONCIATION

1 . . . mamwazel . . vot pair etala mayzohn. .
2 oh byooroh. .
3 voolay parlay . . mair
4 dayrohnzhay. .
5 . . keleur. .
6 pazavohn weeteur. . .
8 . . . . shairsh

Faire means "to make" or "to do"

One great simplicity in French is that the one present tense translates both the simple and progressive forms in English. So **vous parlez anglais** can mean "you speak English" or "you are speaking English".

Enough for now. During the next six lessons, we 'll see some of these points put into practice.

Remember : don't try to do too much !

8th LESSON

A visit

1 — -Good morning (good day) miss. Is your father at home (at the house) ?
2 — -No, sir ; he is at the office.
3 — [Do] you want to speak to my mother ?
4 — -No, don't disturb her.
5 — At what time [does] he come back normally ?
6 — -Oh, not before 8 o'clock (hours).
7 — -[Do] you want the address of his office ?
8 — -(If you) please. -Wait, I [am] looking for it.

NOTES

(1) We have seen that there are fewer prepositions in French. Thus *à la* can mean, depending on the preceding verb "to the", "at the" or "in the". We say *à la* if the noun is feminine — *à la maison* : at home and *au* if the noun is masculine — *au bureau* : at the office.
(2) *Je ne fume pas* : I don't smoke. *Pas* by itself means "not" : *pas aujourd'hui* : not today — *pas après dix heures* : not after 10.00
(3) Remember, the present tense *(temps présent)* in French translates **both** of our present tenses : *je cherche* : I look **and** I'm looking.

9 Voilà. Sept rue Marbeuf, dans le huitième **(4)**.
10 — -Merci beaucoup, mademoiselle. Au revoir.
11 — -De rien, monsieur. Au revoir.
12 A quelle heure. . . ? Il est huit heures. . "Est-ce que vous avez l'heure s'il vous plaît ?"

PRONONCIATION

9 set roo mahbeuf. . weetiem
10 orevwar. . . .
12 eskevoozavay leur. . .

EXERCICES

1. Est-ce que votre mère est à la maison ? – **2.** Ne la dérangez pas s'il vous plaît. – **3.** Voilà l'adresse : il habite dans le sixième. – **4.** Merci beaucoup, monsieur. -De rien, mademoiselle. – **5.** A quelle heure est-ce qu'il rentre ? – **6.** Pas avant huit heures.

Fill in the blanks :

1 Ma mère est . .. . et mon père est .. ..

My mother is in the house and my father is at the office.

2 Vous ...... l' .... ?Attendez, je .. ..

You want the address ? Wait, I'm looking for it.

9 — There [it is] 7 rue Marbeuf, in the 8th [district].
10 — -Thank you very much, miss. Goodbye.
11 — -You're welcome, sir. Goodbye.
12 — At what time . . . ? It's 8 o'clock. . . [Do] you have the time (hour) please ?

NOTES (suite)

(4) Paris is divided into 20 districts called *arrondissements* numbered from the first *le premier* to the twentieth *le vingtième.* It is usual not to say the word *arrondissement* after the figure. *Elle habite dans le treizième* : She lives in the thirteenth (district).

EXERCISES

1. Is your mother at home ? — **2.** Don't disturb her please. — **3.** There is the address : he lives in the sixth (district). — **4.** Thank you very much, sir. Don't mention it, miss. — **5.** At what time does he come home ? — **6.** Not before 8.00

3 . ... est-ce-qu'il ...... ?

At what time does he come back ?

4 Je vais .. .... , puis .. .. et après je ....

I'm going to the café, then to the shop and after I'm going back.

5 Vous voulez ...... à .. mère ? -Non, ne .. dérangez pas.

You want to speak to my mother ? -No, don't disturb her.

NEUVIEME (9ème) LEÇON

(Numbers in the text preceded by N- refer to notes in the "Revision et Notes" Lesson).

Très simple !

1 Ce monsieur s'appelle Henri Laforge et cette **(1)** dame est sa **(N-1)** femme.
2 Ils sont‿à la mairie pour chercher une carte d'identité **(2)** pour leur fils, Jean.
3 – Cet‿enfant, **(1)** il a quel âge ? -Il a huit‿ans **(3)**, monsieur.

PRONONCIATION

1 . . . sa famm
2 eel sontala mayree. . feess, zhohn
3 setohnfohn. . . weetohn

Fill in the blanks

1 à la maison - au bureau. — **2** voulez - adresse - la cherche. — **3** A quelle heure - rentre ? — **4** au café - au magasin - rentre. — **5** parler - ma - la.

REMEMBER TO READ THE NUMBERS AT THE BEGINNING OF EACH LESSON AND AT THE TOP OF EACH PAGE.

9th LESSON

Very simple !

1 — This gentleman is called (calls himself) Henri Laforge and this lady is his wife.
2 — They are at the Town Hall to get (look for) an identity card for their son John (Jean).
3 — -This child, how old is he (he has what age) ? -He is (has) eight years [old] sir.

NOTES

(1) "This" or "that" is *ce* for a masculine noun and *cette* for a feminine noun. *Ce garçon* : this boy — *cette femme* : this woman. (However if a masculine noun begins with a vowel, or a mute "h", we write *cet* — *cet ami* : this friend ; *cet homme* : this man). You see, it really is important to learn the genders !

(2) Everybody in France must carry an identity card with him. (They are always demanded when cashing cheques, for example). They are sometimes referred to as *une pièce d'identité.*

(3) In French, you **have** your age : *elle a dix ans* : she is 10 years old ; *quel âge a cet enfant ?* : how old is this child ?. We must always add *ans* (years) after the age : *vingt ans* : 20 years old.

4 — -Et il s'appelle Laforge. Est-ce qu'il est votre enfant ?
-Oui monsieur.

5 — -Bien. Et il habite chez **(4)** vous ? -Mais évidemment ! Il a huit‿ans !

6 — -D'accord. Je fais mon travail, c'est tout.

7 Est-ce que vous ‿ avez le formulaire B-52 ?

8 — -Oui monsieur, nous l'avons. -Et l'imprimé A-65 ?

9 — -Ça aussi, nous l'avons. -Ah bon ? Mais est-ce que vous ‿ avez son extrait de naissance ?

10 — -Bien sûr. Nous‿avons même **(5)** une photo.

11 — -Très bien. Alors je vous fais la carte. Voilà. Ça fait cent vingt (120) francs.

12 — -Oh zut **(6)** ! J'ai oublié mon portefeuille !

PRONONCIATION

5 eel abeet shay voo
6 . . . traveye, say too. .
7 . . bay sankont deu.
8 . . a swassont sank
9 sa ohssee. . . ekstray de naysohnss
11 sohn van frohn
12 zoot. . zhay oobliay mohn portefoy

EXERCICES

1. Quel âge a cet enfant ? Il a neuf ans. — **2.** Ce monsieur s'appelle Henri et cette dame s'appelle Marie. — **3.** J'habite chez un ami. — **4.** -Deux cafés et une bière. -Ça fait dix francs. — **5.** Oh zut ! J'ai oublié une photo !

4 — -And he is called (calls himself) Laforge. Is he your child ? -Yes, sir.
5 — -Fine. And he lives with you ? -But obviously ! He is (has) eight !
6 — Ok. I'm doing my job, that's all.
7 — Do you have (the) form B-52 ?
8 — -Yes sir, we have it. - And the printed [form] A-65 ?
9 — -That also, we have it. -Oh really ? But do you have his birth certificate (extract) ?
10 — -Of course. We have even a photo.
11 — -Very well. So I'll do (am doing) [for] you the card. Here it is. That makes 120 francs.
12 — -Oh damn ! I've forgotten my wallet !

NOTES (suite)

(4) *Chez* means basically "home of" : *chez moi* : my place ; my home (some English families call their houses *Chez nous* : our place). It can also mean "the shop of" ; *chez le boulanger* : at the baker 's. We will often come across it.
(5) *même* has several meanings : here it means "even". Followed by *que* it means "the same as". Notice it now and we'll look at it in more detail after.
(6) *Zut !* a mild expletive to express annoyance. It is not offensive.

EXERCISES

1. How old is this child ? He is nine. — **2.** This gentleman is called Henry and this lady is called Mary. — **3.** I live at a friend's. — **4.** Two coffees and a beer — That makes 10 francs. — **5.** Oh, damn ! I have forgotten a photo !

Fill in the blanks :

1 .. monsieur, ... dame et ... enfant sont allemands.

This gentleman, this lady and this child are German.

2 ..... Henri et .. femme. Comment .. .. ?

Here is Henry and his wife. How's things ?

DIXIEME (10ème) LEÇON

Bonsoir, Monsieur Duclos

1 Monsieur Duclos rentre chez lui à sept‿heures tous (1) les soirs.
2 D'habitude, il achète quelque chose (2) à manger au supermarché et il monte à son appartement.
3 D'abord, il décroche le téléphone parce qu' (3) il n'aime pas être dérangé (N-2).
4 Puis il dîne, fume une cigarette et allume (4) la télévision.

PRONONCIATION

1 . . . rontr shay looee. . too lay swar
2 dabeetyood. . kelkeshowz a mohnzhay
3 dabor. . daykrosh le telayfon parskeel nemm pa et dayronzhay
4 . . . eel deen

3 .... dame ? Elle . cinquante ...

How old is this woman ? She is fifty years old.

Fill in the blanks

1. Ce - cette - cet — 2 Voici - sa - ça va. — 3.Quel âge à cette - a - ans.

10th LESSON

Good evening, Monsieur Duclos

1 Monsieur Duclos goes back [to] his place at 7.00 every (all the) evening(s).

2 Usually, he buys something to eat at the supermarket and he goes up (mounts) to his apartment.

3 First of all, he disconnects the telephone, because he doesn't like to be disturbed.

4 Then he dines, smokes a cigarette and turns on (lights) the television.

NOTES

(1) *Tout* : all, every is an adjective so it must "agree" with its noun. — *tous les soirs* : every evening (**un** soir) ; — *toutes les femmes* : all the women (une femme) ; — *Tout le monde* (lit. all the world) means "everybody".

(2) *quelque* : some, a few. It, too, must agree : *quelques hommes. quelqu'un* : somebody ; *quelque chose* : something. *quelque part* : somewhere.

(3) *parce que* : because , *Pourquoi ?* : Why ?

(4) Literally "to light the television" ! — *Allumer le gaz* : to light the gas — *Allumer la radio :* to turn on the radio. — On the radio, television : *A la radio, à la télévision.*

5 Il regarde les‿actualités **(5)** et peut-être un film.
6 Après, il lave ses‿assiettes et se couche à dix‿heures.
7 Il aime cette vie tranquille et paisible.
8 Mais ce soir, il n'y a pas de film à la télévision et il pense aller au cinéma.
9 Il y a un film d'horreur au Gaumont et un film politique au Paramount...
10 – Non ! Je pense que je vais écouter la radio. C'est plus calme **(6)**.

PRONONCIATION

5 . . . . peutet. . eun feelm
6 apray. . lav. . . deezeur
7 set vee tronkee ay payzeebl. .
8 . . . . . . ponss allay oh sineyma. .
9 . . . oh gohmohn. . . oh paramoont.
10 . . . . say plyoo kalm

IL AIME CETTE VIE
TRANQUILLE ET PAISIBLE.

EXERCICES

1. Il allume la télévision et il regarde les actualités. – **2.** Elle achète quelque chose à manger au magasin tous les soirs. – **3.** D'habitude, il rentre chez lui à sept heures. – **4.** Il n'y a pas de film à la télévision ce soir.– **5.** Je n'aime pas être dérangé.

5 He watches the news and perhaps a film.
6 After, he washes his plates and goes to bed at 10.00.
7 He likes this quiet and peaceful life.
8 But this evening, there is not a film on (at) the television, and he thinks of going (to go) to the cinema.
9 There is a horror film at the Gaumont and a political film at the Paramount.
10 – No ! I think I'm going to listen to the radio. It's more calm.

NOTES (suite)

(5) *actuel* is what we call a "false friend" : it looks like an English word and means something else. – *actuel* : current, present. – *les actualités* or - *les informations* : the current events, hence : the news.
(6) Some adjectives end in "e" in the masculine form so they **do not change** in the feminine. Another common example is *jeune* : young.

THERE MAY SEEM TO BE A LOT OF DETAILS, BUT DON'T TRY TO REMENBER THEM ALL. ANYTHING IMPORTANT IS ALWAYS REPEATED SEVERAL TIMES IN DIFFERENT SITUATIONS. RELAX AND ENJOY IT !

EXERCISES.

1. He turns on the television and watches the news. – **2.** She buys something to eat at the shop every evening. – **3.** Usually, he comes home at 7.00. – **4.** There is no film on the television this evening. – **5.** I don't like to be disturbed.

Fill in the blanks :

1 Il .... , ... une cigarette et .... la télévision.

He has dinner (dines), smokes a cigarette and watches the television.

2 Ce soir .. . ' . . ... de film . .. télévision ;

This evening there is no film on the television

3 mais .. . . une bonne émission . .. .

but there is a good programme on the radio.

ONZIEME (11ème) LEÇON

Un peu de révision

1 — -A quelle heure est le film ce soir ? -A huit heures et demie.
2 — -Et qu'est-ce que c'est **(1)** ? -C'est un film espagnol.
3 — -Et c'est **(N-3)** bien ? - Je ne sais pas, je ne connais **(2)** pas le metteur en scène.
4 — -Ah bon ? Alors, qu'est-ce qu'il y a **(1)** à la radio ?
5 — -Rien d'intéressant. -Bon, je vais lire un roman !

PRONONCIATION

rayveezeeohn

2 . . keskesay. . seteun feelm
3 ay say. . konnay ;
4 keskeelya . . . radeeoh. .
5 antairessohn. . . rohmohn. .

4 . ' . . . . . , il achète . . . . manger

First of all, he buys something to eat

5 et . . . . il . . . . appartement.

and then he goes up to his apartment.

Fill in the blanks

1 dîne - fume - regarde — **2** il n'y a pas - à la. — **3** il y a - à la radio. — **4** D'abord, - quelque chose à — **5** puis - monte à son.

11th LESSON

A little revision

1 — -At what time is the film this evening ?
2 — -At half past eight (eight hours and a half).
2 — -And what is it ? -It's a Spanish film.
3 — -And is it (it is) good ? -I don't know : I don't know the director (putter on stage).
4 — -Oh really ? Well, what is there on the radio ?
5 — -Nothing (of) interesting. - Good, I'm going to read a novel !

NOTES

(1) These strange-looking expressions are in fact both easy to pronounce and extremely useful : — *Qu'est-ce que c'est ?* : What's this, what's that ? — *Qu'est-ce qu'il y a...?* : What is there...? — *Qu'est-ce qu'il y a sur le piano ?* : What is there on the piano ? By itself, *qu'est-ce qu'il y a ?* means "what's the matter ? " when addressed to a person.

(2) We say : *je sais* (I know) for a thing, and *je connais* for a person or a place — *Je connais sa mère* : I know his mother. *Je connais cette ville* : I know this town — *Il sait beaucoup de choses* : He knows many things.

6 Un jour, à Lyon, un jeune homme monte dans (3) un bus,
7 et commence à mâcher du chewing-gum.
8 Il y a une vieille dame assise (4) en face.
9 Elle regarde le jeune (5) pendant (6) cinq minutes et elle dit :
10 – -C'est inutile d'articuler comme ça, jeune homme,
11 – je suis complètement sourde !

PRONONCIATION

6 . . . leeohn. . .
7 masshay. . shooing geum
8 veeay. . asseez on fass.
10 set inooteel dartikyoolay. . .
11 soord.

EXERCICES

1. Qu'est-ce que c'est ? C'est un livre allemand. – **2.** Je ne connais pas sa mère mais je connais son père. – **3.** Qu'est-ce qu'il y a à la télévision ? - Rien d'intéressant. – **4.** Il regarde la télévision pendant trois heures tous les jours. – **5.** -Pardon monsieur, . . -C'est inutile de parler, je suis sourd.

Fill in the blanks :

1 Qu' . . . . ' . . . a sur . . table ?

. ' . . . un livre.

What's on the table ? It's a book.

6 One day, in Lyons, a young man gets onto (in) a bus
7 and begins to chew (some) chewing-gum.
8 There is an old lady sitting opposite.
9 She looks at the young (person) for 5 minutes and she says :
10 — -It's useless to articulate like that, young man,
11 — I'm completely deaf !

NOTES (suite)

(3) When a verb expresses movement into a place, we use *dans* (in). — *Elle entre dans le salon* : she goes (or comes) into the front room. French is less demanding for specifying whether a verb should be "go" or "come".
(4) The past participle is also an adjective, so it must "agree" : — *Il est assis* : he is seated ; — *elle est assise* : she is seated.
(5) An adjective used to describe a person can stand alone : — *Un sourd* : a deaf man ; — *une sourde* : a deaf woman. — *Un riche* : a rich man ; — *une noire* : a black woman. this is also possible in the plural, like in English : — *les pauvres :* the poor.
(6) *Pendant* : for or during. — *Pendant le dîner* : during dinner ; — *pendant vingt minutes :* during 20 minutes.

EXERCISES

1. What is it ? It's a German book. — **2.** I don't know his mother but I know his father. — **3.** What is on television ? Nothing interesting. — **4.** He watches television for three hours every day. — **5.** Excuse me, sir,. . . - It's useless speaking, I am deaf.

2 Je .... la radio .. soir.

I'm going to listen to the radio this evening.

3 Qu' ... . ' ... ? . ' ... ma carte d'identité.

What's that ? It's my identity card.

4 Elle .... le .... cinq minutes.

She watches the young (man) for five minutes

DOUZIEME (12ème) LEÇON

Un tour dans Paris

1 — Bonjour mesdames, bonjour mesdemoiselles, bonjour messieurs **(1)** ! Je suis votre guide.
2 — Alors, commençons ici par la place du Panthéon : à ma droite, vous voyez le Panthéon même **(2)**,
3 et à ma gauche, l'église de Saint-Etienne du Mont.
4 — -Pardon monsieur, dit un touriste, mais où. . . ?

PRONONCIATION

1 . . .maydam. .maydemwazel. .vot geed
2 . plass du pontayohn. . drwat. .
3 . . gohsh. .

5 Qu' ... . ' .. . a ? .... , ... !

What's the matter ? Nothing, nothing !

Fill in the blanks

1 est-ce qu'il y - la - C'est — **2** vais écouter - ce — **3** Qu'est-ce que c'est ? C'est — **4** regarde - jeune homme - pendant — **5** est-ce qu'il y ? Rien, rien.

12th LESSON

A tour in Paris

1 — Good morning ladies, good morning young ladies, good morning gentlemen ! I'm your guide.
2 — So let's begin here by the place du Panthéon : on (to) my right, you see the Panthéon itself
3 — and on (to) my left, the church of Saint-Etienne du Mont.
4 — -Excuse me, sir, says a tourist, but where. . . ?

NOTES

(1) The word for "sir" or "gentleman" is *monsieur* : otherwise "my sire". Likewise "lady" is *ma - dame,* so if we speak in the plural, the possessive adjective must agree *messieurs.* This type of introduction, however, is rather formal.

(2) Here is another meaning of *même. — moi-même :* myself ; — *elle-même* : herself *lui-même* : himself ; — *vous-même* : yourself. If we attach it to a proper noun : *Londres même,* we mean London, as opposed to its suburbs. — *Le Panthéon même ,* the Panthéon, as opposed to the place du Panthéon.

— Tout‿à l'heure, **(3)** répond le guide.

5 — Le Panthéon était d'abord une église et ensuite. . .

6 — -S'il vous plaît, monsieur, dit le même touriste, mais où sont. . . ?

7 — Mais laissez-moi terminer, je vous‿en prie **(4)**, répond le guide.

8 — -Mais monsieur, c'est très‿important !

9 — -Eh bien, qu'est-ce que vous voulez savoir **(5)** ?

10 — -Où sont les toilettes ? !

PRONONCIATION

4 . . . . tootaleur raypohn
5 . . . onsweet. . .
7 .lessay-mwa terminay
8 . . .trayzamportahn
9 keske. .savwar
10 . . twalett.

QU'EST-CE QUE VOUS VOULEZ SAVOIR ?

EXERCICES

1. Monsieur Legros habite Paris même. – **2.** -Oh, excusez-moi, monsieur ; – Je vous en prie. – **3** Je vais vous le dire tout à l'heure – **4.** Qu'est-ce que vous voulez savoir ? – **5.** Pardon, monsieur, où est l'église de Saint-Etienne du Mont ?

-Later, replies the guide.

5 — The Panthéon was first a church, and then. . .

6 — -Please, sir, says the same tourist, but where are. . ?

7 — But let me finish, if you please (I pray you) !, answers the guide.

8 — -But sir, it's very important !

9 — -Oh well, what do you want to know ?

10 — -Where are the toilets ? !

NOTES (suite)

(3) A curious expression, because it can mean both "earlier" and "later". The context will make the meaning clear.

(4) An emphatic way of saying "please" — *Je vous en prie* can also be used to reply to someone who thanks you, or who apologises to you : — *Oh, excusez-moi, monsieur ; —Je vous en prie.* — Oh, I 'm sorry, sir ; — Don't mention it.

(5) We have seen *je sais* : I know (something). This is the infinitive. This irregular verb goes : *je sais, il (ou elle) sait, nous savons, vous savez, ils (ou elles) savent* (the -ent of the third person plural is always silent). This is the origin of the English word "savvy" meaning "knowledge".

IT'S A LITTLE DIFFICULT AT FIRST TO GET USED TO THE IDEA OF DIFFERENT GENDERS, BUT YOU CAN SEE HOW IMPORTANT IT IS ; **ALWAYS** *LEARN A NOUN WITH ITS GENDER.*

EXERCISES

1. Mr. L. lives (in) Paris itself. — **2.** Oh, excuse me miss ! Don't mention it. — **3.** I will tell you (it) later. — **4.** What do you want to know ? — **5.** Excuse me, sir, where is the church of S.E.D.M. ?

2ème EXERCICE – Put in the correct indefinite article (*un* or *une)*

1 .... heure
2 .... église
3 .... guide
4 .... bureau
5 .... maison
6 .... adresse
7 .... cinéma
8 .... radio
9 .... carte
10 .... photo
11 .... téléphone
12 .... vie
13 .... film
14 .... bus
15 .... télévision

TREIZIEME (13ème) LEÇON

La belle musique

1 – -Est-ce que vous‿aimez cette chanteuse **(1)** ?
2 – -Bof **(2)**, elle a une assez belle **(N-4)** voix. . .
3 mais je trouve que ses chansons sont‿idiotes **(3)**;
4 les paroles sont bêtes et la musique est triste.

PRONONCIATION

1 . .shonteuz. .
2 . . assay bel vwa
3 . .shohnsohn. .ideeot

LES FRANÇAIS AIMENT LES VOITURES RAPIDES !

2nd EXERCISE

1. une heure — **2.** une église — **3.** un guide — **4.** un bureau. — **5.** une maison. — **6.** une adresse. — **7.** un cinéma. — **8.** une radio. — **9.** une carte. — **10.** une photo. — **11.** un téléphone. — **12.** une vie — **12.** un film. — **14.** un bus. — **15.** une télévision.

13th LESSON

Beautiful music

1 — -Do you like this singer ?
2 — -Oh, she has a pretty enough voice
3 — but I find that her songs are idiotic ;
4 — the words are stupid and the music is sad.

NOTES

(1) Masculine nouns that end in "eur" (see line 10) are made feminine by adding "euse" to the root word. So, a saleswoman will be *une vendeuse.*

(2) *"Bof"* ! is a vocabulary in itself : it is a French institution and expresses a basic lack of enthusiasm : — *Vous aimez ce vin ? — Bof !* Do you like this wine ? — Well, I suppose it's alright but. . . Do you get the idea ?

(3) Remember the plural "s" is silent ! However we pronounce the "t" : — *un idiot* [idioh] *; une chanson idiote* [idiot].

5 De toute façon **(4)**, j'aime seulement la musique classique.
6 — -Vous n'aimez pas du tout **(5)** la musique moderne ?
7 — -Si, mais seulement quand les chansons sont‿intelligentes et belles.
8 — -Qui aimez-vous par exemple ? - J'aime **(6)** bien Coco et les Clowns **(7)**.

9 — Une affiche dans la vitrine **(8)** d'un ma-magasin :
10 — "Nous cherchons un vendeur **(1)** : jeune ou vieux ; plein temps ou temps partiel ; expérimenté ou débutant".
11 — Et, en-dessous, au crayon : "Mort ou vivant".

PRONONCIATION

5 De toot fassohn. . seulmohn
7 sontantelizhohnt
8 . . . . . lay kloon
9 afeesh. .vitreen ;
10 vohndeur. .vyeu. .plahn tohn. .tohn parsee-el, eksperimontay oo debyootohn. .
11 on desoo, oh krayohn 'mor oo vivohn'

EXERCICES

1. Dites-moi, Jean, vous aimez ce chanteur ? – Bof ! – **2.** Et vous, Pierre ? -Moi ? Pas du tout ! – **3.** – J'aime bien la musique classique, mais j'aime aussi la musique moderne. – **4.** De toute façon, ses chansons sont bêtes. – **5.** Elle n'aime pas du tout le vin.

5 – Anyway (in any fashion), I like only (the) classical music.
6 – -You don't like at all modern music ?
7 – -Yes [I do], but only when the songs are intelligent and beautiful.
8 – -Whom (do) you like, for example ? – I like (well) Coco and the Clowns.
9 – A sign in the window of a shop :
10 – "We [are] looking [for] a salesman : young or old ; full time or part time ; experienced or beginner".
11 – And, underneath, in pencil : "Dead or alive".

NOTES (suite)

(4) *façon* means a fashion, a way of doing something.
– *Ne le faites pas de cette façon* : Don't do it that way.
– *De toute façon :* in any case, anyway (a fashion in dress is *une mode* [mod]).
(5) Notice the construction of the sentence : *du tout* must follow directly *pas : – Vous l'aimez ? – Pas du tout ! :* – Do you like him (or it) ? – Not at all !
(6) We have said that forming questions with *est-ce que* was very common but not elegant ; here is the other form, and very simple it is. We simply invert the verb and the pronoun : *vous aimez. .. aimez-vous. . ?* This works for all forms and tenses.
(7) Notice the pronounciation [kloon].
(8) window : *une fenêtre ; – une vitrine* a shop-window *faire du lèche-vitrine* (lit. shop-window licking) : go window-shopping.

EXERCISES

1. Tell me, J. (Do) you like this singer ? – Bof (In French in the text !) – **2.** -And you, P. ? –Me ? Not at all ! – **3.** –I like classical music a lot, but I also like modern music. – **4.** –In any case, his/her songs are stupid. – **5.** –She doesn't like wine at all.

Fill in the blanks :

1 ..... - .... ce magasin ? ... . !

Do you like this shop ? Not at all !

2 .. .. , il aime .... le bon vin.

Anyway, he only likes good wine.

3 ... chansons sont .... et la musique est .....

Her songs are sad and the music is beautiful.

QUATORZIEME (14ème) LEÇON

REVISION ET NOTES

1 My father is *mon père* ; my mother is *ma mère* ; my brother is *mon frère* ; my sister is *ma soeur.*
The possession-word thus changes if the singular noun is masculine or feminine. For the plural, the word is *mes* irrespective of the gender : *mes parents, mes cigarettes.*

For "your", "our" and "their", we have one singular form and one plural form, irrespective of gender : *votre carte* (your card) ; *votre père ; vos parents ; notre radio ; notre appartement ; nos amis ; leur adresse ; leur maison ; leurs photos.* (this plural "s" is silent unless the noun begins with a vowel : *leurs‿amis).*

"His" and "her" (its) is slightly different from English, where we say "his" if the **possessor** is masculine and "her" if she is feminine.
In French, this does not count. The words for his/her/its are adjectives and must **agree with the noun they qualify.**

4 Elle . une .... voix.

She has quite a pretty voice.

5 Il n'aime ... . musique moderne.

He doesn't like modern music at all.

Fill in the blanks

1 Aimez-vous - Pas du tout. — **2** De toute façon. . . seulement — **3** Ses - tristes - belle. — **4** a - assez jolie — **5** pas du tout la.

14th LESSON

So *son bureau* can mean : his **or** her office ; we use *son* because *bureau* is masculine. In the same way *sa photo* can be his **or** her photo.
The plural is *ses* : *ses romans* : his or her novels.

(There is one exception to these rules of agreement : if the noun qualified begins with a vowel, we use the masculine adjective to make pronunciation easier). e.g. : *sa amie* would be difficult to pronounce (rather like "a apple") ; so we say *son amie* and *mon amie* and allow the context to show whether the friend is male or female !

2 In the last week, we have seen many different verbs, the infinitives of which end in *-er* . This is the largest category of French verbs, with literally thousands of "members". Let's look at an example :

fumer (to smoke) *je fume ; il/elle fume ; nous fumons ; vous fumez ; ils fument* (the final *-ent* is silent)
This is the pattern for all these verbs. Do you remember

these ?
rentrer ; acheter , monter ; décrocher ; déranger ; manger ; allumer ; regarder ; laver ; se coucher ; aimer ; penser ; écouter :
Look back at Lesson 10 and review them.

The past participle - which corresponds to the English "I have seen " - is simply : *fumé, dérangé* pronounced the same as the infinitive. *Il n'aime pas être dérangé* : He doesn't like to be disturbed. Choose four of the above verbs and write out the forms with : *je ; il/elle ; nous ; vous* and *ils/elles.* (Remember : the final *-ent* is silent).

3 We have seen two ways of saying "it is" : *c'est* and *il est.*
Here is the difference : we use *c'est* to explain what a thing (or who a person) is.
Qu'est-ce que c'est ? C'est une photo de famille.
What is it ? It's a family photo.
Regardez, c'est mon frère. Look, that's my brother.
or to say :
it's me : *c'est moi*
it's you : *c'est vous.*

QUINZIEME (15ème) LEÇON

Les petites annonces

1 Recherche jeune fille pour garder mes‿enfants le soir.
2 Téléphoner **(1)** le matin au 20. 31. 56 **(2)**

PRONONCIATION

1 zheun fee. . mayzohnfohn
2 van, trontayun, sankont seess

or if the noun is qualified by an adjective :
c'est un bon ami, he's a good friend.
(the plural is *ce sont. Ce sont mes bons amis :* They are my good friends.
il est is used to refer to a noun just mentioned :
Où est mon portefeuille ? Il est sur le piano.
Where is my wallet ? It's on the piano.
(if the noun is feminine, we say *elle est).*
Où est l'église ? Elle est en face du Panthéon.
Where is the church ? It's opposite the Panthéon.

or if we are talking about the weather :
il pleut : it's raining
il fait beau : it's fine.

or telling the time :
il est huit heures et demie : it's half past eight.

So much for the rules : in time you will "feel" the correct usage. Remember, don't try to do too much at once.

Learn each noun with its gender !

15th LESSON

(The) Small advertisements

1 Looking [for] young girl (for) to look after (keep) my children [in] the evening.
2 Telephone [in] the morning to 20.31.56.

NOTES

(1) The infinitive is sometimes used on notices, etc. as an imperative : — *Ne jeter rien à terre :* Don't throw anything on the floor.
(2) The French habit is to give their telephone number as a real number, rather than as individual figures. This takes some getting used to, so let's start today !

3 Je vends **(N-1)** un canapé et deux fauteuils modernes. Prix à débattre.
4 A louer. Petit studio. Calme et clair. Salle de bains.
5 Ecrire à Mme DELAYE, 3 boulevard Malesherbes, Paris huitième.

6 -Bonjour Madame. Je vous‿appelle au sujet de votre annonce.
7 -Très bien. Comment vous‿appelez-vous ? **(3)**
8 -Je m'appelle Martine Lenoir, Madame.
9 -Et quel âge avez-vous, Martine ?
10 -J'ai quatorze‿ans, Madame.
11 -Oh, mais vous‿êtes beaucoup trop jeune !
12 Je suis désolée **(4)**. Au revoir.

PRONONCIATION

3 vohn. .fotoy. .pree
4 a looay petee. .sal de ban
5 malzerb
6 oh soozhay de votranonss
10 katorzohn
11 voozet bowkoo troh
12 dayzolay

EXERCICES :

1. Je n'ai pas d'argent pour téléphoner. – **2.** Il y a un petit studio à louer dans le huitième. – **3.** Bonjour ! Je m'appelle Pierre Lefèvre ! – **4.** Mais vous êtes beaucoup trop jeune ! – **5.** Comment vous appelez-vous ?

3 I am selling a sofa and 2 modern armchairs. Price to [be] discussed.
4 To rent. Small studio. Quiet (calm) and light (clear). Bathroom.
5 Write to Mme DELAYE, 3 boulevard Malesherbes, Paris 8th

6 -Good morning, madam. I [am] calling you about the advertisement.
7 -Very well. What is your name (How do you call yourself) ?
8 -My name is (I call myself) Martine Lenoir, Madam.
9 -And how old are you, Martine (what age have you) ?
10 -I am (have) 14 years [old], Madam.
11 -Oh, but you are much too young !
12 I am very sorry. Goodbye.

NOTES (suite)

(3) – *Je m'appelle ; il (elle) s'appelle ; nous nous appelons ; vous vous appelez ; ils s'appellent.* This is called a "reflexive" verb : the subject and the object are the same.
– *Elle se regarde* : She looks at herself. The infinitive is preceded by *se* . – *se regarder ;* – *s'appeler.*

(4) – *Je suis désolé* (if a man is writing ; *désolée* if a woman). A polite expression meaning : I'm terribly sorry.
– *Excusez-moi* : Excuse me ; I'm sorry. – *Pardon ;* Pardon.

EXERCISES

1. I haven't any money to telephone. – **2.** There is a little studio to rent in the 8th. (district) – **3.** Hello ! My name's (I am called) P.L. – **4.** But you are much too young ! – **5.** What is you name ? (What are you called ?).

Fill in the blanks :

1 .... appelez-vous ?

What is your name ?

2 .... âge .... - .... , mademoiselle ?

How old are you, miss ?

3 Je suis ...... ; mon père n' ... pas . .. .

I'm terribly sorry ; my father isn't in.

4 Je vous .... votre annonce.

I am calling you about your advertisement.

SEIZIEME (16ème) LEÇON

Des achats . . . !

1 -Bonjour, madame. Je cherche un piège à rats **(1)**. Vous‿en **(1)** avez un ?
2 -Bien sûr, monsieur. Attendez une minute, je vais‿en **(2)** apporter un.

PRONONCIATION

1 pee-ezh a ra. voozonavay eun
2 . .zhe vayzon aportay eun

5 Je cherche une ..... fille .... mes enfants

I'm looking for a young girl to look after my children.

C'EST UNE PHOTO DE FAMILLE.

Fill in the blanks

1 Comment - vous — **2** Quel - avez-vous — **3** désolé ; - est - à la maison. — **4** - appelle au sujet de - — **5** jeune - pour garder.

16th LESSON

Purchases . . . !

1 -Good morning, madam. I am looking [for] a rat-trap. [Do] you have one ?

2 -Of course, sir. Wait a minute, I'm going to bring one.

NOTES

(1) – *Une bouteille de vin :* a bottle of wine ; – *une bouteille à vin :* a wine bottle. The second construction explains the **purpose** of the object ; – *une brosse à dents :* a toothbrush ; – *un verre à champagne :* a champagne glass.

(2) *en :* This little word means "of it" or "of them". – *Vous avez des cigarettes ? – J'en ai deux :* Do you have any cigarettes ? – I have two. Its use is idiomatic and we will see some more examples later.

3 -Dépêchez-vous, madame. J'ai un train à prendre.

4 -Un train ? Oh, monsieur, je suis désolée,
5 je n'ai pas‿un modèle assez grand **(3)** !

---

6 Un douanier arrête un voyageur à la sortie de la douane **(4)** :

7 -Bonjour monsieur. Ouvrez votre sac, s'il vous plaît.

8 Le voyageur ouvre son sac. . . qui est plein de diamants.

9 -Ces diamants sont pour mes lapins, dit le voyageur.

10 -Pour vos lapins, vous dites ? s'exclame le douanier.

11 -Parfaitement. S'ils ne veulent **(5)** pas de diamants, ils n'auront **(6)** rien à manger !

PRONONCIATION

3 . . .eun tran
6 dooaniay. .vwoyazheur. .dooann
8 . . . .plan de deeamohn
9 say. . . .lapan
10 . . .seksklam
11 parfetmohn seel ne veul. .norohn

EXERCICES

1. Nous cherchons notre sac. – **2.** Il va en apporter un, je pense. – **3.** Si vous ne voulez pas de café, nous avons du thé [tay] – **4.** Je n'ai pas un modèle assez grand. – **5.** Ces diamants sont pour mes lapins.

3 -Hurry (yourself), madam. I have a train to catch (take).
4 -A train ? Oh sir, I'm very sorry.
5 I don't have a model big enough !

6 A customs officer stops a traveller at the exit of the customs (hall).
7 -Good morning, sir. Open your bag, please.
8 The traveller opens his bag. . . which is full of diamonds.
9 -These diamonds are for my rabbits, says the traveller.
10 -For your rabbits, you say ? exclaims the customs officer.
11 -Exactly (perfectly). If they don't want diamonds, they will have nothing to eat !

NOTES (suite)

(3) Notice the word-order : — *je n'ai pas un sac assez grand :* I don't have a bag big enough.
(4) *La douane :* customs, the customs hall, or shed. — *un douanier :* a customs officer — *un policier :* a police officer. A custom in the sense of a tradition : — *une coutume.*
(5) *—Je veux ; il (elle) veut ; nous voulons ; vous voulez ; ils veulent.* The infinitive of this verb is *vouloir :* to want. *—Il veut partir :* he wants to leave.
(6) This is our first encounter with the future tense. We will learn more about it later.

EXERCISES

1. We are looking for our bag. — **2.** He is going to bring one, I think. — **3.** If you don't want coffee, we have tea. — **4.** I don't have a model big enough. — **5.** These diamonds are for my rabbits.

Fill in the blanks :

1 Vous .... une cigarette, . ' .. vous plaît ? J ..

.. deux.

Do you have a cigarette, please ? I have two.

2 .... une minute ; je .... .. apporter un.

Wait a minute ; I'll just go and bring one.

3 .. est .. brosse . ..... ?

Where is my tooth-brush ?

4 Il ouvre ... sac .... chercher un briquet.

He opens his bag to find a lighter.

DIX-SEPTIEME (17ème) LEÇON

Une conversation au téléphone (1)

1 -Allo ? **(1)** . . . Oui, c'est moi. Qui est à l'appareil ?

PRONONCIATION

konvairsasseeohn
1 . . . . .kee etalaparay

5 **. . .** livres sont **. . . .** **. . .** enfants.

These books are for my children.

Fill in the blanks

1 avez - s'il - en ai. — **2** Attendez - vais en. — **3** Où - ma - à dents.
4 son - pour . — **5** Ces - pour mes.

17th LESSON

A conversation on the telephone (1)

1 Hello ? Yes, it's me. Who's speaking (on the apparatus) ?

NOTES

(1) *Allô* ? is only used on the telephone, it is not a greeting. To greet someone, we say *bonjour* (or *bonsoir* if it is the evening).
Bonne nuit means "good night" ; *Qui est à l'appareil ?* is also telephone vocabulary for "Who's speaking ?".

2 . . Ah, bonjour Sophie. . . Bien, et vous ? . . . Oh, quel **(2)** dommage !

3 J'espère que ce n'est pas grave ? . . . . . . Heureusement.

4 Jacques ? . . . . . . oh, il va assez **(3)** bien, mais il a beaucoup de travail en ce moment.

5 . . .Des vacances ? Ne me **(4)** faites pas rire ! Nous n'avons pas ‿ assez **(3)** d'argent. Et vous ?

6 . . . Comme tout le monde . . . . . Avec plaisir. Quand ? Samedi **(N-2)** prochain ?

7 Attendez, je vais voir. Ne quittez pas.

8 Non, samedi, ma mère vient dîner à la maison.

9 Dimanche ? Je pense que nous sommes libres **(5)**. Oui, dimanche est parfait.

10 A huit heures. D'accord. Soignez-vous ! Merci, au revoir.

J'ESPÈRE QUE CE N'EST PAS GRAVE ?

PRONONCIATION

2 . . . .kel domahzh
3 . . .grahv. .eureusmohn
4 onsemomohn
6 toolemond. .plezeer. .kon. .samdi proshan
7 . . . .keetay
8 vee-en
9 . . .leebr. . .parfay
10 weeteur. .swanyayvoo

2 Ah, hello Sophie . . Well, and you ? Oh, what [a] pity !
3 I hope that it's not serious ? . . . – Fortunately.
4 Jack ? . . oh, he's quite well, but he has a lot of work at (in) the moment.
5 . . . Holidays ? Don't make me (to) laugh ! We don't have enough money. And you ?
6 . . . Like everybody . . .With pleasure. When ? Next Saturday ?
7 Wait, I'm going to look. Don't go away.
8 No ; [on] Saturday, my mother [is] coming to dine at home.
9 Sunday ? I think that we are free. Yes, Sunday is perfect.
10 At 8.00 Fine. Look after yourself ! Thank you. Goodbye.

NOTES (suite)

(2) *Quel livre voulez-vous ?* : Which book do you want ?
– *Quelle heure est-il ? :* What time is it ?
– *Quels livres aimez-vous ?* : Which books do you like ?
– *Quelles cigarettes fumez-vous ?* : Which cigarettes do you smoke ?
All these forms are pronounced the same.
– *Quel ; quelle ; quels ; quelles :* which ? or what ?
In exclamations, it means What a . . . ! – *Quelle ville !* : What a town !
– *Quel nom !* : What a name !
– *Quel dommage* : What a pity !
(3) *Assez* has two principal meanings : before an adjective or adverb, it means "quite" : – *Il est‿assez grand* : he's quite big – *elle chante assez bien :* she sings quite well. Before a noun, it means "enough" : –*je n'ai pas‿assez de temps :* I don't have enough time.
(4) With an affirmative imperative, "me" is *moi* and comes after the verb, joined to it by a hyphen : – *parlez-moi* : speak to me ! – *aimez-moi :* love me ! "He" becomes *lui* – *Dites-le lui :* Tell him.
With a negative imperative, the pronouns come before the verb. "Me" is me. – *Ne me regardez pas :* Don't look at me.
(5) *Ces livres sont gratuits :* These books are free (i.e : they cost nothing). – *il n'est pas libre ce soir :* he is not free this evening (i.e : he is busy) – *Du temps libre :* free time
Some shops in France have a sign saying : *Libre service* which means that you are free to browse.

EXERCICES

1. Il a beaucoup de travail en ce moment. – **2.** Samedi, ma mère vient à la maison. – **3.** Je pense que je suis libre dimanche. – **4.** Ne quittez pas, je vais voir. – **5.** Comme tout le monde, nous n'avons pas assez d'argent.

Fill in the blanks :

1 Vous n' .... pas ..... ? .... !

You are not free ? What a pity !

2 Ne .. faites pas .... !

Don't make me laugh !

3 Mon mari .. .. bien mais il a .... travail.

My husband is quite well but he has a lot of work.

DIX-HUITIEME (18ème) LEÇON

Une conversation au téléphone (II)

1 Allô, Anne-Marie ? . . C'est Sophie. Comment‿allez-vous ?

2 Moi, j'ai la grippe . . . . . Non, ce n'est pas trop grave.

PRONONCIATION

1 . . .komontalayvoo
2 . . .greep

EXERCISES

1. He has a lot of work at the moment. — **2.** (On) Saturday, my mother is coming to the house. — **3.** I think that I am free (on) Sunday — **4.** Don't hang up, I'll go and see. — **5.** Like everybody, we haven't enough money.

4 J' ...... que .. n' ... pas ..... .

I hope that it's not serious.

5 .... - .... libre .... ?

Are you free next Saturday ?

Fill in the blanks

1 êtes - libre - Quel dommage — **2** me - rire — **3** va assez - beaucoup de — **4** espère - ce - est - grave — **5** Etes-vous - samedi prochain.

18th LESSON

A conversation on the telephone (II)

1 Hello, Anne-Marie ? . . . It's Sophie. How are you ?
2 Me, I have the flu' . . . No, it's not too serious.

3 Et comment va Jacques ? . . . . Vous prenez des vacances bientôt **(1)** ?

4 Non, malheureusement, ça coûte trop cher.

5 Dites-moi, est-ce que vous voulez venir dîner un soir ?

6 Disons samedi prochain . . . Tant pis **(2)**. Eh bien, dimanche ? . . . Ca vous va ? **(3)**

7 Parfait. Venez vers huit‿heures. Pas trop tôt.

8 . . .Oui, oui. Je prends beaucoup de médicaments, beaucoup trop **(4)** !

9 Allez, dites bonjour à Jacques pour moi.

10 Je vous‿embrasse **(5)**. Au revoir. A dimanche.

PRONONCIATION

3 . . . .byantoh
4 malereuzmohn. .koot
5 deetmwa
6 tohnpee
7 . .vair. . .troh toh
10 zhevoozombrass.

3 And how is (goes) Jack ? [Are] you taking holidays soon ?
4 No, unfortunately. It costs too much (expensive).
5 Tell me, do you want to come to dinner (to dine) one evening ?
6 [Let's] say next Saturday. . . Bad luck. Well, Sunday ? Does that suit you ? (that goes you ?).
7 Perfect. Come around (towards) 8.00. Not too early.
8 . . Yes, yes. I [am] taking a lot of medicines, far too many !
9 O.K. (go), say hello to Jack for me.
10 Lots of kisses (I kiss you). Goodbye. Until (to) Sunday.

NOTES

(1) *Tôt* : early. – *Venez tôt :* come early. *Tard :* late. – *Il se couche tard :* He goes to bed late. To be early : *être en avance,* to be late : *être en retard. Bientôt :* soon – *A bientôt ! :* See you soon !
(2) An idiom meaning "hard luck" "there's nothing we can do". – *Ils ne viennent pas. Tant pis :* they're not coming. Shame.
(3) *Comment va Jacques ? :* How is Jack ? – *Vous‿allez bien ? :* Are you well ? –*Ca vous va ? :* Does that suit you ? – *Ce chapeau vous va bien :* This hat looks good on you, suits you nicely. – *Ca me va :* That's fine by me.
(4) In French, we make no difference between "much" and "many" : – *beaucoup d'argent :* much money ; *beaucoup de voitures :* many cars. Before *beaucoup,* we often use an expression you have seen : *il y a :* there is/there are ; *beaucoup de* : a lot of ; *beaucoup :* a lot ; *vous fumez beaucoup ! :* you smoke a lot ! ; *beaucoup trop :* far too much/many.
(5) It is a custom in France for friends to kiss each other on both cheeks as a polite greeting (men usually shake hands) so it is not unusual to finish a letter or a phone-call to a friend with : *je vous embrasse :* I kiss you.

DON'T TRY TO LEARN ALL THESE NEW EXPRES–SIONS AT ONCE ; WE WILL SEE THEM AGAIN IN LATER LESSONS.

EXERCICES

1. Il fume beaucoup trop ! – **2.** Est-ce que vous voulez venir dîner ? – **3.** Venez à huit heures et demie. Ça vous va ? – **4.** Dites bonjour à votre mari pour moi. – **5.** Ca coûte trop cher !

Fill in the blanks :

1 Je prends .... médicaments ; beaucoup ....!

I'm taking a lot of medicines ; far too many !

2 Il ...... toujours .. ..

He always arrives late.

3 Ne ..... pas .... tôt. Ca .... .. ?

Don't come too early. Does that suit you ?

DIX-NEUVIEME (19ème) LEÇON

Deux conversations au restaurant

1 -Qu'est-ce que vous mangez ? Ca sent bon !
2 -C'est une daube **(1)** de boeuf. Vous en **(2)** voulez ?

PRONONCIATION

1 . . .sa sohn bohn. .
2 . .dowb de beuf

EXERCISES

1. He smokes far too much ! – **2.** Do you want to come to dinner (to dine) ? – **3.** Come at 8.30. Does that suit you ? – **4.** Say hello to your husband for me. – **5.** It costs too much !

4 . . . . beaucoup . ' enfants dans cette école.

There are a lot of children in this school.

5 Comment . . . . . - . . . . et comment . . votre

. . . . ?

How are you, and how is your husband ?

Fill in the blanks

1 beaucoup de - trop. – **2** arrive - en retard. – **3** venez - trop - vous va ? – **4** il y a - d' – **5** allez-vous - va - mari.

19th LESSON

Two conversations at the restaurant.

1 What are you eating ? It smells good !
2 It's a beef stew. [Do] you want some ?

NOTES

(1) A *daube* is a rich stew, made with wine, meat and vegetables. – *un boeuf :* an ox ; – *du boeuf :* beef ; – *un agneau* : a lamb ; – *de l'agneau* : lamb (meat) ; – *un veau* [voh] : a calf ; – *du veau* : veal and, in case you thought it was too easy, – *un cochon* : a pig ; – *du porc* : pork.

(2) – *Je veux du beurre* : I want some butter ; – *J'ai du beurre ; vous en voulez ?* : I have some butter ; do you want some ? *En* avoids the repetition, in the second part of the sentence, of *du beurre. Du, de la* , and *des* can never stand by themselves.

3 -Non merci. Je n'ai pas faim **(N-3)**. J'ai déjà mangé.
4 -Alors, prenez un verre de vin.
5 -Non merci ; je n'ai pas soif non plus. Mais je vais prendre un café.
6 -Bien. Garçon ! Deux cafés et l'addition, s'il vous plaît.

7 -Je ne vais pas prendre de vacances cette année.
8 Ca coûte beaucoup trop cher. Et vous ?
9 -Moi **(3)** je vais en **(4)** Grèce en septembre pour deux semaines.
10 -En Grèce ? Vous‿avez de la chance ! Je suis jaloux.

11 janvier ; février ; mars ; avril ; mai ; juin ;
12 juillet ; août ; septembre ; octobre ; novembre ; décembre.

PRONONCIATION

3 fan. .dayzha mohnzhay
5 swaf nohn plyoo
6 . . .ladeeseeohn
9 . .gress. .septombr. .
10 . . . . .shonss. .zhaloo
11 zhonveeay ; fevreeay ; marss, avreel ; may ; zhwan
12 zhweeyay ; oot ; septombr ; oktobr ; novembr ; dessombr ;

EXERCICES

1. Je n'ai pas faim. J'ai déjà mangé. – **2.** Prenez un verre de vin ! Non merci. – **3.** Vous avez soif ? Oh oui, beaucoup ! – **4.** Qu'est-ce que vous mangez ? Ca sent très bon. – **5.** Garçon ! Un café et l'addition, s'il vous plaît !

3 No, thank you. I'm not hungry (I have not hunger) I have already eaten.
4 Well, have (take) a glass of wine.
5 No, thank you. I'm (have) not thirsty either. But I will (going to) have (take) a coffee.
6 Good. Waiter ! 2 coffees and the bill, please.

7 I'm not going to take holidays this year.
8 It costs much too much (expensive). And you ?
9 Me, I'm going to (in) Greece in September for 2 weeks.
10 To (in) Greece ? You're lucky! (you have luck) I'm jealous.

11 January ; February ; March ; April ; May ; June;
12 July ; August ; September ; October ; November ; December.

NOTES (suite)

(3) This is a colloquial way of speaking ; if another person has been mentioned in the conversation, and we wish to refer to oneself, we use this structure to add emphasis. – *Moi, je m'appelle Jean* : As for me, my name's John.

(4) -*Vous le trouvez en Grèce*: you find it **in** Greece ; – *Elle va en Grèce* : she is going **to** Greece. However, if the country has a plural name (the Netherlands, the United States, etc...) we use *aux* after *aller*. – *Ils vont aux Etats-Unis :* They go/ are going to the United States.

EXERCISES

1. I am not hungry. I have already eaten. – **2.** Have a glass of wine ! No thank you. – **3.** Are you thirsty ? Oh yes, very (a lot). – **4** What are you eating ? It smells very good. – **5.** Waiter ! A coffee and the bill please !

Fill in the blanks :

1 J'ai .. vin. Vous .. .. ?

I have some wine. Do you want some ?

2 ... , je vais .. Italie et ... Etats-Unis cette .....

As for me, I'm going to Italy and to the United States this year.

3 Vous .... ? Alors, ... un verre .. vin.

You're thirsty ? Well, have a glass of wine.

4 .. ' ... - .. ... vous ...... ? .. boeuf ?

What are you eating ? Beef ?

VINGTIEME (20ème) LEÇON

Encore (1) un peu de révision

1 Aujourd'hui, nous‿allons revoir (2) quelques‿expressions utiles :
2 -Venez vers huit‿heures, d'accord ?
-Parfait.

PRONONCIATION

onkor. .reveezeeon
1 revwar. .kelkezekspresseeohn

5 Ils ne .... pas .... vacances .. ..

They aren't going to take holidays in August.

JE N'AI PLUS FAIM.
J'AI DÉJÀ
MANGÉ.

Fill in the blanks

1 du - en voulez. – **2** Moi, - en - aux - année – **3** avez soif ? - prenez - de. – **4** Qu'est-ce que - mangez - Du. – **5** vont -prendre de - en août.

20th LESSON

A little more (again a little) revision

1 Today we are going to see again some useful expressions.

2 Come around (towards) 8.00, OK. ? -Perfect.

NOTES

(1) When we like a play or a band in France we shout *encore !* – meaning "again" ! "more" ! – *Encore du vin ? :* Some more wine ? – *Vous‿en voulez encore ? :* You want some more of it ? – *Encore un peu s'il vous plaît* : A little bit more, please.

(2) English tends to modify its verbs by using "postpositions" (look at, look after, look for, etc...) ; French adds a prefix to the verb : – *voir* : to see ; *revoir :* to see again ; *brancher* : to plug in ; *débrancher :* to unplug. This is part of the "genius" of the language : we will show you many more examples.

3 -Elle est malade et elle prend beaucoup de médicaments.
4 -Je cherche un nouveau stylo. Vous‿en avez un ?
5 Il n'a pas faim et il n'a pas soif : il a déjà mangé.
6 -Qui est‿à l'appareil ? Oh, c'est Sophie. Comment‿allez-vous ?
7 -Ma femme **(3)** a beaucoup de travail en ce moment.
8 -Des diamants pour vos lapins ? Ne me faites pas rire !
9 -Vous voulez un verre de vin ? -Avec plaisir.
10 -Comment vous‿appelez-vous ? Je m'appelle Sophie Delaye.
11 -Je suis désolé, je suis pris **(4)** samedi soir. -Eh bien tant pis !
12 -Cette nouvelle robe vous va très bien.

PRONONCIATION

4 steelo
6 . . .laparay

EXERCICES

1. J'ai du vin ici. Est-ce que vous en voulez ? – **2.** Encore un petit peu, s'il vous plaît. – **3.** Ce nouveau chapeau et cette nouvelle robe sont très jolis. – **4.** Mon mari est pris ce soir. -Quel dommage ! – **5.** Comment s'appelle sa femme ? – **6.** Je veux revoir cet exercice, s'il vous plaît.

3 She is ill and she [is] taking a lot of medicines.
4 -I'm looking for a new pen. [Do] you have one?
5 He is (has) not hungry and he is (has) not thirsty ; he has already eaten.
6 -Who is on the phone ? Oh, it's Sophie. How are you ?
7 My wife has a lot of work at (in) the moment.
8 Diamonds for your rabbits ? Don't make me (to) laugh !
9 -[Do] you want a glass of wine ? -With pleasure.
10 -What is your name ? -My name is Sophie Delaye.
11 -I'm very sorry , I'm taken [on] Saturday evening. - Oh well, hard luck !
12 -That new dress suits you very well.

NOTES (suite)

(3) —*Une femme* : a woman ; *ma femme* : my wife. We have a similar problem with *une fille* : a girl ; *sa fille* : his daughter. The context should make the sense clear : *(un homme, un mari* : a man, a husband ; *un garçon, un fils* : a bov, a son).
(4) This is the **past participle** of the verb *prendre* : to take.

EXERCISES

1. I have some wine here. Do you want some ? — **2.** A little more, please. — **3.** This new hat and this new dress are very pretty. — **4.** My husband is busy this evening. What a pity ! — **5.** What's his wife called ? — **6.** I want to see this exercise again please.

2ème EXERCICES Put in the correct indefinite article (un une)

1 .... fauteuil
2 .... salle de bains
3 .... douanier
4 .... sac
5 .... femme
6 .... voyageur
7 .... monde
8 .... grippe
9 .... verre
10 .... addition
11 .... brosse à dents
12 .... livre
13 .... agneau

VINGT-ET-UNIEME (21ème) LEÇON

REVISIONS ET NOTES

1 *Vendre* (to sell) ; *prendre* (to take) ; *attendre* (to wait for). These verbs - which we have already used - are part of a second category of verbs : those whose infinitives end in *-re.*
Here is how they look :
je vends , il (elle) vend ; nous vendons ; vous vendez ; ils vendent.
Remember that the final *s* and the *-ent* are silent ; but there is a difference in pronunciation between the "he" and the "they" forms. *il vend* [eel vohn] ; *ils vendent* [eel vohnd]
If the verb begins with a vowel, of course, we make a liaison with the "s" of *ils, elles.*
elle attend [el attohn] ; *elles‿attendent* [elzattohnd].
The past participle of these verbs usually ends in *-u : vendu , attendu.*

2nd EXERCISES (un or une)

1. un fauteuil — 2. une salle de bains — 3. un douanier. — 4. un sac — 5. une femme. — 6. un voyageur. — 7. un monde. — 8. une grippe — 9. un verre. — 10. une addition. — 11 une brosse à dents. — 12. un livre. — 13. un agneau.

21st LESSON

Let's remind ourselves of two irregular verbs we have seen :
savoir (to know) ; *je sais ; il (elle) sait ; nous savons ; vous savez ; ils savent.*
prendre (to take) ; *je prends ; il (elle) prend, nous prenons, vous prenez ; ils prennent* (past participle : *pris).*

2 The days of the week are : *lundi ; mardi ; mercredi ; jeudi ; vendredi ; samedi ; dimanche ,*
Notice that, unless they are used at the beginning of a sentence, they are not spelled with an initial capital letter.
We do not need a preposition to express "on. . . ."
– *Il vient jeudi* : He's coming on Thursday.
– *Téléphonez-moi mardi :* Phone me on Tuesday.
If we want to say : he works Saturdays, we put the definite article before the noun, thus :
il travaille le samedi. (no final "s" because proper nouns in French are never pluralised).

– *A samedi ! :* Until Saturday ! (See you on Saturday)
– *Bon week-end ! :* Have a nice week-end !

3 *Avoir faim* – certain expressions which in English use "to be" are constructed with *"avoir"* (to have) in French. Thus :
– *Avez-vous faim ? :* Are you hungry ?
– *Elle n'a pas soif :* She is not thirsty.
– *Vous avez de la chance :* You are lucky.
– *Quel âge a votre enfant ? :* How old is your child ?

Here are some new ones :
Elle a peur la nuit : She's frightened at night.

VINGT-DEUXIEME (22ème) LEÇON

Les trois jeux nationaux (1)

1 Il y a trois grands jeux d'argent en France :
2 Le Loto, la Loterie Nationale et le Tiercé.
3 Les deux premiers sont des jeux de hasard
4 et le dernier est‿un jeu où on **(N-1)** parie sur des chevaux.
5 Ils‿ont tous **(2)** lieu une fois par semaine

PRONONCIATION

1 trwa zheu nassionoh
2 lottoh, tyersay
3 . . .zheu de azar
4 . . .shevoh
5 . . .tooss lyeu

Vous avez raison : You are right.
Il a tort [tor] : He's wrong
Excusez-moi, j'ai sommeil [sommey] *: Excuse me, I'm sleepy.*

4 Numbers
un (1) – deux (2) – trois (3) – quatre (4) – cinq (5) – six [seess] (6) – sept [set] (7) – huit (8) – neuf (9) – dix [deess] (10) – onze (11) – douze (12) – treize (13) quatorze (14) – quinze (15) – seize [sez] (16) – dix-sept [deesset] (17) – dix-huit [deezweet] (18) – dix-neuf (19) – vingt [vahn] (20).

22th LESSON

The 3 National games

1 There are 3 big money games in France.
2 The Loto, the National Lottery and the Tiercé.
3 The first two are games of chance
4 and the last is a game where one bets on horses
5 They all [of them] take (have) place one time a week

NOTES

(1) Most nouns and adjectives form the plural by adding "s" (not pronounced). However those ending in *-eu -au -eau* add a (silent) x:
un jeu – des jeux ; un château – des châteaux.
Similarly, those nouns (or adjectives) ending in *-al* change to *-aux* [oh] *:*
un cheval – des chevaux ; un journal – des journaux ; la police nationale – les musées (museums) *nationaux.*
Other exceptions will be pointed out later.

(2) If *tous* comes before a plural noun, it means "all. ." and is pronounced [too]. If it comes after a verb, it means "all of them" "every one" and is pronounced [tooss] :
tous les journaux : all the newspapers ;
Venez tous à huit heures : All of you come at 8.00.

6 On achète des billets de Loterie à des guichets **(3)**
7 ou, comme pour le Loto, au tabac.
8 Si vous voulez jouer au **(4)** Tiercé,
9 vous‿allez dans‿**(5)** un café spécial
10 qui s'appelle un P.M.U. **(N-2) (6)**
11 Tous ceux qui jouent espèrent faire fortune !

PRONONCIATION

6 . . .geeshay
10 . . .pay em oo
11 too se. .zhoo essper

TOUS CEUX QUI JOUENT ESPÈRENT FAIRE FORTUNE !

EXERCICES

1. Le Tiercé a lieu le dimanche. – **2.** Ma soeur joue du piano et moi de la guitare. – **3.** J'espère gagner beaucoup d'argent. – **4.** On achète les billets dans un tabac. – **5.** Ce monsieur s'appelle Duclos.

6 One buys Lottery tickets at ticket offices
7 or, as for the Loto, at the tabac.
8 If you want to play (at) the Tiercé
9 you go in [to] a special café
10 which is called a "P.M.U.".
11 All those who play hope to make [their] fortune !

NOTES (suite)

(3) *Un guichet* is a versatile word, its sense depending on where you are : in a bank, it is the cashier's window ; in a train station, it is the ticket office ; in a theatre, it is the box-office. If you hear it, start looking for some kind of window or counter !

(4) *Jouer* : to play. For games and sports, we say *au* (or *à la*) :
Il joue au football : he plays football
but for instruments, we say *du* (or *de la*)
Elle joue du piano ; il joue de la guitare.
Un joueur (une joueuse) : a player.

(5) Aller au théâtre : to go to the theatre
Aller en Grèce : to go to Greece
Aller dans un café, un bar, etc. . : to go into a café, or a bar.
The use of *dans* reinforces the idea of "inside" "into".

(6) In America, there is a betting system called the "Pari mutuel" which is based on the French system called *Pari Mutuel Urbain :* Mutual urban betting. – *parier* : to bet ; *un pari :* a bet (Notice that the French capital has nothing to do with this system !)

EXERCISES

1. The Tiercé takes place on Sunday. – **2.** My sister plays the piano and me [I play] the guitar. – **3.** I hope to win a lot of money. – **4.** One buys tickets in a "tabac". – **5.** This gentleman is called Duclos.

81 quatre-vingt-un (katrevan-eun)

Fill in the blanks :

1 En France, ... beaucoup .. tennis.

In France, one plays a lot of tennis.

2 . . . . trois grands ....

There are three big national games.

3 Ils ... . une fois ... semaine.

They all take place once a week.

VINGT-TROISIEME (23ème) LEÇON

Le Loto

1 — -Qu'est-ce que vous faites là Jean ?
2 — -Je fais mon Loto. C'est‿un jeu très‿intéressant.
3 — Regardez : vous prenez cette carte et vous choisissez **(N-3)** une série de chiffres.
4 — Par exemple, ici, j'ai le cinq, le vingt-deux, le quarante-trois et le quarante huit **(N-4)**
5 — Ensuite, vous mettez une croix sur ces chiffres
6 — et vous donnez la carte au patron du tabac.

4 Les deux .... sont des .... de ....

The first two are games of chance.

5 Si vous ...... jouer, vous .... et vous .....

.... un café.

If you want to play, you wait and you go to a café.

Fill in the blanks

1 on joue - au- . — **2** Il y a - jeux nationaux. — **3** ont tous lieu - par - . — **4** premiers - jeux - hasard. — **5** voulez - attendez - allez dans.

23rd LESSON

The Loto

1 — What are you doing there, John ?
2 I [am] doing my Loto. It's a game [which is] very interesting
3 Look : you take this card and you choose a series of figures.
4 For example, here I have (the) 5, (the) 22, (the) 43 and (the) 48.
5 After, you put a cross on these figures.
6 and you give the card to the boss of the "tabac".

PRONONCIATION

3. . .shwazissay. . .shifr
4 . .karront
5 onsweet. .krwa

7 — -Et alors ? -Ben (1) vous‿attendez les résultats.
8 — Si vous‿avez choisi les bons (2) chiffres, vous gagnez.
9 — -Et vous‿avez gagné ? - Non, pas‿encore.
10 — -Bon, moi je vais jouer : je choisis le seize ;
11 — ensuite le treize, le quatorze et le vingt.

PRONONCIATION

7 bahn
8 shwazee. .ganyay
9 . . .ganyay
10 . . .sez
11 trez, katorz. .vahn

EXERCICES

1. Qu'est-ce que vous faites là ? – **2.** Vous choisissez la bonne réponse. – **3.** C'est un jeu qui est très intéressant. – **4.** Il va jouer du piano ce soir. – **5.** Qu'est-ce que je fais ? Ben, j'attends.

Fill in the blanks :

1 ..... le ...... , le .... et le .....

Play the 13, the 14 and the 20.

7 And then (so) ? -Ehm, you wait [for] the results
8 If you have chosen the right (good) figures, you win.
9 -And have you won ? -No, not yet.
10 -Well (me), I'm going to play : I choose the 16,
11 after the 13, the 14 and the 20.

NOTES

(1) *Ben* [bahn] is not really a noun, but a sound. Its meaning is something like "Well. . ." "You know. ."
It is not particularly elegant, but very common and useful. (It's a contraction of *"Eh bien".)*

(2) *Un bon vin :* a good wine. *Cette soupe est très bonne :* This soup is very good
Est-ce-que vous‿avez le bon numéro ? : Do you have the right number ?
Voilà la bonne réponse : There's the right answer.
Wrong is *faux* (feminine : *fausse)*
un faux numéro : a wrong (phone) number.
Bad is *mauvais (mauvaise) :*
un mauvais‿élève : a bad pupil.

IL VA JOUER DU PIANO CE SOIR.

EXERCISES

1. What are you doing there ? – 2. You choose the right answer – **3.** It's a game which is very interesting. – **4.** He is going to play the piano this evening. – **5.** What am I doing ? Well, I'm waiting.

85 quatre vingt-cinq (katrevan-sank)

2 Si vous avez ...... les .... ' vous ....

If you choose the right figures, you win.

3 Et vous .... ? Pas ....

And have you won ? Not yet.

4 Vous ...... une ..... et vous ...... la carte .. patron.

You put a cross and you give the card to the boss.

VINGT-QUATRIEME (24ème) LEÇON

Le passe-temps numéro un

1 – Il y a un quatrième jeu que (N-5) nous avons oublié.
2 – C'est un jeu qui vient du Sud (1) de la France ;
3 – Le jeu de boules, ou la "pétanque" !
4 – Partout où il y a un peu d'espace (2),
5 vous voyez des joueurs de boules

PRONONCIATION

Passtohn
2 . . .vyehn. .syood
3 . . .bool. .paytonk
4 Partoo. .ayspass

5 .. ' ... - .. ... vous .... ? Je

.... le seize.

What do you choose ? I choose the 16.

Fill in the blanks

1 Jouez - treize - quatorze - vingt. — **2** - choisi - bons chiffres - gagnez. — **3** - avez gagné - encore. — **4** - mettez - croix - donnez - au. — **5** Qu'est-ce que - choisissez ? - choisis.

24th LESSON

The number one pastime

1 — There is a fourth game which we have forgotten
2 — It is a game which comes from the South of France ;
3 — the game of bowls, or (the) "pétanque" !
4 — Everywhere where there is a little space
5 — you see players of bowls

NOTES

(1) *Le nord :* [nor] *; l'ouest* [west] : west ; *l'est* [lest] ; east ; *le sud :* south. The South of France is often called *le Midi* (literally : midday).

(2) *Un peu de* : a little. . . *un peu de lait :* a little milk.
Vous voulez du sucre ? Un peu, s'il vous plaît
Do you want some sugar ? A little, please.
peu de (without *un)* : little, few
peu de temps : little time ; *il y a peu de gens qui l'aiment :* few people like it/him/her.
much - many - a lot of : *beaucoup de.*

6 – qui jouent dans les parcs ou sur la place du marché.
7 – C'est‿un jeu qui demande beaucoup d'habileté,
8 – beaucoup de concentration... et un peu de passion.
9 – Mais‿il y a un autre passe-temps en France.
10 – Les gens le font ; ils‿en parlent, ils le vivent à chaque **(3)** moment.
11 – C'est la passion nationale numéro un : bien manger **(4)**.

PRONONCIATION

6 ...park. .marshay
7 ..demohnd. .abiltay
8 ...konsontrassiohn. .passeeohn
10 ...parl. .veev. .shak

EXERCICES

1. C'est un jeu qui vient du Sud de la France. – **2.** Vous voyez des joueurs partout. – **3.** J'aime beaucoup de sucre et un peu de lait dans mon café. – **4.** C'est un jeu que j'aime beaucoup. – **5.** Il y a peu de gens qui le font.

Fill in the blanks

1 C'est un jeu ... demande un ... .. concentration.

It's a game which demands a little concentration.

6 – who play in (the) parks or on the market-place.
7 – It is a game which requires (ask for) a lot of skill
8 – a lot of concentration. . . and a little passion.
9 – But there is another pastime in France.
10 – (The) people do it, they talk about it , they live it at every moment.
11 – It is the number one national passion : eating (to eat) well.

NOTES (suite)

(3) *Chaque :* each, every
Chaque jour, elle fait la même chose : Every day, she does the same thing.

(4) The infinitive, e.g. *manger,* is also used where English would use a gerundive,"eating."
Défense de fumer : No smoking
J'aime marcher : I like walking.

EXERCISES

1. It's a game which comes from the South of France. – **2.** You see players everywhere. – **3.** I like a lot of sugar and a little milk in my coffee. – **4.** It's a game which I like a lot. – **5.** Few people do it.

2 Voilà un livre ... j'aime ....

There's a book which I like a lot.

3 .. voit des .... de boules ....

One sees bowls-players everywhere.

4 .... il va .. cinéma.

He goes to the cinema every Tuesday.

VINGT-CINQUIEME (25ème) LEÇON

Deux histoires drôles

1 — Après une audition, un producteur dit à une chanteuse :
2 — -Mademoiselle, votre chanson est comme l'épée de Charlemagne **(1)**.
3 — Toute fière, la fille dit -Ah bon ? Comment cela ?
4 — -Eh bien elle est longue, plate et mortelle **(2)** !

5 — Deux‿alpinistes sont bloqués dans une tempête de neige.

PRONONCIATION

Deuzeestwar drowl
1 . . .ohdeesseeon
2 . . .epay. .sharlemanye.
3 toot fyair. .fee. .
4 . . .long, plat
5 . . .blockay. . .tompet. .nezh. . .

5 Il aime beaucoup ...... et ..... aux boules.

He loves eating and playing bowls.

Fill in the blanks

1 - qui - peu de - . — **2** - que - beaucoup - — **3** On - joueurs - partout. — **4** Chaque mardi - au - . — **5** manger - jouer -.

25th LESSON

2 funny stories

1 — After an audition, a producer says to a singer :
2 — -Miss, your song is like Charlemagne's sword.
3 — All proud, the girl says -Oh really ? How [is] that ?
4 — Well, it's long, flat and deadly !
5 — Two climbers (alpinists) are blocked in a snowstorm.

NOTES

(1) *L'ami de Pierre :* Peter's friend ; *la voiture de ma femme :* my wife's car ; *La photo de la maison :* the photo of the house.
(2) The masculine forms of these adjectives are *long* [lohn], *plat* [plah] and *mortel.*

6 — Après douze heures ils voient **(3)** arriver un Saint-Bernard
7 — avec un tonneau de cognac autour du cou **(4)**.
8 — -Regardez cela ! **(5)** -dit un des hommes
9 — Voilà le meilleur ami de l'homme !
10 — -Oui, dit l'autre -et regardez la taille du chien qui le porte !

11 — "Tout est bien qui finit bien" !

PRONONCIATION

6 . . .vwa. .san bernar
7 . . .tonnow
9 . . .meyeur.
10 . . .tie. .shee-ehn
11 . . .finee.

EXERCICES

1. Ce livre est long et il n'est pas très intéressant. — **2.** Ecoutez ça ! C'est Georges qui arrive. — **3.** Elle a un chapeau sur la tête et une écharpe autour du cou. — **4.** Vous voyez ceci ? C'est le stylo de Michel. — **5.** Voilà le meilleur ami de l'homme.

Fill in the blanks :

1 La plaine est ...... et ..... .

The plain is long and flat.

2 Il a un parapluie . .. .

He has an umbrella in his hand.

6 – After 12 hours, they see a Saint-Bernard arriving
7 – with a barrel of brandy around it's (the) neck.
8 – Look [at] that ! -says one of the men
9 – There is man's best friend !
10 – Yes, says the other -and look at the size of the dog which [is] carrying it !
11 – "All's well that ends well" (All is well which finishes well).

NOTES (suite)

(3) *Voir* : to see. *Je vois, vous voyez, il/elle voit, nous voyons ils voient* [vwah]. Past participle : *vu.*

(4) *Il a une épée à la main :* he has a sword in his hand.
Elle a un chapeau sur la tête : she has a hat on her head.
autour de : around
J'ai une écharpe autour du cou : I have a scarf around my neck.

(5) *Ceci-cela :* this-that. This book : *ce livre ;* Look at this : *Regardez ceci ;* Listen to that : *Ecoutez cela.*
Ceci and *cela* have only one form each. They are not used to speak of people, nor before nouns. (*cela* is usually always shortened to *ça* in conversation. You know the expression : *Comment ça va ? :* How are you ? In line 3, we see another idiomatic usage *"Comment cela (ça)" ?* This is like our "How come" ?

VOICI LE MEILLEUR AMI DE L'HOMME.

EXERCISES

1. This book is long and it is not very interesting. – **2.** Listen to that ! It's George(s) who is arriving. – **3.** She has a hat on her head and a scarf around her neck. – **4.** You see this ? It's Michael's pen. – **5.** There is man's best friend.

3 " .... est bien ... . bien".

All's well that ends well.

4 Elle est la meilleure amie .. ..

She's my wife's best friend.

VINGT-SIXIEME (26ème) LEÇON

Que fait (1) Monsieur Duclos le matin ?

1 — Nous ‿ avons parlé de ce que (N-5) fait M. Duclos le soir.
2 — Regardons-le maintenant le matin, quand le réveil sonne.
3 — D'abord, il se lève (2). . . très lentement.

PRONONCIATION

2 mantenohn. .matahn. .revay
3 . . . .lontemohn

5 *Put in the correct indefinite article (un or une)*

— chanson ; — chien ; — jeu ; — billet ; — cheval.

Fill in the blanks

1 - longue - plate -. — **2** - à la main - — **3** Tout - qui finit - . — **4** - de ma femme - . — **5** une chanson; un chien ; un jeu ;un billet; un cheval.

26th LESSON

What does M. Duclos [do] [in] the morning ?

1 — We have spoken of what (that which) M. Duclos does [in] the evening.
2 — [Let's] look [at] him now [in] the morning, when the alarm-clock rings.
3 — Firstly, he gets (himself) up. . .very slowly.

NOTES

(1) *Qu'est-ce que vous faites ? :* What are you doing ?
We told you earlier that there were several ways of asking a question, and *(qu')est-ce que* was very common and somewhat "familiar". We so far have seen other ways, and a more "elegant" way of saying : *qu'est-ce que vous faites ?* is the inversion : *que faites-vous ?*
Qu'est-ce que faït M. Duclos ? thus becomes *Que fait M. Duclos ?*
Qu'est-ce que vous mangez ? Que mangez-vous ? : What are you eating ?
The two forms have exactly the same meaning.

(2) We have already seen a couple of reflexive verbs. Let's revise : *se lever :* to get up — *je me lève ; il/elle se lève ; vous vous levez ; nous nous levons ; ils se lèvent* [lev].
Notice that these verbs in this text must be reflexive in French :
se lever, to get up ; *s'habiller :* to get dressed ; *se raser :* to shave, etc. . Another habit to get used to.

4 — Il va à la salle de bains et se lave **(3)** le visage
5 — . . . à l'eau **(4)** froide, pour se réveiller.
6 — Ensuite, il se rase et se brosse les dents.
7 — De retour dans sa chambre, il commence à s'habiller.
8 — Les jours de travail, il met une chemise blanche **(5)**, une cravate bleue
9 — et un costume gris foncé **(6)**.
10 — Il met des chaussettes et des chaussures noires,
11 — et un imperméable s'il pleut.
12 — Enfin, il prend sa serviette et descend dans la rue.

PRONONCIATION

4 . . .lav. .veezazh
5 . .low frwad. .revayay
6 . . .raz. . .dohn
7 . . .sabiyay
8 . . .may. . .kravat
9 . .gree fonssay.
10 . .may. . .nwar
11 . . .ampermayabl seel pleu
12 . . .prohn. .daysohn

EXERCICES

1. -Que faites-vous ? -Je me rase. — **2.** Regardons ce que fait M. Duclos le soir. — **3.** Elle se lave et se brosse les dents. . . très lentement. — **4.** -Que mangez-vous ? -Un poulet à la crème. — **5.** De retour dans sa chambre, il s'habille.

4 – He goes to the bathroom and washes (himself the) his face. . .
5 – (at the) in cold water, to wake (himself) up.
6 – Next, he shaves (himself) and brushes (himself) his teeth.
7 – Back (of return) in his room, he begins to dress (himself).
8 – [On] work-days he puts [on] a white shirt, a blue tie
9 – and a dark-grey suit.
10 – He puts [on] socks and black shoes,
11 – and a raincoat if it is raining.
12 – Finally, he takes his brief case and goes down in [to] the street.

NOTES (suite)

(3) In the *25ème leçon*, we saw how to say : she has a hat on her head : *elle a un chapeau sur la tête.* Here, we see another example of how the parts of the body are not "personalised" with the possessive adjective (my, her, etc..).
Elle se lave le visage : she washes her face.
Je me brosse les dents : I am brushing my teeth.
The French suppose that if we have already mentioned the subject of the sentence, it is superfluous to specify on **whose** head the hat appears. Economical !
(4) *A l'eau chaude :* in hot water. *Ecrire à l'encre verte :* to write in green ink *Poulet à la crème* : chicken in cream sauce. *Danser à la russe :* to dance in the Russian manner. We have examples in American cooking (chicken à la King, for example) of this gallicism.
(5) The masculine form is *blanc* [blahn].
(6) Light (not heavy) is *léger,* but for a colour, we say *clair ;* similarly dark (of a room etc.) is *sombre* but for a colour, we say *foncé* (feminine forms : *légère* [layzhair] *; claire ; sombre ; foncée).*

EXERCISES

1. -What are you doing ? -I am shaving. – **2.** Let's look at what M. Duclos does (in) the evening. – **3.** She washes, and brushes her teeth...very slowly. – **4.** What are you eating ? A chicken in cream (sauce). – **5.** Back in his room he dresses.

Fill in the blanks :

1 Que ...... - .... ce .... ? Je vais dîner ....

Georges.

What are you doing this evening ? I'm going to dinner at George's.

2 Regardons- .. : il .. .... et .. ....

Let's look at him : he is washing and shaving.

3 Il prend .. serviette et .... la rue

He takes his brief case and goes down into the street.

VINGT-SEPTIEME (27ème) LEÇON

Les commerçants

1 – Quand vous voulez (N-6) du pain, vous‿allez chez le boulanger (1).
2 – Là, vous trouvez non seulement des baguettes (2)
3 – mais‿aussi des croissants, des tartes et des gâteaux (3).

PRONONCIATION

Lay komersohn
1 . . .pan. .boolonzhay
2 . . .baget
3 . . . .gatoh

4 Il ... une .... , une cravate .....

et des .... noires.

He puts on a white shirt, a blue tie and black shoes.

5 Elle .. .... toujours . . ' ... froide

She always washes in cold water.

Fill in the blanks

1 - faites-vous - soir - chez- — **2** -le - se lave - se rase. — **3** sa - descend - dans - — **4** met - chemise blanche - bleue - chaussures.— **5** se lave - à l'eau-.

27th LESSON

(the) Tradesmen

1 — When you want bread, you go to the baker's.
2 — There, you find not only "baguettes"
3 — but also croissants, tarts and cakes.

NOTES

(1) In English, we can say : I go to the baker's **or** to the bakery. The same distinction exists in French.
For the first, we say *chez le boulanger* and for the second *à la boulangerie.* We recommend using *chez* because it familiarises you with this extremely common idiom.

(2) A *"baguette"* is a long, thin, crusty loaf baked fresh every day. One can also ask for *"un pain"* (a thicker baguette) or *"un pain de campagne"* (country bread). The word for loaf *(miche)* is never used when ordering in a baker's.

(3) *un gâteau — des gâteaux ; un bateau* (a boat) — *des bateaux*

4 — Si vous avez besoin (4) de viande, vous allez chez le boucher.
5 — Vous pouvez (5) y (6) acheter toutes sortes de viandes et de volailles ;
6 — et si vous avez envie (N-6) de bon jambon, ou de pâté
7 — ou d'autres produits du porc, vous allez chez le charcutier (7).
8 — Le lait, le beurre, la crème et les oeufs (8) :
9 — on les trouve à la crèmerie (1).
10 — Chez l'épicier, il y a des conserves, du thé, du vin. . .
11 — Et quand vous avez mangé tout ce que vous avez acheté. . .
12 — vous allez à la pharmacie - pour acheter de l'Alka-Seltzer !

VOUS Y TROUVEREZ TOUTES SORTES DE VIANDES ET VOLAILLES.

PRONONCIATION

4 . . .bezwan. .veeond. . .booshay
5 . . . .voleye
6 . . .onvee. .zhombohn
7 . .prodwee. .por. . .sharkooteeay
8 . .lay. .krem. .layzeu
10 . . .eppeesseeay. .konsairv. .tay
11 . . .monzhay tooske. .ashtay
12 . .farmassee

4 – If you (have) need (of) meat, you go to the butcher's.
5 – You can buy there all sorts of meats and poultry ;
6 – and if you (have) want (of) good ham or (of) pâté
7 – or other pork products, you go to the "charcutier".
8 – Milk, butter, cream and eggs :
9 – they are found (one finds them) at the creamery.
10 – At the grocer's, there are tinned foods, tea, wine. .
11 – And when you have eaten everything (all) that you have bought. . .
12 – you go to the chemist's -to buy (of) Alka-Seltzer !

NOTES (suite)

(4) Here is another idiom with *avoir (Leçon 21 N3) :*
avoir besoin de : to need.
Elle a besoin de vacances : She needs a holiday
J'ai besoin d'une allumette : I need a match ; *un besoin* : a need.

(5) *Pouvoir :* to be able - can ; *je peux ; il/elle peut ; vous pouvez nous pouvons ; ils peuvent* [perv] (irregular).

(6) We have already seen how *en* is used to avoid repeating a noun
Vous avez des cigarettes ? J'en ai deux.
In the same way, *y* is used to avoid repeating a place-name or location :
Vous connaissez Paris ? – J'y vis : I live here/there -
We'll see *y* in more detail later.

(7) Untranslatable, despite the "pork-butcher's" of so many dictionaries : perhaps the nearest equivalent is an American "delicatessen".
A *charcutier* sells pork products, salads, "quiches". . .and so much more !

(8) Notice the irregular pronunciation [layzeuh] ; another word with the same pronunciation is *un boeuf* [beuf] : an ox - *des boeufs* [beuh]

EXERCICES

1. Je veux du lait, du beurre, et des oeufs, s'il vous plaît. – **2.** Allez chez le boulanger et achetez deux baguettes. – **3.** Que faites-vous quand vous avez mangé ? -Je me couche ! **4.** Vous y trouvez toutes sortes de viandes et volailles. – **5.** Il ne peut pas trouver de jambon.

Fill in the blanks :

1 C'est .... vous avez mangé, mon enfant ?

This is all you have eaten, my child ?

2 Elle . ... de ....

She needs a holiday.

VINGT-HUITIEME (28ème) LEÇON

REVISION ET NOTES

1 *On* is extensively used in French, often when in English we could use the passive voice.
On dit qu'en France . . . It is said that, in France. . .
On chante souvent cette chanson. . . . This song is often sung.
On le trouve chez l'épicier. . . It can be found at the grocer's
Or when the person who is the subject is unknown.
On vous demande au téléphone : Someone is asking for

EXERCISES

1. I want some milk, some butter and some eggs, please. – **2.** Go to the baker's and buy 2 baguettes. – **3.** What do you do when you have eaten ? -I go to bed ! – **4.** You find there all sorts of meat and poultry. – **5.** He can't find any ham.

3 Il fait chaud. J' .. .. ' une glace.

It's warm (weather). I feel like an ice-cream.

4 Ils .. .. venir avant .... heures.

They cannot come before eight o'clock.

5 .... le charcutier .. trouve du ...... et du pâté.

At the "charcutier's" one finds ham and pâté.

Fill in the blanks

1 - tout ce que - – **2** - a besoin - vacances - – **3** - ai envie d'– – **4** - ne peuvent pas -huit - – **5** Chez - on - jambon.

28th LESSON

you on the phone. And in modern **spoken** French, *on* is used instead of *nous.*
On arrive à huit heures : We're arriving at eight.
You will get the feel of it after a few more examples.

2 L'alphabet [alfabey] français

A [ah] B [bay] C [say] D [day] E [euh] F [eff]
G [zhay] H [ash] I [ee] J [zhee] K [ka] L [el]
M [em] N [en] O [oh] P [pay] Q [kiou] R [air]

S [ess] T [tay] U [iou] V [vay] W [doublevay]
X [eeks] Y [eegrek] Z [zed]

3 Here is the last group of French verbs : those which end in -IR.
Choisir : to choose ; *je choisis ; il/elle choisit ; nous choisissons ; vous choisissez ; ils choisissent* [shwazeess]
finir : to finish
je finis ; il/elle finit ; nous finissons ; vous finissez ; ils finissent [feeneess].
Conjugate these verbs :
dormir (to sleep) ; *sentir* (to feel/to smell)
servir (to serve) ; *définir* (to define)

4 **Numbers** (continued)
20 : *vingt* – 21 : *ving-et-un* – 22 : *vingt-deux* etc...
30 : *trente* – 40 : *quarante* [karont] – 50 : *cinquante* [*sankont*] – 60 : *soixante* [swassont]

A different system applies for 70, 80, et 90 :
70 : *soixante-dix* (60 + 10) so we continue to add to the 10 – 71 : *soixante-et-onze* – 72 : *soixante-douze* – 73 : *soixante-treize,* etc. . .
80 : *quatre-vingt* (4 x 20) so we continue to add to the 20 – 81 : *quatre-vingt-un* – 82 : *quatre-vingt-deux,* etc. .
90 : *quatre-vingt-dix* (4 x 20 + 10) – 91 : *quatre-vingt-onze.* – *92 : quatre-vingt-douze* – 93 : *quatre-vingt-treize,* etc. . .

Don't worry about the spelling for the time being and remember that reacting to numbers automatically takes a lot of practise.

5 who. . . which (that) . . . In English, the use of this relative pronoun depends on whether the preceding noun is animate (who) or inanimate (which or that). In French, the use of the relative depends on whether the noun is the subject or the object of the sentence ; whether it is animate or not is irrelevant.

SUBJECT : *QUI* OBJECT : *QUE*

The bread **which** is in my plate. The bread : subject : *qui.*
Le pain **qui** *est dans mon assiette.*
The bread which I am eating. The bread : object : *que.*
Le pain **que** *je mange.*
The man (whom) I know : *l'homme que je connais.*
The man who is speaking : *l'homme qui parle.*
Any difficulty we might have comes from the English tendency to leave out the object relative pronoun (the man I know, etc..) and sometimes we are not sure about the subject and the object. French is so much clearer.
NEVER omit the relative pronoun in French.

-ce que — -ce qui : what (that) depending again on whether WHAT is subject or object of the verb following :

Vous mangez **ce que** *vous achetez* : you eat what you buy
Dites-moi **ce qui** *vous intéresse :* tell me what interests you
Don't worry about these points of grammar : they are guidelines to aid your assimilation : they are **explanations** not **instructions.**

6 *vouloir* : to want

je veux [veuh] *; il/elle veut ; nous voulons ; vous voulez ; ils veulent* [verl].

avoir envie de ; j'ai envie de, etc.. expresses the feeling that one wants something for one's pleasure ; it conveys the English idiom "I feel like.."
Je veux une réponse ! : I want an answer !
J'ai envie d'une glace : I feel like an ice-cream
J'ai envie d'un bain : I'd like a bath, etc. .
(when offering something, we always use : *vouloir*)
Voulez-vous du café ? etc. . .

VINGT-NEUVIEME (29ème) LEÇON

Questions ridicules

1 — -Lequel (1) est le plus lourd (N-1) : un kilo de plomb ou un kilo de plumes ?
2 — -Ben, un kilo de plomb, bien sûr.
3 — Le plomb est plus lourd que les plumes !
4 — -Mais non ! un kilo, c'est‿un kilo. Ils‿ont le même poids (2).

5 — -Qu'est- ce que vous pensez de mon nouveau petit‿ami ? (3)
6 — -Il est sans doute plus‿intelligent que le dernier
7 — et il est plus beau (4) et plus gentil aussi.
8 — Mais. . . il a un petit défaut : il bégaie (5)

NOUS AVONS UNE TRÈS BELLE VOITURE AMÉRICAINE.

PRONONCIATION

1 . . .lekel. .loor. .plohn. .plyoom
4 . . .pwa
5 . . .noovow peteetamee
6 . .derneeay
7 . . .boh. .zhontee
8 . . .dayfoh. .begay

29th LESSON

Ridiculous questions

1 — Which is the heavier (the most heavy), a kilo of lead or a kilo of feathers ?
2 — Hemm, a kilo of lead, of course.
3 — (The) lead is heavier (more heavy) than (the) feathers !
4 — (But) no ! a kilo is a kilo. They have the same weight.

5 — What do you think of my new boy-friend (little friend) ?
6 — He's without doubt more intelligent than the last [one]
7 — and he is more handsome and kinder too.
8 — But . . he has a small failing : he stammers

NOTES

(1) *lequel de ces livres voulez-vous ?* : which one of these books do you want ?
Laquelle de ces montres préférez-vous ? : Which of these watches do you prefer ?
Lequel, laquelle (plural *lesquels*) is used to discover a person's choice or preference.
(2) *poids :* weight - is a singular noun despite the final *s.* Like in English (series ; means ; etc.) French has a few such singular nouns. Of course, they do not alter in the plural.
(3) You are probably beginning to "feel" the position of the adjective in French by now. Usually, we place it after the noun. However here are some which we place before :
grand (big) - *petit* (small) - *long* (long) - *haut* [oh] (high) - *joli* (pretty) - *beau* (beautiful, handsome) - *jeune* (young) *vieux* [vieuh] (old) - *bon* (good, kind) - *mauvais* (bad) . Continuous contact will make this become a reflex.
(4) *Beau* in the feminine is *belle.* Since we put it before the noun, there is a third form which is used if a masculine noun begins with a vowel : *un bel appartement.*
(5) *Bégayer* : to stammer, behaves like *payer* : to pay.
je paie ; il/elle paie ; nous payons; vous payez ; ils/elles paient [*pay*].

9 – -Oui, d'accord, mais seulement quand il parle !

10 – -Alors ma chérie (6), j'ai deux pommes.
11 – Laquelle voulez-vous ? -La plus grosse !

PRONONCIATION

11 lakel

EXERCICES

1. Laquelle de ces deux pommes voulez-vous ? – **2.** Vous payez l'addition à la caisse, * monsieur. – **3.** Elle est plus belle que ma soeur. – **4.** Nous avons une très belle voiture américaine. – **5.** Qu'est-ce qu'ils pensent du nouveau film ?

* la caisse : the cash-desk.

Fill in the blanks :

1 ...... est le .... de ces deux ?

Which is the heavier of these two ?

2 Cet exercice est .... que le ....

This exercise is longer than the last (one).

3 Ils ont un ... appartement et une ....

They have a beautiful apartment and a large house.

9 – Yes, O.K, but only when he talks !

10 – Well, my darling, I have two apples
11 – Which [one] do you want ? The biggest (more big)!

NOTES (suite)

(6) A term of affection which is used less indiscriminately than in English : *mon chéri ; ma chérie.*
We begin a letter with *Cher . . . (Chère) . . .* (Dear).

EXERCISES

1. Which of these two apples do you want ? – **2.** You pay the bill at the cash-desk, sir. – **3.** She is more beautiful than my sister. – **4.** We have a very beautiful American car. – **5.** What do they think of the new film ?

4 Ils ont le .... non !

They have the same weight. Of course not !

5 Qu'est-ce qu' ... . de .. .. petite amie ?

What do they think of this new girl-friend ?

Fill in the blanks

1 Lequel - plus lourd -. – **2** - plus long - dernier. – **3** - bel - grande maison. – **4** - même poids - Mais - – **5** - ils pensent - sa nouvelle.

TRENTIEME (30ème) LEÇON

Chez Monsieur Duclos.

1 — L'appartement de Monsieur Duclos est composé de deux pièces **(1)**,
2 — d'une cuisine et d'une salle de bains.
3 — Il se trouve dans‿un vieil **(2)** immeuble dans la banlieue parisienne.
4 — Il y a six‿étages . . et une concierge ! **(3)**
5 — Il vous‿ouvre la porte et vous‿arrivez dans l'entrée.
6 — A droite, il y a la cuisine et, à côté, la salle de bains.
7 — Plus loin, on voit la pièce principale, le salon **(4)**
8 — qui est meublé **(5)** avec beaucoup de goût **(6)**.

GOÛTEZ CE GÂTEAU !
IL EST DÉLICIEUX.

PRONONCIATION

1 . . . .pee-ess
2 . . .kweezeen
3 . . .vyayimmeubl. .bonlyeu
4 . .seezaytahzh. .konsee-airzh
5 . .ontray
6 . .akotay. .
7 . .lwan. .vwa. .salohn
8 . .meublay. .goo

30th LESSON

[At] M. Duclos '

1 — The apartment of M. Duclos is composed of 2 rooms
2 — (of) a kitchen and (of) a bathroom.
3 — It is located (finds itself) in an old building in the suburbs of Paris.
4 — There are 6 floors . .and a "concierge" !.
5 — He opens the door [for] you and you arrive in the entrance [hall].
6 — To (at) [the] right there is a kitchen and, next to it, (to side) the bathroom.
7 — Further, one sees the main room, the living room
8 — which is furnished with much taste.

NOTES

(1) *Une pièce* here means a room in general ; *une chambre* is a bedroom. *Une salle* is used to mean a large room in a public building, or in compound nouns like *salle de bains* or *salle à manger* (dining room).
Il habite un deux-pièces is a familiar way of saying he lives in a two-roomed apartment.
(2) *Vieux* in the feminine is *vieille,* and before a masculine noun beginning with a vowel, *vieil.*
mon vieil ami : my old (male) friend (see Lesson 29 note 4)
un immeuble is a block of flats.
(3) *Une* (or *un)* *concierge* is a French institution. It is a person who is paid to look after the building, distribute mail.. .. and keep out unwelcome visitors ! They have a reputation for gossip, whose justification we will not enter into here...
(4) This is the correct word for the front room of a house or flat ; however, most younger people say : *un living !*
(5) *Un meuble :* a piece of furniture ; *des meubles :* furniture
un appartement non meublé : an unfurnished flat
(6) *goûter* . to taste. *Goûtez cette soupe ! :* Taste this soup !
un goût : a taste
La soupe a un goût étrange : the soup has a strange taste. It also means a taste in the sense of preference. In cafés, you will see the word *déguster* : *Dégustez nos vins .* This more formal word indicates physical tasting **and** appreciation.
Une dégustation de vin : a wine-tasting

9 — Il y a deux beaux fauteuils et un canapé confortable **(7)**.
10 — Au milieu de la pièce, il y a une table basse **(8)**.
11 — Derrière, sur les murs, il a pendu des jolis tableaux.
12 — Les fenêtres du salon donnent sur une petite cour.

PRONONCIATION

9 . . .fohtoy. .kanapay
11 . . .pondyoo. .tabloh
12 . . . . .koor

EXERCICES

1. Ils habitent dans un vieil immeuble dans la banlieue parisienne. – **2.** Goûtez ce gâteau ! Il est délicieux. – **3.** Il y a un salon, une chambre et une salle à manger. – **4.** Je vais acheterun joli meuble pour ma cuisine. – **5.** Sur les murs, ils ont pendu des jolis tableaux.

Fill in the correct prepositions :

1 . . . . la porte

Behind the door

2 . . . . de la pièce

In the middle of the room

9 – There are two handsome armchairs and a comfortable couch.
10 – In the middle of the room, there is a low table
11 – Behind, on the walls, he has hung pretty paintings.
12 – The windows of the living-room give on [to] a small court yard.

NOTES (suite)

(7) *Confortable* (notice the spelling) is never applied to a person, like in English : *Are you sitting comfortably ?*
In French, we say : *Etes-vous bien assis ?*
I am comfortable here : *je suis bien ici*

(8) *Basse* in the masculine is *bas* [ba]

EXERCISES

1. They live in an old building in the Paris suburbs. – **2.** Taste this cake ! It's delicious. – **3.** There is a living-room, a bedroom and a dining-room. – **4.** I'm going to buy a (piece of) pretty furniture for my kitchen. – **5.** On the walls, they have hung pretty paintings.

3 ... les murs

On the walls

4 . .... de la cuisine

Next to the kitchen

5 ....

Further

6 .... la banlieue

In the suburbs

7 . ...

On the right

TRENTE ET UNIEME (31ème) LEÇON

Chez M. Duclos (suite)

1 — Dans sa chambre, M. Duclos a un grand lit,
2 — une armoire où il range - parfois - ses vêtements **(1)**
3 — et une table de nuit ; un réveil électrique est posé dessus **(2)**.
4 — Tout‿autour de la chambre, il y a des photographies
5 — des beaux paysages de France.
6 — M. Duclos est citadin mais il rêve de vivre à la campagne **(3)**

PRONONCIATION

1 . . . .lee
2 . . .armwar. . parfwa. .vetmoh
3 . . .nwee. . .dessyoo
4 . . .fohtografee
5 . . .payeezazh
6 . . .seetadan. .kompanye

8 . ...

On the left

Fill in the blanks

1 Derrière – **2** Au milieu – **3** Sur – **4** A côté – **5** Plus loin – **6** Dans – **7** A droite – **8** A gauche

---

31st LESSON

At M. Duclos (continued)

1 – In the bedroom, M. Duclos has a large bed,
2 – a wardrobe where he puts away -sometimes- his clothes
3 – and a night-table ; an electric alarm clock is placed on [it].
4 – All around the bedroom there are photographs
5 – of (the) beautiful landscapes of France
6 – M. Duclos is [a] city dweller but he dreams of living (to live) in the country.

NOTES

(1) We saw, in the last lesson, that *un meuble* is a piece of furniture. Here is another example of the logic of French when dealing with what in English are collective nouns : *Les vêtements :* clothes ; *un vêtement :* a piece of clothing *les‿informations* : the news information ; *une information :* a news item, a piece of information.
We'll point out more of these as we go along.

(2) *Sur la table :* on the table ; *sous la chaise* : under the chair. When *sur* is not followed directly by a noun, we say *dessus.* Do not confuse this preposition with the adjective *sûr,* which means "sure" or "safe". (We have seen *bien sûr).* The pronunciation is the same.

(3) *La ville :* the town ; *en ville :* in town (or city). *La campagne :* the country (side) ; *un paysage :* a landscape. The geographical country is *un pays* [payee] (although the French also use this word to describe a region).

7 – Néanmoins, il a des voisins sympathiques **(4)**.
8 – L'appartement au-dessus **(2)** appartient à un homme d'affaires
9 – qui voyage beaucoup et qui n'est jamais chez lui **(N-2)**
10 – et en-dessous **(2)** vit un vieil homme sourd.
11 – Donc M. Duclos n'a jamais de problèmes de bruit !

PRONONCIATION

7 Nayonmwan. .vwazan sampateek
8 . . .ohdessyoo aparteean
9 . . .vwayahzh. .zhamay
10 . . .vee eun vyayom soor
11 . . . .brwee

EXERCICES

1. Ses voisins sont très sympathiques. – **2.** En France, il y a des paysages magnifiques. – **3.** Elles rêvent de vivre à la campagne. – **4.** N'avez-vous jamais de problèmes de bruit ? – **5.** Où est-ce que vous rangez vos vêtements ?

Fill in the blanks :

1 .... de la chambre

All around the room

2 L'appartement .. - ......

The flat above

7 — Nevertheless, he has nice neighbours.
8 — The flat above belongs to a businessman
9 — who travels a lot and is (not) never at (his) home,
10 — and below lives an old, deaf man.
11 — Thus, M. Duclos (not) never has problems of noise !

NOTES (suite)

(4) A very important and common word which translates as nice, kind, pleasant, etc. (but not "sympathetic"!). In familiar parlance, people contract it to *sympa* . There is a famous radio programme (and bumper sticker) *Les routiers sont sympas* (Truck drivers are nice guys).

EXERCISES

1. His neighbours are very nice. — **2.** In France, there are magnificent landscapes. — **3.** They dream of living in the country. — **4.** Don't you (n)ever have problems of noise ? — **5.** Where do you put away your clothes ?

EN FRANCE, IL Y A DES PAYSAGES MAGNIFIQUES.

3 L'étage .. ..

The floor below

4 ... table avec .. livre posé ......

A table with a book (placed) on it

TRENTE-DEUXIEME (32ème) LEÇON

Le métro

1 — La meilleure façon de visiter Paris, c'est à pied (1)
2 — mais si vous voulez aller d'un endroit à un autre rapidement (2)
3 — faites comme (3) les Parisiens : prenez le métro.
4 — Le système est très efficace et en plus il n'est pas cher.
5 — Le prix de votre ticket ne dépend (4) pas de la longueur du trajet :

PRONONCIATION

1 . . .mayeur fassohn. .setapeeay
2 . . .ondrwa
4 . . .trayzefeekass. .onplyooss
5 . .pree. .teekay.daypohn

5 Elle . ' est ...... chez .... .

She is never at home

Fill in the blanks

1 tout autour — **2** en dessus — **3** au dessous — **4** une - un - dessus — **5** n' - jamais - elle.

32nd LESSON

The metro (Underground)

1 — The best way (fashion) to visit Paris (it) is on foot
2 — but if you want to go from one place to another quickly
3 — do like the Parisians [do] : take the metro.
4 — The system is very efficient and what's more (in more), it is not expensive.
5 — The price of your ticket does not depend on (of) the length of the journey :

NOTES

(1) *en voiture* : by car ; *en bus :* by bus *; en avion :* by plane ; *à pied :* on foot.

(2) By now you have probably realized how to form adverbs : we *add -ment* to the feminine form of the adjective.
lent (slow) *lentement* : slowly
heureux (happy) *heureusement* : happily, fortunately
There are a few irregular forms which we will look at later.

(3) *comme* : like, as *Faites comme moi* : Do as I do *Il parle français comme un Français* : He speaks French like a Frenchman. *Elle est belle comme une fleur :* she is as beautiful as a flower.

(4) *dépendre :* to depend behaves like *vendre* : to sell. *je dépends il/elle dépend ; nous dépendons ; vous dépendez ; ils dépendent* [dehpond]
Notice the postposition : *de*
Il dépend de ses parents : he depends on his parents.

6 – il coûte le même prix pour deux stations **(5)** que pour dix.
7 – Les trains roulent **(6)** tous les jours, de cinq heures et demie
8 – jusqu'à une heure du matin.
9 – Pour aller de Vincennes au Quartier Latin, prenez la ligne numéro un.
10 – Vous changez à Châtelet et vous descendez à Saint-Michel.
11 – "La deuxième voiture, c'est le métro !"

PRONONCIATION

7 . . . too lay zhoor
8 . . .zhooska
9 . . .vansen. .karteeay latan
11 . . . vwatyoor

EXERCICES

1. Ils veulent y aller à pied. – **2.** Les Parisiens prennent le métro tous les jours. – **3.** Faites attention : En Angleterre, on roule à gauche ! – **4.** Nous changeons notre voiture la semaine prochaine. – **5.** Le métro est ouvert jusqu'à une heure du matin.

Fill in the blanks :

1 Il parle .. français ....

He speaks French like I do.

2 Ceux-ci coûtent le .... prix ... ceux-là

These ones cost the same price as those ones.

6 — It costs the same price for 2 stations as for 10.
7 — The trains run (roll) every day, from 5.30
8 — to 1.00 in (of) the morning.
9 — To go from Vincennes to the Latin Quarter, take (the) line number one.
10 — You change at Châtelet and you get off (descend) at Saint-Michel.
11 — "The second car (it) is the metro!"

NOTES (suite)

(5) *Une station de métro* : a metro station **but** *une gare* : a train station. *La Gare du Nord* : Paris North Railway Station. When asking for a metro station, we usually ask for just the name (see Lesson I). The metro and buses are run by the R.A.T.P. (*Régie Autonome des Transports Parisiens).*

(6) *rouler* means literally to roll :
Il roule ses cigarettes : He rolls his cigarettes.
It is also used as we use "run" or "drive" in English :
En France, on roule à droite : In France, people drive on the right.
Vous roulez trop vite ! : You're driving too fast !

EXERCISES

1. They want to go there on foot. — **2.** The Parisians take the metro every day. — **3.** Be careful : in England, they drive (one drives) on the left ! — **4.** We are changing our car next week. — **5.** The metro is open until one o'clock in the morning.

3 Il est .... et, ... il . ' est ... cher.

It is efficient and, what's more, it is not expensive.

4 Elle parle .... ' .... et

....

She speaks slowly, clearly and distinctly. (*)

TRENTE-TROISIEME (33ème) LEÇON

Quelques questions

1 Que font les Parisiens quand‿ils veulent voyager rapidement ?
2 Pourquoi le métro est-‿il bon marché **(1)** ?
3 Combien de billets y-a-t-il **(N-3)** dans un carnet ? (réponse phrase 10 !)
4 Comment va-t-on de Vincennes au Quartier Latin ?
5 Quel est le nom de la station où on change de ligne ?

PRONONCIATION

3 . . .eeyateel
4 . . .vaton
Oh geeshay

5 Il ..... le train ici, il ...... à Châtelet et il .... à Vincennes.

He takes the train here, he changes at Châtelet and he gets off at Vincennes.

(*) clear : *clair* ; distinct : *distinct*

Fill in the blanks

1 le - comme moi. — **2** - même - que. — **3** efficace - en plus - n - pas. — **4** lentement - clairement - distinctement. — **5** - prend - change - descend.

33rd LESSON

A few questions

1 What do the Parisians [do] when they want to travel quickly ?
2 Why is the metro cheap ?
3 How many tickets are there in a "carnet" ? (answer sentence 10 !)
4 How [does] one go from Vincennes to the Latin Quarter ?
5 What is the name of the station where one changes (of) line ?

NOTES

(1) *bon marché* literally is a good market, i.e. not expensive, so, as an adjective, *bon marché* means cheap (the opposite is *cher* : expensive, dear).
bon is an irregular adjective (like good in English). Its comparative is *meilleur* and its superlative *le meilleur,* so cheaper is *meilleur marché.*
Ce magasin est meilleur marché que l'autre : this shop is cheaper than the other ; *bon marché* **has no feminine nor plural form**

Au guichet

6 (Un touriste demande **(2)** un ticket)
7 — -Un aller-retour **(3)** pour la Gare de l'Est s'il vous plaît
8 — -Mais monsieur, il n'y a pas de billets aller-retour
9 et d'ailleurs **(4)** le ticket coûte toujours le même prix ;
10 mais prenez plutôt **(5)** un carnet **(6)** de dix tickets.
11 — D'accord. Ça fait combien ? **(7)**

PRONONCIATION

7 . .allay retoor
9 . .die-eur
10 . .karnay . .dee. .

COMBIEN DE PLACES
Y-A-T-IL DANS VOTRE
VOITURE ?

EXERCICES

1. Que faites-vous le samedi ? - Je travaille. — **2.** Ces billets d'avion coûtent très cher ! — **3.** Comment allez-vous de Paris à Lyon ? En train ? — **4.** Téléphonez chez Jean et demandez Michel. Il vous attend. — **5.** Combien de places y-a-t-il dans votre voiture ?.

At the ticket office

6 (A tourist [is] asking [for] a ticket)
7 – A return to (for) the East Station, please.
8 – But sir, there are no return tickets
9 and, moreover the ticket costs always the same price
10 But take rather a "carnet" of 10 tickets.
11 – O.K. How much is that ?

NOTES (suite)

(2) *demander* means only "to ask for" (to demand is *exiger* [egzeezhay]). Notice the lack of postposition :
Vous demandez M. Dupont ? : You're asking for M. Dupont ?

(3) *un ticket* is used for a bus or metro ticket **only**, otherwise we use billet [beeyay] *un (billet) aller-retour* : a return (ticket) - literally "to go, to return". a one-way (ticket) is *un (billet) aller-simple* [sampl]

(4) *ailleurs* [eye-eur] means elsewhere, somewhere else.
Je n'en ai pas ; essayez ailleurs : I don't have any ; try somewhere else. *D'ailleurs* means furthermore or moreover, but is much more common than these two words in English.

(5) *plutôt* : rather - *Il fait plutôt chaud* : it's rather hot.
But after an imperative verb it means "instead" or "why don't you. .? " *Allez plutôt chez Fournier ; c'est meilleur* : Why don't you go to Fournier's ; it's better. – *Essayez plutôt ceci* : try this instead.

(6) *un carnet* : a small exercise-book ; *un carnet d'adresses* : an address-book ; *un carnet de chèques* [shek] : a check book. In the metro, it means a booklet of ten tickets. Buying them like this saves you about 20%. You say : – *Un carnet, s'il vous plaît.*

(7) *Ça fait combien ?* or *ça me fait combien ?* are very common idiomatic ways of saying *combien ça coûte ?*
You use them to ask for a bill, or when the cashier has totalled your purchases, etc. . .

EXERCISES

1. What do you do on (the) Saturday ? — I work. – **2.** These plane tickets cost a lot ! (very dear !) – **3.** How do you go from Paris to Lyons ? By train ? – **4.** Telephone John's and ask for Michael. He's waiting for you. – **5.** How many seats (places) are there in your car ?.

Fill in the blanks :

1 .... à John. Il est .... en français.

Ask John instead. He's better at (in) French.

2 Pourquoi le métro ... - .. .. ici ?

Why is the metro cheaper here ?

3 Comment .. - . - .. .. Quartier Latin ?

How does one get to the Latin Quarter ?

TRENTE-QUATRIEME (34ème) LEÇON

La galerie d'art

1 Un vieux colonel fait le tour d'une galerie avec un guide.
2 Il s'arrête **(1)** devant un tableau et il déclare :
3 — Celui-ci **(2)** c'est‿un Monet. Je le reconnais **(3)**.

PRONONCIATION

. . .dar
1 . . .kolonel
3 Selyooee-see. .monay. .rekonay

4 . . . . de lettres . . . - . - il dans ce mot ?

How many letters are there in this word ?

5 Je n' . .´ . . pas : essayez . . . .

I don't have any : try somewhere else.

Fill in the blanks

1 Demandez plutôt - meilleur. — **2** est-il meilleur marché - ? — **3** va-t-on au - ? — **4** Combien - y a-t- - ? — **5** en ai - ailleurs.

34th LESSON

The Art Gallery

1 An old colonel [is] doing the tour of an art gallery with a guide.
2 He stops (himself) in front of a picture and he declares :
3 — This [one] here (it) is a Monet. I recognize it.

NOTES

(1) *arrêter* : to stop something - or somebody - *Elle arrête sa voiture* : she stops her car. *s'arrêter* : to stop. *Le bus s'arrête devant l'église* : the bus stops in front of the church *(un arrêt* [array] *de bus* : a bus-stop).
This use of the reflexive form is much more common than in English.

(2) *celui-ci ; celui-là* : this one here ; that one there.
You must imagine someone pointing to one then to the other : we call these "demonstrative" pronouns.
The feminine forms are *celle-ci* and *celle-là.* We will look at the plural and other uses in later lessons. The construction of the sentence in line 3 is an alternative to that in line 5. The first is more idiomatic.

(3) *reconnaître* : to recognize *je reconnais ; il/elle reconnait ; nous reconnaissons ; vous reconnaissez ; ils/elles reconnaissent* [rekoness] - past participle *reconnu.*

4 Timidement, le guide dit : -Vous vous trompez (4), mon colonel (5),
5 celui-ci est un Seurat (2), celui-là est un Monet.
6 – Oui, bien sûr, dit le connaisseur, un peu gêné (6).
7 Il s'arrête devant une statue ; tout de suite (7), il dit :
8 – Très bien : cette statue est un Degas !
9 – Pas du tout, mon colonel ; celle-ci est un Rodin.
10 – D'accord, mais regardez-moi (8) ça : c'est certainement un Picasso.
11 – Eh bien non, mon colonel ; celui-là, c'est un miroir !

12 celui-ci ; celui-là ; celle-ci ; celle-là.

EST-CE QUE ÇA VOUS GÈNE SI JE FUME ?

PRONONCIATION

4 Timeedmohn. .trompay
5 . .seura. .selyooee-la
6 . .zhenay
7 . .statyoo. .toot-sweet
8 . .dayga. . .selsee. .rohdan
10 . .sertenmohn
11 . . .meerwah

4 Timidly, the guide says : -You're making a mistake, (my) colonel.

5 this [one] here is a Seurat ; that [one] there is a Monet.

6 – Yes, of course, says the connaisseur, a little embarrassed.

7 He stops (himself) in front of a statue ; at once, he says :

8 – Very well ; this statue is a Degas !

9 – Not at all (my) colonel ; this [one] here is a Rodin.

10 – O.K., but look (me) [at] that : it's certainly a Picasso

11 – Well, no, (my) colonel ; that [one] there (it) is a mirror !

12 This [one] here ; that [one] there (masculine form) ; this [one] here ; that [one] there (feminine form).

NOTES (suite)

(4) *se tromper* : to make a mistake, to confuse.
Il se trompe de veste : he takes the wrong jacket.
Si je ne me trompe pas : If I'm not mistaken.
Here, the guide tells the colonel that he is confusing two painters (you are wrong : *vous‿avez tort).*

(5) In the French army, one always put *"mon"* before the rank mentioned, except for *sergent* and *caporal* ; *mon capitaine, mon lieutenant,* etc . . *un soldat* : a soldier ; *l'armée* (f.) : the army. *Le service militaire* : military service -

(6) *gêner* is a word with many meanings, here we see it as "to be embarrassed, put out". We find it in expressions like :
Est-ce que ça vous gêne si je fume ? : does it bother you if I smoke ? or *Est-ce que le bruit vous gêne ? :* Does the noise bother you ? We will point out other uses as they come up.

(7) Notice the pronunciation : [toot-sweet]. This simply means "straight away" "at once" Immediately *: immédiatement.*

(8) An emphatic, idiomatic way of attracting someone's attention. You could say *Regardez ça !* adding *moi* makes the imperative more forceful. It is commonly found with this verb and with *écouter* (to listen). *Ecoutez-moi cette lettre !* : Would you listen to this letter !

EXERCICES

1. Je commence à huit heures et je m'arrête à quatre heures et quart. – **2.** Michel ! Venez ici tout de suite ! – **3.** Regardez-moi ça ! C'est un Picasso - Pas du tout ! – **4.** Celui-ci, c'est mon frère et celui-là c'est mon meilleur ami. – **5.** Est-ce que ça vous gêne si je fume ?

Fill in the blanks

1 Vous .... ' étage ; il habite au ....

You've got the wrong floor ; he lives at the sixth.

2 ..... - .. c'est un .... et ..... - ..

c'est une statue.

This one here is a painting and that one there is a statue.

3 Le bus . ' .... sa porte.

The bus stops in front of his (her) door.

TRENTE-CINQUIEME (35ème) LEÇON

REVISION ET NOTES

1 *Comparaison d'adjectifs.* Whereas English has two ways of making comparisons - er -est ; more -most, French has only one :
grand : big, tall ; *plus grand* : bigger ; *le plus grand :* the biggest.
intéressant : interesting ; *plus intéressant ; le plus intéressant. – Ce livre est plus intéressant que l'autre :* this

EXERCISES

1. I begin at 8.00 and I stop at 4.15 – **2.** Michel ! Come here at once !. – **3.** -Would you look at that ! It's a Picasso. -Not at all !. – **4.** This one here is my brother and that one there is my best friend. – **5.** Does it bother you if I smoke ?

4 J'espère ... la fumée ne ....

I hope the smoke doesn't bother you.

5 Est-ce-que vous .... - .. ?

Do you recognize this one here ?

Fill in the blanks

1 - vous trompez d - sixième. – **2** Celui ci - tableau - celle-là. – **3** - s'arrête devant - – **4** - que - vous gêne pas. – **5** - reconnaissez - celui-ci.

35th LESSON

book is more interesting than the other one.
Il est plus fort que moi : he is stronger than me,
mais je suis plus intelligent que lui : but I am more intelligent than him. (Notice that, in English, when we are comparing only two things, we must use the **comparative** : Which is the bigger of these two ? etc. . French does not make this distinction : *Lequel est le plus lourd des deux ?* : Which is the heaviest of the two ? Another simplification !)

Elle est aussi intelligente **que** *sa soeur* : she is as intelligent as her sister.
less expensive ; the least expensive : *moins cher ; le moins cher.* [mwahn share]
We will look at any irregular forms as and when they occur.

2 *Lui* is also an "indirect object pronoun" ; the others are *me - vous - nous* and *leur.* Let's see how they are used :
Elle me donne un livre : she gives me a book.
Il leur explique la phrase : he explains the sentence to them.
Vous lui parlez trop vite : you are speaking to him/to her too quickly.
Do you see that, in each case, the pronoun in English is followed by "to" ? We call this an "indirect object". We place the French pronoun before the verb except when the verb is an affirmative imperative :
Donnez-moi un gâteau ! : give me a cake !
Pronoun-order is quite a complex subject in French so we prefer to tackle it gradually, getting your intuition to work for you. By the end of the course, however, you will have seen all the examples necessary to assimilate the rule.

3 Forming questions :
We mentioned at the beginning of this course that the question-form *-est-ce que / -qu'est-ce que,* although extremely frequent, was considered somewhat "inelegant". We still recommend that you use it when you begin to formulate questions yourself, but we have

---

TRENTE-SIXIEME (36ème) LEÇON

Les secrétaires

1 Une femme téléphone au bureau de son mari

taken this opportunity to show you how *-est-ce que* is replaced in more formal language.

The inversion of verb and subject pronoun :
Est-ce qu'ils sont anglais ? *Sont-ils anglais ?*

Est-ce que vous avez l'heure ? *Avez-vous l'heure ?*

The inversion of il y a
If we tried to pronounce *y a- -il,* , it would be rather unpleasant (try it ! ee-a-eel) so we add a letter t before the last word for euphony : *y a-t-il*. The t has no meaning.
Est-ce qu'il y a un bus ce soir ? *Y a-t-il un bus ce soir ?*

Combien de tickets est-ce qu'il y a ? *Combien de tickets y a-t-il ?*

We find this "euphonic t" each time that a final and an initial vowel would otherwise have to be pronounced together :
Est-ce qu'elle va en Egypte ? *Va-t-elle en Egypte ?*

This type of language is considered rather stuffy when spoken in everyday conversation, but it is quite normal - **even obligatory** - when written. Because of the formalism of French, there is a wider gap between the written and spoken languages than exists in English. Our course tries to marry the two where possible, but emphasizing **usage** and the **spoken** language.

36th LESSON

(The) secretaries

1 A woman telephones to the office of her husband.

2 — Je voudrais **(1)** parler à M. Martin. -Il est absent.
3 Est-ce que je peux prendre un message ?
4 — S'il vous plaît. Je pars en voyage **(2)**, alors dites-lui
5 que j'ai repassé **(N-1)** ses chemises, j'ai fait le lit,
6 j'ai envoyé les enfants chez sa mère
7 et j'ai laissé un repas **(3)** froid dans le frigo **(4)**.
8 — Très bien madame. Je vais lui dire. Qui est à l'appareil ?

9 Une femme rencontre par hasard la secrétaire de son mari.
10 — Je suis très heureuse de vous connaître, mademoiselle.
11 Mon mari m'a dit si peu **(5)** de choses sur vous.

PRONONCIATION

2 . .voodray. .martan. .etabsohn
3 . .peu. . .mesahzh
4 . .par
7 . .lessay. .freegoh
9 . .parazar

2 – I would like to speak to M. Martin. -He is absent.
3 Can I take a message ?
4 – [Yes], please. I (am) leaving on a trip so tell him
5 that I have ironed his shirts, I have made the bed,
6 I have sent the children to his mother's
7 and I have left a cold meal in the fridge.
8 – Very well madam. I will (am going to) tell him. Who is speaking ?

9 A woman meets by chance the secretary of her husband.
10 – I am very happy to meet (know) you, miss.
11 My husband has told me so few things about (on)you.

NOTES

(1) This is our first encounter with the conditional form :
Je veux : I want - *Je voudrais* : I would like - *Voulez-vous. . .?* Do you want . . .? - *Voudriez-vous. . .?* : Would you like. . .?
(2) *Un voyage* : a trip ; *un trajet* : a journey - *voyager* : to travel ; *un agent de voyage* : a travel agent ; *partir en voyage* : to go on a trip ; *en voyage d'affaires* : on a business trip.
(3) *Un repas* : a meal. The principal meals are :
le petit déjeuner : breakfast ; *le déjeuner* : lunch and ; *le dîner* : dinner. ; *déjeuner* : to have lunch ; *dîner* : to have dinner.
(4) This is a familiar word for *le réfrigérateur* (like "fridge" and "refrigerator " in English).
(5) Much, many : *beaucoup ;* little, few *: peu.*
There is little hope : *il y a peu d'espoir.*
There are few people here : *il y a peu de gens ici.*
so little, so few *: si peu de ;* so much, so many *: tellement.*
We can appreciate that the French make no distinction here between countable and uncountable nouns.

Do you find that you are beginning to understand things without needing long, detailed explanations ? We hope so !

EXERCICES

1. Voudriez-vous parler à M. Martin ? S'il vous plaît. – **2.** Il y a tellement de bruit chez lui ! – **3.** Nous avons si peu de temps !. – **4.** Est-ce que vous aimez voyager ? -Oui, beaucoup. – **5.** Je voudrais prendre le petit déjeuner à huit heures.

Fill in the blanks

1 Il y a .... gens et .. .. place !

There are so many people and so little room !

2 Est-ce que vous .... demain ?

Are you leaving on a trip tomorrow ?

3 Nous .... à la banque hier [ee-air]

We phoned the bank yesterday.

TRENTE-SEPTIEME (37ème) LEÇON

Une soirée (1) au théâtre

1 Jean et Marie-Claude vont‿au théâtre pour voir une pièce **(2)**

PRONONCIATION

. . .swaray oh tayatr

EXERCISES

1. Would you like to speak to M. Martin ? (Yes) please. — **2.** There is so much noise at his place ! — **3.** We have so little time ! — **4.** Do you like travelling ? -Yes, very much. — **5.** I would like to have (take) breakfast at 8.00.

4 et ils .... un carnet de chèques.

and they sent us a cheque-book.

5 Michel . dit : "Je suis très .... de ....

.... , Monsieur.

Michel said : "I am very happy to meet you sir".

Fill in the blanks

1 - tellement de - si peu de. — **2** - partez en voyage. — **3** - avons téléphoné . — **4** - nous ont envoyé. — **5** - a - heureux - vous connaître.

37th LESSON

An evening at the theatre

1 Jean and M-Claude go to the theatre (for) to see a play.

NOTES

(1) *Le soir :* the evening (i.e. from 6 p.m. to 10 p.m.)
La nuit : the night. *Le matin* : the morning
Il se lève tôt le matin : he gets up early in the morning.
La soirée : the evening **plus** the activities involved : the sense is wider than the word *"soir"*.
Dans la matinée : in the morning.
Téléphonez-moi en fin de matinée : telephone me towards the end of the morning.
(2) *Une pièce* : here is another meaning.
Une pièce de théâtre : a play. *Une pièce de monnaie* : a coin.

2 qui s'appelle "L'amour, toujours l'amour".
3 Ils‿arrivent au théâtre à huit‿heures et quart **(N-2)**,
4 un quart d'heure avant le lever **(3)** du rideau.
5 L'ouvreuse **(5)** leur montre les fauteuils et Jean lui donne un pourboire.
6 La pièce commence : deux comédiens **(5)** entrent en scène :
7 – Je vous‿aime Gisèle. Vous m'entendez, je vous‿aime **(N-3)**.
8 – Ah bon ? Mais je ne vous‿aime pas. J'aime Pierre.
9 – Pourquoi ? -Parce qu'il me donne des bijoux **(6)**
10 et vous ne me donnez rien.
11 A ce moment, Jean commence à ronfler très fort. Il dort **(7)**.

PRONONCIATION

4 . .levay. .reedoh
5 . . .poorbwar
6 . .komedeean entr. .sen
9 . . parskeel. .beezhoo
11 . . .ronflay. . .dor

EXERCICES

1. Frère Jacques, Frère Jacques, dormez-vous ? – **2.** A quelle heure vous levez-vous le matin ? – **3.** Il leur montre les places, – **4.** et ils lui donnent un pourboire. – **5.** Ils ne me donnent jamais rien. – **6.** Montrez-lui le billet.

2 which is called "Love, always love".
3 They arrive at the theatre at 8.15 (8 hours and [a] quarter)
4 a quarter of an hour before curtain-up. (the lifting of the curtain).
5 The usherette shows then the seats (armchairs) and Jean gives her a tip.
6 The play begins : two actors come (enter) on stage.
7 – I love you, Gisèle. You hear me ? I love you.
8 – Oh really ? But I don't love you. I love Pierre.
9 – Why ? -Because he gives me jewels
10 and you don't give me anything. (nothing).
11 At this moment Jean begins to snore very loudly (strong). He [is] sleeping.

NOTES (suite)

(3) *Lever* : to lift, to rise. *Se lever* : to get up.
Le lever du soleil : the sun rise.

(4) *Une ouvreuse* is the woman in a theatre or cinema who shows you to your seat. It is usual to give her a tip *(un pourboire* literally "to drink", cf. German trinkgeld) See next lesson for what can happen if this tradition is ignored !

(5) When we have to refer to a group containing both masculine **and** feminine nouns, the masculine form takes precedence. Here, for example, we have *un comédien* and *une comédienne* but we say *deux comédiens* (the word means "an actor" ; "a comedian" ; is *acteur comique*). The same for the agreement of adjectives : *Le mari et la femme sont très gentils.*

(6) Another irregular plural. The singular is *bijou.* There are seven nouns like this -two more common ones are *genou* : a knee *(les genoux)* and *chou :* cabbage *(les choux).*

(7) *Dormir* : to sleep. *Je dors ; tu dors ; il ou elle dort ; nous dormons ; vous dormez ; ils dorment.*
s'endormir : to fall asleep.

EXERCISES

1. Brother John, Brother John, are you sleeping ? – **2.** (At) what time do you get up in the morning ? – **3.** He shows them the seats, – **4.** and they give him a tip – **5.** They never give me anything. – **6.** Show him/her the ticket.

Fill in the blanks

1 Il ne ... . rien.

He never gives her (or him) anything.

2 Je .... ai donné notre adresse.

I gave them our address.

3 Il s' .... au théâtre.

He always fall asleep in the teatre.

4 ... fils et .. fille sont ...... et .....

His (her) son and his (her) daughter are tall and good-looking.

TRENTE-HUITIEME (38ème) LEÇON

Vengeance...

1 Jean-Pierre Legros est‿un monsieur bien (1) difficile !
2 Un jour, il va voir un film de suspense.
3 Il paie et il entre ; l'ouvreuse lui montre sa place (2).
4 – Ah non ! dit‿-il. C'est trop loin de l'écran.

PRONONCIATION

Vonzhonss
2 . .soospenss
3 . .pay
4 . .aykron

5 Elle ... répond : "Je ne .... aime pas".

She answers him : "I don't love you."

Fill in the blanks

1 - lui donne jamais - . — **2** - leur - . — **3** - endort toujours - — **4** Son - sa - grands - beaux. — **5** - lui - vous.

38th LESSON

Vengeance

1 J.P. Legros is a very difficult gentleman !
2 One day, he goes to see a murder mystery (suspense film).
3 He pays and he goes in ; the usherette shows (to) him his place.
4 – Ah no ! says he. It's too far from the screen.

NOTES

(1) Another way of saying :. *un monsieur très difficile.*
C'est bien loin or *c'est très loin :* it's very far.

(2) Remember that, grammatically, we don't know whether it is the man's place or the woman's place. *Son/sa* agrees with the gender of the noun possessed and not the sex of the possessor.
son fils : his **or** her son.
The context tells us to whom the object belongs.

5 Elle lui montre une autre place. -Mais je suis trop près !
6 Essayant **(3)** de rester calme, l'ouvreuse indique un autre fauteuil,
7 mais là, il y a une dame avec un énorme chapeau.
8 Enfin, il trouve une bonne place au milieu de la salle . . .
9 et il donne une pièce de vingt centimes à l'ouvreuse **(4)**.
10 Elle la **(5)** regarde avec un air de **(6)** mépris et lui dit :
11 — C'est le mari qui est l'assassin !

PRONONCIATION

5 . . .pray
6 Essayohn. .andeek
8 . . .meelyeu. .
9 . . .sonteem
10 . . .maypree
11 . . .assassan

VOUS PAYEZ À LA CAISSE ET VOUS ENTREZ ICI.

EXERCICES

1. Vous payez à la caisse et vous entrez ici. — **2.** Essayant de rester calme, elle lui montre une autre place. — **3.** Je suis trop près de l'écran et trop loin de la porte. — **4.** Elle a l'air très intelligente, qu'est-ce que vous en pensez ? — **5.** C'est lui qui est le directeur.

5 She shows (to) him another place. - But I'm too close !

6 Trying to remain calm, the usherette indicates another seat.

7 but there, there is a woman with an enormous hat.

8 At last, he finds a good place in the middle of the hall. . .

9 and he gives a 20 centime - coin to the usherette

10 She looks at it with an air of contempt and says to him :

11 – It is the husband who is the murderer(assassin)!

NOTES (suite)

(3) This is the present participle of *essayer.*
Most present participles of all three categories of verbs end in *-ant :*
aller : allant (going) ;
vendre : vendant (selling)
finir : finissant (finishing).

(4) The French currency unit is the *franc* [frohn] divided into one hundred *centimes.*
3 F 25 : *trois francs vingt cinq* or just *trois vingt cinq.*
20 centimes is certainly not a generous tip ! In a restaurant if you see *Prix nets,* it means that the service-charge is included.

(5) *la* i.e. *la pièce.* She looks at it (masc.) - she looks at him *: elle* **le** *regarde.*

(6) *Vous avez l'air fatigué :* you look tired.
Il a l'air très content : he seems very happy.
Avec un air de : with an air of
Il a l'air intelligent : he looks intelligent.

EXERCISES

1. You pay at the cash (desk) and you enter here. – **2.** Trying to remain calm, she shows him another place. – **3.** I am too close to the screen and too far from the door. – **4.** She looks very intelligent, what do you think ? – **5.** It's he who is the director.

Fill in the blanks :

1 Il ... donne ... .; elle .. regarde.

He gives her a coin ; she looks at it.

2 Vous .... . ' ... triste. -Moi ? Pas .. ....

You look sad. Me ? Not at all.

3 ... cadeau coûte ... francs ...... - ....

His/her present costs 10 F 90.

TRENTE-NEUVIEME (39ème) LEÇON

Un argument valable (1)

1 – Vous n'avez pas un franc pour moi, monsieur ?
2 – Un franc ? Bien sûr que non **(2)** !
3 – Oh monsieur, je n'ai rien **(N-4)**, je n'ai pas d'argent,
4 je n'ai pas de maison et n'ai plus d'amis.

Don't forget to read the text aloud : it is important to get the rythm of the language, and to "feel" the liaisons.

4 .... - .... un ..... fauteuil.

Show us another seat/armchair.

5 ...... au café, j'ai rencontré un ami.

Going to the café, I met a friend.

Fill in the blanks

1 - lui - une pièce - la -. — **2** - avez l'air - du tout. — **3** Son - dix - quatre-vingt-dix. — **4** Montrez-nous - autre - . — **5** Allant-.

39th LESSON

A valid argument

1 — You don't have a franc for me, sir, [do you] ?
2 — A franc ? Of course (that) not !
3 — Oh sir, I have (not) nothing ; I haven't any money,
4 I haven't a house and I have no more (of) friends.

NOTES

(1) *Valable* : valid. *Votre billet n'est pas valable* : your ticket is not valid. *valeur* : value. *Un tableau de grande valeur* : a valuable painting.

(2) *Bien sûr* ! : Of course ! *Bien sûr que non !* : Of course not ! The *que* is emphatic. We can also say : *bien sûr que oui.*

5 Je n'ai plus qu'une **(3)** chose au monde. -Quoi **(4)** ?

6 — Ce petit revolver ; alors, vous n'avez toujours pas un franc ?

A la fortune du pot

7 — Je vous‿ai invité **(5)** à dîner, mon cher ami, mais regardez :

8 je n'ai plus rien dans mon garde-manger ;

9 plus **(6)** de sucre, plus de pain, plus de riz, plus de biscuits,

10 plus de conserves . . .tenez **(7)**. .si . . il y a quelque chose :

11 une énorme toile d'araignée ! Bon appétit **(8)** !

PRONONCIATION

5 . . plyookyoon shohz
6 . .revolvair
fortyoon. .poh
8 . .gard-monzhay
9 . . . .ree. .biskwee
11 . .twal daranyay. .apaytee

5 I have only (no more than) one thing in (at) the world. - What ?
6 — This little revolver ; so, you still haven't a franc ?

(At the) Pot-luck

7 — I have invited you to dine, my dear friend, but look :
8 — I have nothing more (no more nothing) in my larder :
9 [no] more (of) sugar, [no] more (of) bread, [no] more (of) rice, [no] more (of) biscuits,
10 [no] more (of) tinned food. .wait a minute !. (hold) . .yes, there is something
11 an enormous spider's web ! Bon appétit !

NOTES (suite)

(3) *J'ai seulement cinq minutes* : I have only five minutes or *Je n'ai que cinq minutes.*
The two sentences mean the same.
Elle n'a qu'un mari ! : She has only one husband !
Je n'ai plus que : I have only . .left
Je n'ai plus que dix francs : I have only ten francs left.

(4) Like saying "What ?" in English, this could be considered impolite or abrupt. More politely we would say *Qu'est-ce que c'est ? ".* If you wish someone to repeat what they have said, you would say *Pardon ?* [pah-dohn], with a rising intonation.

(5) *J'ai invité Jean ; je l'ai invité.* So, our word order is subject - object - auxiliary -verb.
Elle nous a dit. . . : she told us. .
Ils leur ont donné . . : they gave them. .

(6) *Il n'y a plus de sucre* [pliou] means there is no more sugar. *Donnez-moi plus de sucre* [plious] : give me **more** sugar. In order to avoid a possible confusion ; the French themselves often use . *davantage : Davantage de sucre, s'il vous plaît :* more sugar, please.

(7) *Tenir :* to hold ; *je tiens ; tu tiens ; il/elle tient ; nous tenons ; vous tenez ; ils tiennent* [tyenn] *; j'ai tenu* : I (have) held. *Tenez ! :* Hold on ! Wait a minute !

(8) A ritual before beginning a meal in most European countries, you wish your fellow eaters a good appetite. This custom is absent from Anglo-Saxon culture. One wonders why. . .

EXERCICES

1. Est-ce que vous avez deux maris, ma chère amie ?– **2.** Bien sûr que non ! Je n'ai qu'un mari !. – **3.** Il nous a invités à déjeuner vendredi prochain. – **4.** Je n'ai plus d'argent ! Qu'est-ce que je vais faire ? – **5.** Il n'a plus qu'une chose au monde. -Qu'est-ce que c'est ?

Fill in the blanks :

1 Je . 'ai .... .. sucre, ... pain, ... !

I have no more sugar, no more bread, no more anything !

2 Dépêchez-vous ! Ils . ' ... ... dix minutes !

Hurry up ! They only have ten minutes !

3 Je . ' .. .. dix francs dans ma poche.

I have only 10 francs left in my pocket.

QUARANTIEME (40ème) LEÇON

La rue Mouffetard

1 Le dimanche matin, Madame Martin va au marché de la rue Mouffetard.
2 C'est‿un très vieux marché en bas d'une (1) petite rue étroite.

PRONONCIATION

. .mouftar
2 . .on ba . .aytrwat

EXERCISES

1. Do you have 2 husbands, my dear friend ? — **2.** Of course not ! I have only one husband ! — **3.** He has invited us to lunch next Friday. — **4.** I have no more money ! What am I going to do ? — **5.** He has only one thing left in the world. -What is it ?

4 Ils .... de venir tôt.

They told us to come early.

5 Je . ' .. .. à .... donner.

I have nothing left to give you.

Fill in the blanks

1 -n' - plus de - plus de - plus rien. — **2** - n'ont que -. —**3** -n'ai plus que -. — **4** - nous ont dit - . — **5** - n'ai plus rien - vous -.

40th LESSON

The rue Mouffetard

1 On (the) Sunday morning, Mme Martin goes to the market of the rue Mouffetard.
2 It is a very old market at the bottom of a small, narrow street.

NOTES

(1) *Bas* (f. *basse)* : low. *En bas de :* at the bottom of. *En haut de :* at the top of - *Au milieu de :* in the middle of. *Autour de :* around (these forms are invariable).

3 Il y a toujours beaucoup de monde (2) et c'est très vivant.
4 On y trouve des gens qui jouent de l'accordéon ou de la guitare
5 et d'autres (3) qui distribuent des tracts politiques et des journaux. .
6 et il y a aussi des gens qui achètent des fruits et des légumes.
7 Tous ces gens se parlent (4) en même temps !
8 Madame Martin s'arrête devant l'éventaire d'un marchand de primeurs.
9 — Quelle est la différence entre ces deux sortes de haricots ?
10 — Ceux-ci (5) sont cultivés en France et ceux-là sont‿importés.
11 — Je vais prendre les moins chers. Avez-vous aussi des carottes ?
12 — Oui, bien sûr. Celles-ci sont très bonnes. Je vous‿en mets un kilo ? (6)

QUE FAITES-VOUS LE DIMANCHE MATIN ?
40

PRONONCIATION

3 . . . .veevohn
4 . . .geetar
5 . .distreebyoo. .trakt
6 . . .laygyoom
8 . . .ayvontair. . .marshohn. .preemeur
9 . .de areekoh
10 Se-see. .se-la amportay
11 . .mwa. . .
12 . .voozonmay. .

3 There are always lots of people (world) and it is very lively.
4 One finds (there) people who play (of) the accordeon or (of) the guitar
5 and others who distribute political tracts and newspapers . .
6 and there are also people who buy fruit and vegetables.
7 All these people talk [to] each other at the same time !
8 Mme Martin stops in front of the stand of a greengrocer.
9 – What is the difference between these two sorts of beans ?
10 – These here are grown (cultivated) in France and those there are imported.
11 – I will (am going to) take the least expensive. Have you as well any carrots ?
12 – Yes, of course. These are very good. I will put (you) one kilo (of them) ?

NOTES (suite)

(2) We have seen a couple of idiomatic uses of *le monde* (the world) :
Tout le monde : everybody
Il y a beaucoup de monde (≠ très peu de monde) : a lot of people, crowded.
Dans le monde : throughout the world.
Une seule chose au monde : one single thing in the world.
(Le Monde is also the name of the most influential French daily newspaper).

(3) *Autre* (other) must always be followed by a noun (*un autre journal - un autre endroit).* If we want to say "others" by itself (e.g. some like bread, and others like toasts), we must say *d'autres.* We will see more differences between the two forms later.

(4) *Il se parle :* he talks to himself **but**
Ils se parlent : they talk to each other.
Il se connait : he knows himself (i.e. faults and virtues)
Ils se connaissent : they know each other.

(5) We have seen *celui-ci* and *celui-là* (f. *celle*), our demonstrative pronouns (Lesson 34 Note 2) ; this is the plural.

(6) This is the type of idiomatic language you are likely to hear in shops and markets. Instead of the formal :
*Je voudrais un kilo de. .*we hear *Mettez-moi un kilo de ..*
The greengrocer does not say :
En voulez-vous un kilo, madame ? but *Je vous en mets un kilo ?*

EXERCICES

1. Tout le monde est content de ce livre. – **2.** On y trouve des gens qui jouent de la guitare. – **3.** Que faites-vous le dimanche matin ? Je vais au marché. – **4.** Quelle est la différence entre ces deux sortes de riz ? – **5.** Tout le monde se parle en même temps !

Fill in the blanks :

1 Il y a .... de .... là-bas.

There are always a lot of people there.

2 Certains aiment le thé, . ' ...... préfèrent le café.

Some (people) like tea, others prefer coffee.

3 .... tous les jours.

We speak to each other every day.

QUARANTE-ET-UNIEME (41ème) LEÇON

Réservons une table

1 – Bonsoir. Est-ce bien **(1)** le restaurant "Aux Savoyards" ? -Oui monsieur.

PRONONCIATION

1 . . .essbyehn. .restorohn oh savwayar

EXERCISES

1. Everybody is happy with this book. — **2.** You find (there) people who play the guitar. — **3.** What do you do on Sunday morning ? -I go to the market. — **4.** What is the difference between these two sorts of rice ? — **5.** Everybody speaks to each other at the same time !

4 A combien sont les carottes ? ...... - .. sont à dix francs.

How much are the carrots ? These ones are at 10 F.

5 Et ...... - .. sont à neuf francs. Je .... en .... un kilo ?

And these ones are at 9 F. You want a kilo ?

Fill in the blanks

1 - toujours beaucoup - monde. — **2** - d'autres -. — **3** Nous nous parlons -. **4** Celles-ci -. — **5** Celles-là - vous - mets -.

41st LESSON

Let's book a table

1 — Good evening. Is this (well) the restaurant "Aux Savoyards" ? -Yes, sir.

NOTES

(1) In this lesson we see two polite uses of the adverb *bien* (well). Make do with recognizing them : they are forms you are likely to hear in polite conversation.
Vous êtes bien M. Duclos ? : You are M. Duclos, aren't you ?
Est-ce bien "Aux Savoyards" ? : This is "Aux Savoyards", isn't it ?
Voulez-vous bien me suivre ? : Would you kindly follow me ?
Vous voulez bien me dire. . . : Kindly tell me. . .

2 — Je voudrais réserver une table pour quatre personnes pour ce soir.
3 — Quatre couverts **(2)**. Vers **(3)** quelle heure voudriez-vous ?
4 — Vers huit heures, si c'est possible.
5 — Désolé, monsieur, mais nous sommes complets **(4)** jusqu'à dix heures.
6 — Ça fait un peu tard **(5)**. Vous êtes sûr que vous n'avez rien ?
7 — Je vous assure. A part une toute petite table
8 qui est près de la cuisine et. .
9 — Ça ne fait rien **(6)**. Je la prends. Je m'appelle Desroches.
10 — Vous voulez bien l'épeler, s'il vous plaît?
11 — D.E.S.R.O.C.H.E.S. -Merci monsieur. A tout à l'heure.

12 ''L'appétit vient en mangeant, la soif s'en va **(7)** en buvant'' Rabelais.

PRONONCIATION

2 . .voodray. . .kat person
3 Kat koovair. .vair. .voodreeay
5 . . .komplay. .
7 . .voozassyoor. a par. .
9 . .prohn
10 . . .laypaylay
11 day-eu-ess-air-oh-say-ash-eu-ess. . .atootaleur
12 . .monzhon. . .byoovohn

EXERCICES

1. Je m'en vais en vacances la semaine prochaine. — **2.** -Elles ne peuvent pas venir. -Ça ne fait rien. — **3.** J'arrive vers neuf heures. — **4.** -Vous êtes bien français ? -Non, désolé ! — **5.** Tous les hôtels sont complets jusqu'à demain.

2 – I would like to reserve a table for 4 persons for this evening.
3 – 4 places. Around what time do you like ?
4 – Around 8.00 if it is possible.
5 – [Very] sorry, sir, but we are full [up] until 10.00 p.m. .
6 – That's getting late. You're sure you have (not) nothing ?
7 – I assure you. Apart [from] a really small table
8 which is near the kitchen and . .
9 – That doesn't matter. I [will] take it. I'm called Desroches.
10 – Would you kindly spell it, please ?
11 – D.E.S.R.O.C.H.E.S. -Thank you, sir. Until later on.
12 "The appetite comes with (in) eating, the thirst goes away with (in) drinking" Rabelais.

NOTES (suite)

(2) *Un couvert* is the place-setting in a restaurant which includes : *le couteau :* the knife - *la fourchette* : the fork - *la cuillère* [kwee-air] : the spoon - *le verre :* the glass - *le sel :* the salt - *le poivre :* the pepper and - *la serviette :* the napkin (we have also seen that this latter can mean brief-case).
(3) *Il vient vers moi :* he comes towards me.
Vers huit heures : around 8.00
(4) *Plein* [plahn] : full (empty : *vide*)
Remplir (conjugated like *finir*) : to fill **but** for theatres, hotels and restaurants we use *complet.* If you see this sign on the door of a hotel, it means "full up".
(5) An idiomatic way of saying : *c'est un peu tard.*
(6) Another idiom, literally "it makes nothing", which means "it's not important" "it doesn't matter". It is invariable.
(7) *Aller :* to go. *S'en aller :* to go away .
je m'en vais ; tu t'en vas ; il/elle s'en va ; nous nous en allons (on s'en va) ; vous vous en allez ; ils/elles s'en vont.
Allez vous -en ! : Go away !
On s'en va dans trois minutes : We're leaving in three minutes.

EXERCISES

1. I'm going away on holiday next week. – **2.** They can't come -Never mind. – **3.** I'm arriving around 9.00 – **4.** You are French, aren't you ? -No, terribly sorry ! – **5.** All the hotels are full until tomorrow.

Fill in the blanks :

1 Elle . ' .. .. huit heures.

She's leaving around eight o'clock.

2 .... - vous sûr que vous . ' .... ?

Are you sure that you have nothing ?

3 . .... une toute petite table, nous sommes ....

Apart (from) a really small table, we are full (up).

4 Voulez-vous .... nom, monsieur ?

Will you kindly spell your name, sir ?

QUARANTE-DEUXIEME (42ème) LEÇON

REVISION ET NOTES

1 **The past tense** : grammar-books give many different names to this tense which expresses two different English concepts. French makes no difference between "I bought" and "I have bought" — thus making life much simpler for us !
You have already come across the tense before. It is formed with **the present tense** *of avoir* and the **past participle** of the verb we wish to use.

The past participles are formed thus :

verbs like *acheter* → *acheté*
verbs like *finir* → *fini*
verbs like *vendre* → *vendu*
Elle a vendu sa voiture : she sold (or has sold) her car.

5 Je .... réserver une table pour .. ....

I would like to reserve a table for this evening.

Fill in the blanks

1 - s'en va vers - —**2** Etes- - n'avez rien ? — **3** A part - complets — **4** - bien épeler votre - — **5** - voudrais - ce soir.

42nd LESSON

Nous avons fini de manger : we (have) finished eating. *Ils ont acheté un tapis :* they (have) bought a carpet.

The negative form is simple :

Nous n'avons pas fini ; ils n'ont pas acheté ; elle n'a pas vendu.
Est-ce qu'elle a acheté la robe jaune ? : Did she buy (or has she bought) the yellow dress ?
Certain verbs have irregular participles : some you will pick up naturally, others you can look up at the end of the book. Here are two common ones to start with : *j'ai eu* : I (have) had ; *il a dit :* he (has) said

NOTE : There is an "historic" tense which has exactly the same use as the one we have just seen, but it is much more literary and not found in conversation and modern writing. We will see it in the next book.

2 *Quelle heure est-il ? :* What time is it ?
To tell the time, we must first announce the nearest hour.

So, for example, 3.00 p.m.

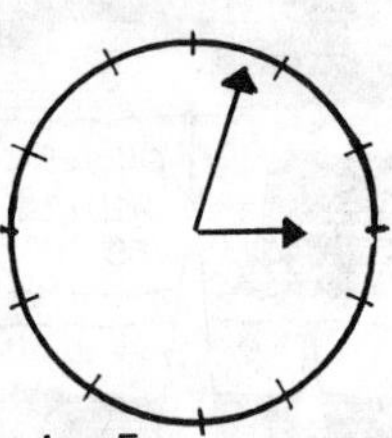

Il est trois heures . . .
Then, the number of minutes past, i.e. 5
Il est trois heures cinq -Simple !
(Notice there is no conjunction between the hour and the minute).

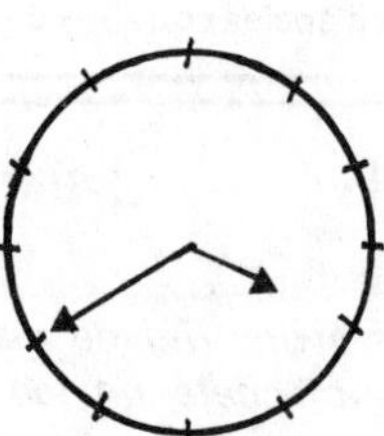

The nearest hour is 4.
Il est quatre heures. . .
Now, we announce the number of minutes to go : 20
Il est quatre heures moins vingt.

For the quarter and three quarter, we say :

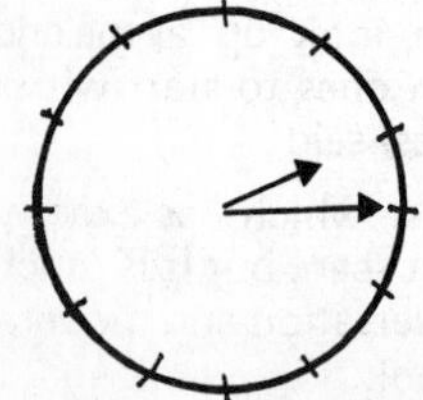

Il est deux heures et quart [kah]

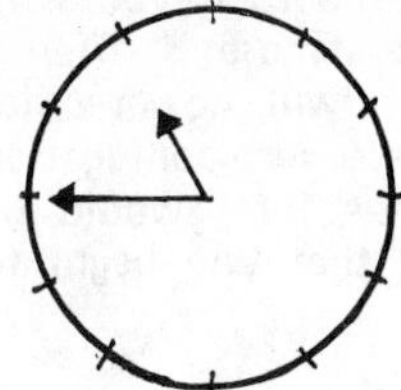

Il est onze heures moins le quart

For the half, we say :

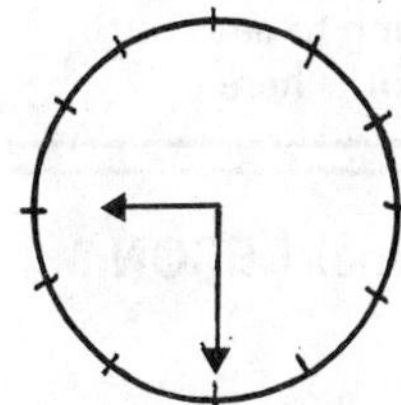

Il est neuf heures et demie.

(a half-hour is written *une demi-heure,* without an "e": *demi* never agrees with its noun before a hyphen.) For public announcements (trains, cinema-times, television programmes, etc. . .) the French use the 24 hour clock, which corresponds a little to our "a.m." and "p.m.". We will see this later.

3 *Je vous aime* is a very formal way of declaring one's love ! In fact, like most other languages (and old English), French has two ways of saying "you". We are learning the polite, formal way *-vous-* which is how you would address anybody you did not know in everyday situations.
The other, familiar form, is *tu* (like our "thou") ; the French themselves often have difficulty knowing when exactly to use it (especially between different generations). Suffice it to say that it is almost always used for one's family and close friends and young children

We do not wish, at this stage, to burden you with another verbal form -especially as its use is often a question of "feeling" a situation. We will, however, (a) include it henceforth when we give a verb-conjugation (b) use it in texts where the *vous* form would be artificial. Like this, you will find that you begin to assimilate it naturally.

4 An important point of grammar to remember is that French negatives are composed of two parts : the *ne* and another particle.
je ne fume pas : I don't smoke
je ne fume jamais : I never smoke
elle n'a rien à manger : she has nothing to eat
il ne travaille plus ici : he no longer works here

QUARANTE-TROISIEME (43ème) LEÇON

Que faites-vous dans la vie ?

1 Quand on quitte l'école de nos jours (1), on a un grand choix d'emplois ;
2 on peut devenir ingénieur ou technicien, médecin ou avocat par exemple.
3 Ces dernières (2) professions nécessitent plusieurs années d'études supérieures
4 à l'université ou dans une grande école (3).

PRONONCIATION

1 .kontonkeet. . .shwa domplwa
2 . . .anzhenyeur. .tekniseeah medsan. .avoka
3 .dairneeair. .nessesseet plyoozee-eurzanay

When speaking quickly, the French often drop the *ne.* Don't imitate them ! Always remember : two parts
ne . . . rien ; ne . . . pas : nothing, doesn't
ne . . . jamais : never ; *ne . . . plus* : no longer, no more.

---

*REMEMBER to read your ASSIMIL every day ;
Only by constant contact can you pick up a language naturally and efficiently.*

43rd LESSON

What do you [do] in (the) life ?

1 When one leaves school nowadays, one has a wide choice of jobs ;
2 one can become [an] engineer or [a] technician, [a] doctor or [a] lawyer, for example.
3 These latter professions necessitate several years of higher (superior) studies
4 at (the) university or at a "grande école".

NOTES

(1) *De nos jours* (lit. of our days) : nowadays
dans le passé (or, more elegantly : *jadis* [zhadeess]) : in the past.
dans le futur (or *dans l'avenir*) : in the future.

(2) *Dernier* : last, latest
Voici les **dernières** *nouvelles* : here is are the latest news
Le **dernier** *homme sur terre :* the last man on earth but
ce dernier (or *ces derniers - ces dernières) :* the latter
ce premier : the former (there is also a feminine form).

(3) A difficult concept to translate, the *grandes écoles* (lit. big schools) are specialized higher educational establishments for training engineers, businessmen or administrators. They are independent of the university system *(l'université* is feminine). *Grande école* is not a "high school" which, in French, is *un lycée* [leesay].

5 D'autres préfèrent devenir journaliste ou professeur.

6 Et n'oublions pas les‿artisans tels **(4)** le menuisier, le plombier ou le maçon.

7 Certaines personnes **(5)** ne peuvent pas supporter **(6)** de travailler à l'intérieur

8 dans des‿usines, des‿ateliers ou des bureaux,

9 alors elles peuvent devenir représentants, ou même chauffeurs de taxi.

10 Et, malheureusement, il y a ceux qui **(N-1)** ne trouvent pas de travail **(7)**, les chômeurs **(8)**.

Définition d'une administration

11 Une administration est‿un service où ceux qui arrivent en retard

12 croisent ceux qui partent en avance.

PRONONCIATION

5 . . .zhoornaleest
6 . . .layzarteezohn tel. .menweezeeay plombeeay. .massohn
7 .sairten
8 . .daizoozeen
9 . . .peuv
10 . . .se kee. .shohmeur
12 .krwahz. .part

EXERCICES

1. -Que font-ils ? -Il est ingénieur et son frère est médecin. — **2.** -Et que fait sa femme ? -Elle est au chômage — **3.** Il a un travail très intéressant ; il est avocat. — **4.** Les artisans sont ceux qui travaillent avec leurs mains. — **5.** Cela nécessite beaucoup de travail.

5 Others prefer to become journalist(s) or teacher(s).
6 And [let's] not forget the artisans such [as] the joiner, the plumber or the mason.
7 Certain persons cannot stand to work inside (at the interior)
8 in factories, workshops or offices
9 so they can become representatives, or even taxi-drivers.
10 And, unfortunately, there are those who do not find a of job - the unemployed.

Definition of an administration

11 An administration is a department where those who arrive late
12 cross those who leave early.

NOTES (suite)

(4) *tel* (f. *telle ;* pl. *tels, telles)* means such ; followed by a list of examples it means **such as** :
Des actrices modernes telle Isabelle Huppert : Modern actresses such as I.H. We will look at other meanings later on.
(5) *Une personne* is **always** feminine, even if describing a man (just accept it !).
(6) *Je ne peux pas le (la) supporter :* I can't stand him (her). *Est-ce que vous supportez le froid ? :* Can you put up with the cold ?
(7) *Il a trouvé du travail :* he has found work
≠*Il n'a pas trouvé* **de** *travail*
Il a trouvé un travail (or un emploi) : he has found a job. *Travailler :* to work (*une oeuvre* is a work of art ; *les travaux* are construction works).
(8) *Un chômeur* : an unemployed person
Etre au chômage : to be unemployed. Why **les** *chômeurs ?* Because we are speaking about them as a whole group.

EXERCISES

1. What do they do ? -He is an engineer and his brother is (a) doctor. — **2.** -And what does his wife do ? -She is unemployed. — **3.** He has a very interesting job ; he is [a] lawyer. — **4.** The artisans are those who work with their hands. — **5.** It necessitates a lot of work.

Fill in the blanks

1 On appelle .... ne trouvent pas de travail les ....

We call those who cannot find work "unemployed"

2 Il y a des .... et des .... Ces .... sont souvent très riches.

There are doctors and lawyers. The latter are often very rich.

3 On peut .... artisan et avoir du ....

You can become [an] artisan and have work.

QUARANTE-QUATRIEME (44ème) LEÇON

M. Duclos accueille (1) un client

1 Notre ami Duclos est cadre (2) dans‿une grande société (3) pétrolière.

PRÉSENTEZ-MOI À VOTRE SOEUR.

PRONONCIATION

akeuy. .kleeohn

4 Je ne peux pas .... personne.

I can't stand this person.

5 .... arrivent .. .. croisent ....

partent .. ..

These who arrive late cross those who leave early.

Fill in the blanks

1 ceux qui - chômeurs. — **2** médecins - avocats - derniers - **3** devenir - du travail. — **4** supporter cette . — **5** Ceux qui - en retard - ceux qui - en avance.

44th LESSON

M. Duclos meets a client

1 Our friend Duclos is [an] executive in a large petrol firm.

NOTES

(1) *Rencontrer :* to meet someone (or something), to come across them. *Une rencontre :* a meeting, an encounter ; *une réunion :* a business meeting
Accueillir (j'accueille, vous accueillez) means to greet. welcome or meet someone. In public buildings, *"accueil"* means **"reception"**.

(2) *Un cadre* is literally the frame of a painting.
We translate it as "executive" here but there is no exact translation. The title corresponds to someone in a middle - management or executive position in a company

(3) *Une société* : a society in the socio-cultural sense or, more commonly, a company, a firm *(une firme)*.

2 Aujourd'hui il est‿à l'aéroport de Roissy pour accueillir un client **(4)** suisse.
3 Il l'attend devant la sortie de la douane.
4 "Le vol Air France six cent soixante-trois en provenance de Genève
5 vient d'arriver **(5)** à la porte numéro six" annonce le haut-parleur.
6 M. Duclos cherche parmi la foule des gens qui sortent de la douane
7 mais il ne reconnaît personne **(6)**. Attendez . . .
8 Là-bas, l'homme en costume gris avec un magazine sous le bras
9 – Ça doit‿**(N-2)** être lui, se dit M. Duclos. -Je vais me présenter.
10 Il avance vers l'homme et, tendant **(8)** la main, lui dit :
11 – Permettez-moi de me présenter, je suis M. Duclos de la société I.P.F. **(7)**
12 – Je ne comprends pas le français, dit l'homme avec un fort‿accent allemand

PRONONCIATION

2 .ohzhourdwee. .eye-ropor. .akeuyeer. .sweess
4 . . .see son
5 .vyehn dareevay. . .oh-parleur
6 . . . .sort
8 . . . .brah
9 Sa dwatetr
10 . . .tohndohn. .man
11 . . . .ee-pay-ef
12 . . .fortaksohn

2 Today, he is at the airport of Roissy to meet a Swiss client.
3 He [is] waiting [for] him in front of the exit of the customs.
4 "AF flight 663 coming from Geneva
5 has just arrived at (the) gate (door) n° 6" announces the loudspeaker.
6 M. Duclos looks among the crowd of people who come out of the customs
7 but he does not recognize anybody. Wait [a minute] . . .
8 Over there, the man in [the] grey suit with a magazine under his (the) arm.
9 – That must be him, says [to] himself M. Duclos. -I will (am going) introduce (present) myself.
10 He advances towards the man and, holding [out] his (the) hand, says to him
11 – -Allow me to introduce myself. I am M. Duclos of (the) I.P.F. (company).
12 – I do not understand French, says the man with a strong German accent.

NOTES (suite)

(4) *Un client (une cliente)* is both a customer and a client.
(5) *Je viens :* I am coming / I come.
Je viens de manger : I have just eaten.
Nous venons d'arriver : we have just arrived.
The structure is idiomatic.
(6) *Je n'ai vu personne :* I saw nobody
Remember, we always need the double negative in French.
Personne n'est là : nobody is there.
Il n'aime personne : he doesn't like anybody.
(7) This is a formal way of introducing oneself ; a more "relaxed" phrase would be : *-Bonjour, je m'appelle Duclos.* Remember that formality is a major feature of the French language.
(8) *tenir :* to hold ; *tendre :* to hold out
(je tends, tu tends, il/elle tend, nous tendons, vous tendez, ils tendent)
Tendez votre assiette : hold out your plate.
past form : *tendu*

EXERCICES

1. Il a un magazine sous le bras. — **2.** -Vous venez d'arriver ? -Oui, j'arrive de Genève. — **3.** Je ne reconnais personne. . .Attendez !Ça doit être lui. — **4.** Présentez-moi à votre soeur. — **5.** L'homme en costume bleu avance vers la porte. — **6.** J'ai rencontré un ami en vacances.

Fill in the blanks :

1 .... - vous quelqu'un ? Non, ...

Do you recognize anyone ? No, no-one

2 Nous .... et nous sommes ....

We have just arrived and we are tired.

3 Mon frère est ..... dans une grande ....

My brother is an executive in a large company.

QUARANTE-CINQUIEME (45ème) LEÇON

M. Duclos trouve son client

1 M. Duclos se sent très gêné à cause de (1) son‿erreur.

PRONONCIATION

1 . .se sohn. .akohzde. .ayreur

EXERCISES

1. He has a magazine under his arm. – **2.** You have just arrived ? Yes, I arrive from Geneva. – **3.** I don't recognize anybody. . Wait ! That must be him. – **4.** Introduce me to your sister. – **5.** The man in a blue suit advances towards the door. – **6.** I met a friend on holiday.

4 .... - ... devant la ......

Wait for me in front of the exit.

5 Vous .... Monsieur Duclos. Permettez-moi de

.. ..

You must be M. Duclos. Allow me to introduce myself.

Fill in the blanks

1 reconnaissez - personne. – **2** venons d'arriver - fatigués – **3** cadre - société – **4** Attendez-moi - sortie – **5** devez être - me présenter.

45th LESSON

M. Duclos finds his client

1 M. Duclos feels (himself) very embarrassed because of his mistake.

NOTES

(1) Because *: parce que ;* because of *: à cause de.*
L'avion est en retard à cause d'une grève : the plane is late because of a strike. *La cause d'un accident* : the cause of an accident.

2 Derrière lui, une voix dit : -Vous me cherchez, peut‿-être ?
3 — Je suis Maurice Chavan. Heureux de vous connaître.
4 — Enchanté **(2)**. Je suis Michel Duclos de la . . .
5 — Je sais, répond le Suisse avec un sourire ironique.
6 — Euh. . . Voulez-vous **(3)** me suivre ? Nous‿allons chercher ma voiture.
7 Les deux‿hommes se dirigent vers les‿ascenseurs.
8 — J'espère que vous‿avez fait un bon voyage ?
9 — Oui, ce n'était pas mal, quoique **(4)** je n'aime pas l'avion.
10 — Voulez-vous **(3)** aller tout de suite à votre hôtel
11 ou voulez-vous passer au bureau d'abord ?
12 — Non, je veux prendre une douche et me raser avant tout.

PRONONCIATION

3 moreess shavohn.
4 Onshontay. .
5 . . .eeroneek
7 . . .deereezh. .layzasonseur
9 . . .kwake
10 . . .toot-sweet. . .

EXERCICES

1. A cause de lui, je suis en retard. — **2.** Voulez-vous bien me suivre, s'il vous plaît ? — **3.** Je suis Michel Duclos. Heureux de vous connaître. — **4.** Je veux me raser avant tout ! — **5.** Il n'a pas fait un bon voyage, il était malade.

2 Behind him, a voice says : -You're looking for me perhaps ?
3 — I am M. Chavan. Happy to meet (know)you.
4 — Delighted. I am M.D. of(the). . .
5 — I know, replies the Swiss with an ironic smile.
6 — Um. .will you (do you want to) follow me ? We are going to get (look for) my car.
7 The two men go (direct themselves) towards the lifts.
8 — I hope you had (made) a good journey ?
9 — Yes, it wasn't bad, although I don't like planes (the plane).
10 — Do you want to go immediately to your hotel
11 or do you want to go (pass by) to the office first ?
12 — No, I want to take a shower and shave (myself) before anything (all).

NOTES (suite)

(2) This exchange illustrates the formal greetings exchanged between two people meeting for the first time. *Enchanté* is not as flowery as it sounds : it simply means : delighted to meet you. French people - especially at formal parties - have a disconcerting habit of simply announcing their name as they shake hands - which at first sounds like a series of arcane salutes : just reply with a smile and your own name !

(3) In this dialogue, we see the two uses of *voulez-vous. . .* The literal meaning (line 10) is clear : it is asking for a preference ; the polite use (line 3) is a way of introducing a suggestion or a request and is the equivalent in English of "Will you. . .? or "Would you mind. .?
Voulez-vous une cigarette ? : Do you want a cigarette ?
Voulez-vous (bien) me suivre ? : Would you follow me, please ?

(4) *quoique* [kwahke] or *bien que :* both mean although. They are followed by a subjunctive which we will see later on.

EXERCISES

1. Because of him, I am late. — **2.** Would you follow me, please ? — **3.** I am Michel Duclos. Pleased to meet you. — **4.** I want to shave before anything ! — **5.** He didn't have a good trip ; he was ill.

Fill in the blanks :

1 .... je n'aime pas . ' ..... , ce . ' était pas mal.

Although I don't like planes, it wasn't bad

2 Je suis Jean Vincent - ....

I'm John Vincent - Delighted to know you.

3 Les deux hommes .. .. l'ascenseur.

The two men go towards the lift.

4 ...... - .... aller .... à l'hôtel ?

Do you want to go immediately to the hotel ?

QUARANTE-SIXIEME (46ème) LEÇON

A l'hôtel

1 Les deux‿hommes arrivent ensemble dans l'entrée (1) de l'hôtel de Meaux.

PRONONCIATION

1 . . .lontray. . .otel de mow

5 .... - .... la fenêtre, s'il vous plaît ?

Will you open the window, please ?

Fill in the blanks

1 Quoique - l'avion - n'. — 2 Enchanté. — 3 - se dirigent vers - — 4 Voulez-vous - tout de suite - — 5 Voulez-vous ouvrir -.

Do you notice that our translations of the exercises are becoming less literal and more idiomatic ?
Don't worry about it ; you are beginning to equate two idioms rather than two sets of words.

46th LESSON

At the hotel

1 The 2 men arrive together in the entrance[hall] of the Hotel de M.

NOTES

(1) *l'entrée :* the entrance, can also mean the lobby or the entrance-hall ; *la sortie :* the exit ; *sortie de secours :* emergency exit ;
entrée libre on a shop-window means (theoretically !) that you are free to go in and just browse.
(On a restaurant menu *l'entrée* is either the appetizer or the main course).

2 C'est‿un hôtel trois‿étoiles situé non loin des Champs-Elysées.
3 La première chose qu'ils voient **(2)** est‿une affiche marquée "Complet"
4 mais ils ne s'inquiètent pas parce que M. Chavan a réservé sa chambre.
5 Ils s'approchent de la réception et le Suisse s'adresse à la réceptionniste :
6 — Bonjour, madame ; j'ai une chambre réservée au nom de Chavan.
7 — Une minute, s'il vous plaît. Quel nom avez-vous dit ? Je ne trouve rien.
8 Oh pardon. Voilà. Une chambre avec salle de bains et w.c. **(3)**
9 réservée pour trois nuits. Signez ici, s'il vous plaît.
10 C'est la chambre trois cent un (301) au troisième étage. Voilà le chasseur.
11 — Merci **(4)** madame ; je préfère porter mes propres **(5)** valises.

VOULEZ-VOUS DES CAROTTES ?
MERCI, JE N'AI PLUS FAIM.

PRONONCIATION

2 . .trwazaytwal. .lwan. .shonzayleezay
3 . . .komplay
4 . .sankee-et
8 . .vay say
9 . .seenyay
10 . .shasseur
11 . . .may prop

2 It is a 3-star hotel situated not far from the C.E.
3 The first thing which they see is a sign marked "Full up"
4 but they don't worry because M. C. has reserved his room.
5 They approach (themselves of) the reception and the Swiss addresses (himself) to the receptionist.
6 – Good morning madam, I have a room reserved in (at) the name of Chavan.
7 – One minute please. What name did you say (have you said) ? I don't find anything (nothing)
8 Oh, pardon. Here. A room with bathroom and w.c.
9 reserved for 3 nights. Sign here, please.
10 It is (the) room 301 on the 3rd floor. Here is the page-boy
11 – [No] Thank you madame ; I prefer to carry my own suitcases.

NOTES (suite)

(2) *il voit* [eel vwa] is singular ; *ils voient* [eel vwa] is plural but both are pronounced the same. Notice carefully the pronunciations of all of these plural verbs (or better still, listen to the recordings).
(3) *les toilettes* : the toilet(s) but in "officialese" (hotels, estate-agents literature, etc. .) we hear W.C. - [vaysay]. It is a little coy if used in every-day speech.
(4) Be careful ! *Merci* means not only "thank you" but also "no thank you". If, at table, you are offered something which you wish to take, you would say *s'il vous plaît ; merci* would be a refusal. Many a foreigner has missed out because of this particularity (you can always nod your head vigourously. .)
(5) *propre :* own (i.e. belonging to that person). It is **always used before the noun.**
Ses propres chaussures : His (her) own shoes
Ma propre voiture : my own car.
If it is placed after the noun, it means. . . clean !
Ses chaussures ne sont pas propres : His/her shoes are not clean.
If you want to say : this is not my own car, you say *ce n'est pas ma propre voiture.*

12 – Vous‿en êtes sûr, Monsieur ? L'ascenseur est‿en panne (6) !

PRONONCIATION

12 . .syoor

EXERCICES

1. Ils voient une affiche "complet" mais ils ne s'inquiètent pas. – **2.** J'ai une chambre réservée au nom de Duclos. – **3.** Mais je ne trouve rien ! – **4.** Ce sont mes propres skis. – **5.** Voulez-vous des carottes ? Merci, je n'ai plus faim.

Fill in the blanks :

1 Ma voiture est .. .. Pouvez-vous m'aider ?

My car has broken down. Can you help me ?

2 Ses .... chaussures sont toujours ....

His/her own shoes are always clean.

3 .. chambre est .... de Chavan.

The room is reserved in the name of Chavan.

12 — You're sure of it, sir ? The lift is not working !

NOTES (suite)

(6) Literally "broken down" *une panne* is a breakdown (mechanical, electrical, etc. .).
You will see it on signs placed on lifts, telephones, cars, etc. .
You may also see *Hors service* which means : not in use, but it is often an euphemism for the same thing !
tomber en panne : to break down

EXERCISES

1. They see a sign "Full up" but they don't worry. — **2.** I have a room reserved in the name of Duclos. — **3.** But I can't (don't) find anything ! — **4.** These are my own skis. — **5.** Do you want some carrots ? [No] thank you ; I'm no longer hungry.

4 Ne vous .... pas ; il n' . . . ... de problème.

Don't worry ; there's no problem.

5 Elle arrive à .... heures .. .. -Vous .. êtes ... ?

She is arriving at 9.30 -You are sure of that ?

Fill in the blanks

1 - en panne - — **2** - propres - propres (sorry !). — **3** La - réservée - au nom - — **4** - inquiétez - y a pas - — **5** - neuf - et demie - en - sûr ?.

QUARANTE-SEPTIEME (47ème) LEÇON

Pas si vite (1)

1 Devant un cinéma, les gens font patiemment la queue
2 attendant leur tour **(2)** malgré la pluie.
3 Tout‿à coup un jeune homme arrive, bouscule quelques personnes
4 et se dirige résolument vers le début de la queue.
5 Une énorme main le saisit par le col de sa veste.
6 – Dites donc, le resquilleur **(3)** ! Vous‿allez faire la queue comme tout le monde. .
7 ou bien . . Le costaud **(4)** n'a pas besoin de terminer sa phrase !

FAITES LA QUEUE ICI,
S'IL VOUS PLAÎT.

PRONONCIATION

1 . .passeeamoh. .keu
2 . .malgray
3 Tootakoo. .booskyool
5 . .sayzee
6 . .reskeeyeur
7 . .kostoh

47th LESSON

Not so fast

1 In front of a cinema, (the) people are patiently queuing (make patiently the queue)
2 waiting their turn despite the rain.
3 Suddenly (all a blow) a young man arrives, jostles a few people
4 and goes resolutely towards the beginning of the queue.
5 An enormous hand seizes him by the collar of his jacket.
6 – Hey, queue-jumper ! You are going to queue-up like everybody
7 or else. .The hefty (man) doesn't need to finish his sentence !

NOTES

(1) Like in English, *vite* (fast) is both adjective and adverb. You can either say *conduire rapidement* or *conduire vite* for to drive quickly, to drive fast.

(2)We insist a lot on learning the gender at the same time as you learn a noun. Here is a good example of why : *un tour* : a turn, a tour.
C'est mon tour : it's my turn
Le Tour de France : The Tour of France bicycle race : a big annual event in France.
However *une tour* means a tower.
La Tour Montparnasse : the Montparnasse Tower
Please try and memorise the gender of new words !

(3) Here, and in the next line, we meet our first slang word : *resquiller* (which some say is a national pastime) consists of queue-jumping, or slipping into a cinema, bus, etc. . without paying ; *un resquilleur (une resquilleuse)* is the person who does this.
Dites-donc means something like : Hey you !

(4) *costaud* as an adjective means strong, hefty, or large and *un costaud* (no feminine. .) describes such a person. Slang *(argot)* or "popular" words are very prevalent in the speech of most people ; perhaps as a way of neutralizing the formalism of French. Such words should be used carefully however by a foreigner.

8 – C'est comme vous voulez, monsieur, répond le jeune
9 mais si je ne passe pas maintenant
10 vous tous (5) vous‿allez attendre longtemps. . .
11 Le projecteur est en panne et je suis le réparateur. !

PRONONCIATION

10 .voo tooss
11 . .prozhekteur

EXERCICES

1. Faites la queue ici, s'il vous plaît. – **2.** Nous attendons tous notre tour. – **3.** Malgré la pluie, je vais au cinéma ce soir. – **4.** Vous n'avez pas besoin de tous ces vêtements. – **5.** C'est comme vous voulez, monsieur.

Fill in the blanks :

1 Le .... ne .... la queue.

The queue-jumper never queues up.

2 Faites comme .... !

Do like everybody else !

3 Heureusement qu'il est .... ; cette valise est lourde !

Fortunately he's hefty ; this suitcase is heavy !

8 — It's as you like, sir, answers the young /man/
9 but if I don't pass now
10 all of you (you all) are going to wait /a/ long time.
11 The projector is broken (down) and I'm the repair-man.

NOTES (suite)

(5) Remember that when *tous* is a pronoun, it is pronounced [tooss].

EXERCISES

1. Queue up here please. — **2.** We are all waiting our turn. — **3.** Despite the rain, I'm going to the cinema this evening. — **4.** You don't need all those clothes. — **5.** It's up to you, sir.

4 ...... le prix, je vais . ' ....

Despite the price, I'm going to buy it.

5 .. .... de France passe devant .. .... Eiffel.

The Tour of France passes in front of the Eiffel Tower.

Fill in the blanks

1 - resquilleur - fait jamais — **2** - tout le monde - — **3** -costaud - — **4** Malgré - l'acheter — **5** Le Tour - la Tour.

QUARANTE-HUITIEME (48ème) LEÇON

Quelques expressions idiomatiques

1 — Ne faites pas de bruit ; je suis en train de **(1)** faire un enregistrement !
2 — Qu'est-ce que c'est que ce machin ? **(2)** C'est pour écrire à l'envers **(3)**.
3 — Laquelle des ces deux cartes postales voulez-vous ? -Ça m'est égal.
4 — Ce n'est pas la peine de crier ; je suis sourd comme un pot.
5 J'espère qu'il a l'habitude de conduire à droite s'il va en France.
6 — Passez-moi un coup de fil **(4)** quand vous avez le temps.
7 — Est-ce que je peux vous poser une question ? -Allez-y. **(5)**

EST-CE-QUE JE PEUX VOUS POSER UNE QUESTION ?

PRONONCIATION

1 . .on trande. .onrezheestremohn
2 . .alonvair
3 . .sa metaygal
4 . .pa la pen. .poh
5 . .labeetyood. .
6 koodefeel
7 . .allayzee

48th LESSON

A few idiomatic expressions

Note : (Because, by its very nature, an idiom is untranslatable, we have tried where possible to give an English equivalent and not to worry about the literal translation).

1 — Don't make any noise ; I'm busy making a recording !
2 — What on earth is that thing ? It's for writing backwards
3 — Which of these 2 post-cards do you want ? -I don't mind
4 — It's useless shouting : I'm as deaf as a post
5 I hope he's used to driving on the right if he's going to France.
6 — Give me a ring when you have time.
7 — Can I ask you a question ? -Go ahead.

NOTES

(1) We said earlier that the present tense in French translates both English present tenses (I work ; I am working). If, however, we wish to insist upon the present aspect of an action — "I'm in the middle of. . ." etc. ., we add *être en train de* before the verb.
Je suis en train d'écrire : I am busy writing.

(2) *machin* and its bed-fellow *truc* - both masculine - are real life-savers : they mean "thingammy-bob" "whatname" "whosis" etc. .and can fill in for any word missing from your vocabulary until you learn the correct one.

(3) *à l'envers* : backwards (for direction, not education)
à l'endroit : the right way around
You're wearing it back to front : *vous le portez à l'envers.*

(4) *Un fil* [feel] is a wire. The plural, of course, has an unpronounced "s" *des fils* [feel] - DO NOT CONFUSE THIS with :
un fils [feess] : a son (plural *des fils* [feess]
Obviously, the context is of capital importance !
Un coup de fil : a buzz, a ring.

(5) *Allez-y* is a very useful expression that can be used whenever you want someone to go ahead and do an action : to cross the road, to walk in front of you, to serve you at table, etc. . It is best translated as "go on" "go ahead"

8 – Qu'est-ce qu'il y a ? Vous êtes malade ?
9 Il vaut **(N-3)** mieux être riche et en bonne santé
10 que d'être pauvre et malade !

PRONONCIATION

9 . .voh myeu

EXERCICES

1. Ils ont cinq enfants : deux filles et trois fils. – **2.** Nous sommes en train d'apprendre le français. – **3.** Elle a l'habitude de faire la cuisine : elle a une grande famille. – **4.** Vous êtes prêt ? Bien, allez-y ! – **5.** Votre pullover [poolovair] est à l'envers !

Fill in the blanks :

1 . . . . . . de ces deux vins voulez-vous ? Ça . ' . . . .

Which of these two wines do you want ? I don't mind.

2 Ce n'est . . . . d'insister ; je n'ai . . . . d'argent.

It's useless insisting : I haven't got any more money

8 — What's up ? Are you sick ?
9 It's better to be rich and in good health
10 than to be poor and sick !

EXERCISES

1. They have 5 children : 2 daughters and 3 sons. — **2.** We are busy learning French. — **3.** She is used to cooking : she has a large family. — **3.** Ready ? Well, go ahead ! — **5.** Your pullover is on back-to-front.

3 Il m'a ..... un .... la semaine dernière.

He gave me a ring last week.

4 Qu'est- .. - ... . ' ... que ce ...... ?

Je ne sais pas.

What on earth is that thing ? -I don't know.

5 Il .... être riche ... pauvre.

It's better to be rich than poor.

Fill in the blanks

1 Lequel - m'est égal. — **2** - pas la peine - plus. — **3** passé - coup de fil . — **4** ce que c'est - machin. — **5** vaut mieux - que.

QUARANTE-NEUVIEME (49ème) LEÇON

REVISION ET NOTES

1 We have already seen that *qui* and *que* are used to express : which that who(m) etc. depending on whether the relative is **subject** *(qui)* or **object** *(que).*
We also know the compound relatives *ce qui* and *ce que.*
Now we have a plural form
ceux qui — ceux que
Ceux qui veulent venir, dépêchez-vous ! : Those who (subject) want to come, hurry up !
Les bleus sont ceux que je n'aime pas : the blue ones are those which I don't like.

2 *devoir : je dois* [dwah] *, tu dois ; il/elle doit ; nous devons ; vous devez ; ils/elles doivent* [dwahv]
This expresses the idea of "must" "to have to".
It is generally followed by an infinitive.
Nous devons partir : we must leave
Il ne doit pas boire : he musn't drink
Ça doit être eux : that must be them.
The past participle is *dû.*
Elle a dû partir means *either* -she had to leave **or** -she must have left. Another simplification. *(devoir* means also "to owe")

3 Another common and idiomatic verb is *valoir* : to be worth. It is usually found in these forms :
Ça vaut cent francs : it is worth 100 F.
Ils ne valent rien : they are worth nothing.
-and in these idioms :
Est-ce que ça vaut la peine ? : Is it worth the trouble ?
Il vaut mieux partir : you had better leave.
Est-ce qu'il vaut mieux acheter un appartement ou en louer un ? : Is is better to buy an apartment or to rent one ?
We will gradually see more and more such idioms but only when they appear in a natural context.

49th LESSON

The "second wave"

So far, your studying has been passive - all we have asked you to do is to read, understand and let the feel of the language sink in.
Tomorrow begins the active phase : it will add about five minutes to your daily study. Here is what we want you to do :
When you have been through Lesson 50 in the usual way, go back to Lesson I. After listening to it again and reading the French text through aloud, cover it up with a piece of paper and try and reproduce it from the translation opposite. Check through afterwards, or stop the minute you block on something and repeat it again. Lesson 51 will send you back to Lesson 2 and so on.

This is the way to consolidate and develop your knowledge, going from the receptive stage to the reproductive stage until finally you reach -in your own time - the creative, or generative stage.
But, above all, enjoy yourself !

CINQUANTIEME (50ème) LEÇON

Une lettre

Chers parents,

1 Me voilà - enfin - en vacances dans le Midi (1).
2 J'ai fait beaucoup de choses et j'ai rencontré plein de (2) gens.
3 Avant hier, j'ai visité la Camargue (3). Quelle merveille (N-1) !
4 J'ai même essayé de monter à cheval...
5 Hélas ! Le résultat n'était pas brillant !
6 Hier, j'ai téléphoné à Oncle Jacques, qui vous embrasse,
7 et aussi j'ai acheté plein de cadeaux pour vous.
8 Malheureusement, j'ai oublié d'apporter mon appareil de photo (4) ;
9 J'ai emprunté celui de Michel, mais il n'a pas marché.
10 Donc, j'ai acheté des cartes postales, c'est mieux (5) que rien.
11 Les vacances arrivent à leur fin : je pars après-demain.

PRONONCIATION

2 Zhay fay. .zhay ronkontray
3 Avonteeyair. .veezeetay. .kamarg. .mervay
4 . . .essayay
5 .Aylass. .rayzoota. .etay. .breeyohn
6 .eeyair. .telefohnay
8 . . .oobleeyay. .apparay
9 . .ompruntay. . .marshay
10 . .ashtay. .

50th LESSON

A letter

Dear parents

1 Here I am - at last - on holiday in the Midi.
2 I have done many things and I have met loads of people.
3 [The day] before yesterday, I (have) visited the Camargue. What [a] marvel !
4 I (have) even tried to ride (mount to) a horse. .
5 Alas ! the result wasn't brilliant.
6 Yesterday, I (have) bought loads of presents for you.
8 Unfortunately I (have) forgotten to take my camera.
9 I (have) borrowed Michel's (the one of M.), but it did not (has not) work.
10 Thus I (have) bought post-cards ; it's better than nothing.
11 The holidays approach (arrive at) their end ; I [am] leaving [the day] after tomorrow.

NOTES

(1) *Le Midi* is not, as one would expect, the middle of France, but the South ! *un accent du Midi* : a southern accent BUT *il est midi :* it is 12.00 midday.
(2) A colloquial way of saying *beaucoup de* (a lot of). It is invariable.
(3) *La Camargue* is a beautifully wild region of lakes and marshes on the Mediterranean coast to the east of Montpellier. It is famous for its white ponies.
(4) There is a series of words in French that we call "false friends" they look like English words but mean something different.
une caméra is a good example : it means : a movie camera. A camera is *un appareil de photo.*
(5) We have already come across this word : it is an irregular comparative of *bien.*
Il joue bien : he plays well ; *elle joue mieux que lui :* she plays better than him.
Don't forget that French uses *bien* for good.

12 Je sais que cette lettre n'est pas très longue
13 mais au moins, ça prouve que j'ai pensé à vous.
14 Je vous‿embrasse bien fort. Votre fils (6) Paul.

PRONONCIATION

13 . .ponssay
14 . .feess

EXERCICES

1. C'est une carte postale, mais c'est mieux que rien. — 2. Hier, nous avons visité la Camargue. — 3. Vous n'avez pas acheté trop de cadeaux, j'espère. — 4. Mon fils a oublié son appareil de photo. — 5. mais il a emprunté celui de son cousin.

Fill in the blanks :

1 J'ai fait .... choses et j'ai ...... beaucoup de ....

I've done loads of things and I've bought a lot of presents.

2 ... frère a .... que moi.

My brother played better than me.

12 I know that this letter isn't very long
13 but at least it proves that I (have) thought of you
14 All my love (I kiss you very strong). Your son Paul.

NOTES (suite)

(6) Remember the pronunciation [feess]

EXERCISES

1. It's a post-card, but it's better than nothing. – **2.** Yesterday we visited the Carmargue. – **3.** You haven't bought too many presents, I hope. – **4.** My son forgot his camera. – **5.** but he borrowed his cousin's.

J'AI MÊME ESSAYÉ DE MONTER À CHEVAL.

3 J' .. .. Oncle Jacques qui vous ....

I phoned Uncle Jack, who sends his love.

4 Les vacances .... à ....

The holidays are approaching their end.

5 J' .. .. mon stylo, donc j' .. ..
..... de Michel.

I forgot my pen so I borrowed Michel's.

CINQUANTE-ET-UNIEME (51ème) LEÇON

R.S.V.P. (1)

1 Et maintenant, quelques questions : où est Paul ?
2 Qu'est-ce qu'il a fait avant - hier ? (2)
3 Est-ce qu'il a visité Montpellier ?
4 A qui est-ce qu'il a téléphoné ?
5 Est-ce-qu'il a pris des photos ? Pourquoi pas ?
6 Qu'est-ce qu'il a essayé de faire en (3) Camargue ?
7 Quand ‿ est-ce que les vacances se terminent ?

---

8 — Quelle dure journée aujourd'hui au bureau !
9 Nous ‿ avons travaillé comme quatre.

PRONONCIATION

air ess vay pay
3 . .monpeleeyay
7 .Konteske. .

Fill in the blanks

1 plein de - acheté - cadeaux. — **2** Mon - joué mieux. — **3** -'ai téléphoné à - embrasse. — **4** arrivent - leur fin. — **5** -'ai oublié - ai emprunté celui.

* * *

Second wave : Première Leçon

Please spend the extra time necessary to do this "second wave" : it's worth the effort !

51st LESSON

R.S.V.P.

1 And now, a few questions : where is Paul ?
2 What did he do [the day] before yesterday ?
3 Did he visit M. ?
4 To whom did he telephone ?
5 Did he take [any] photos ? Why not ?
6 What did he try to do in [the] Camargue ?
7 When do the holidays finish ?

8 — What [a] hard day today at the office !
9 We worked like four.

NOTES

(1) If you have ever received a formal invitation, you will know these letters ***R**épondez* ***S**'il* ***V**ous* ***P**laît* (Please Reply). When writing notes, the French often abbreviate *s'il vous plaît* to *svp*.

(2) As for the present tenses, we are showing the less formal (spoken) way of forming questions. When this has become almost automatic, we will introduce the more elegant form.

(3) *La Camargue* : the Camargue ; *la Bretagne* : Brittany, but we say *Elle va en Bretagne tous les ans* : she goes to B. every year. *Nous prenons nos vacances en Normandie* : We take our holidays in Normandy. When you are *in* a region or **going to** a region, you replace the definite article (*le, la*) by *en*.

10 – Vous devez‿être épuisé !
11 – Pas tellement (4). Nous sommes huit‿au bureau !

12 J'ai téléphoné ; il a acheté ; nous avons oublié

PRONONCIATION

10 . .aypweezay

EXERCICES

1. Est-ce que vous avez visité la Normandie ? – **2.** Est-ce qu'il a essayé ce chapeau ? – **3.** A qui est-ce que vous avez parlé au téléphone ? – **4.** Quelle dure journée ! Je suis épuisé ! – **5.** J'ai tellement de travail aujourd'hui !

Fill in the blanks :

1 L'année dernière, nous .... Bretagne.

Last year, we visited Brittany.

2 ... - .. - ... vous .... votre caméra?

Have you brought your movie-camera ?

3 Ils ... . une maison .. Normandie.

They have bought a house in Normandy.

10 – You must be exhausted !
11 – Not too much. There are eight of us (we are 8) in the office !
12 I (have) telephoned ; he (has) bought ; we (have) forgot(ten).

NOTES (suite)

(4) *Il fait tellement chaud ! :* it is so hot !
Aimez-vous le champagne ? -Pas tellement : Do you like champagne ? -Not so(much). *Il a tellement d'argent qu'il est malheureux :* He has so much money that he is unhappy.

EXERCISES

1. Have you visited (the) Normandy ? – **2.** Has he tried this hat ? – **3.** To whom did you speak on the phone ? – **4.** What a hard day ! I'm exhausted. – **5.** I have so much work today.

4 Nous ...... partir ..... - ....

We must leave the day after tomorrow.

5 .... - .. - ... le film .. commencé ?

When did the film begin ?

CINQUANTE-DEUXIEME (52ème) LEÇON

Un entretien d'embauche

1 — Eh bien, Monsieur Neveu, vous voulez travailler pour nous ?
2 — Oui, ç'est ça. Je n'ai pas d'emploi actuellement **(1)**.
3 — Alors racontez-moi **(2)** ce que vous avez déjà fait.
4 — Oh, j'ai fait beaucoup de métiers dans ma vie ;
5 J'ai conduit **(3)** des camions, j'ai joué du piano dans un cabaret . . .
6 — Oui, très intéressant, mais est-ce que vous avez travaillé dans la haute-couture ?
7 — Ben, en quelque sorte **(4)**. Mais j'ai aussi construit **(5)** des maisons

PRONONCIATION

ontretyen dombohsh
2 omplwa
4 . .meteeyay
5 . .kondwee. .zhooay. .kabaray
6 . .owt kootyoor
7 . .konstrwee

Fill in the blanks

1 - avons visité la - — **2** Est-ce que - avez apporté - — **3** - ont acheté - en - — **4** - devons - après-demain. — **5** Quand est-ce que - a -.

* * *

Second wave : Deuxième Leçon

52nd LESSON

A job interview (hiring)

1 — Well, M. N., you want to work for us ?
2 — Yes, that's right. I don't have a job at the moment.
3 — Well, tell me what you have already done.
4 — Oh, I have done many jobs in my life
5 I have driven lorries, I have played the piano in a cabaret. .
6 — Yes, very interesting, but have you worked in (the) high fashion ?
7 — Well, in a manner of speaking. But I have also built houses

NOTES

(1) Another "false friend" *actuellement* means now, at the moment. The adjective is *actuel* (fem. *actuelle)* : current, present. Actually is *en effet* (and is much less used than in English).

(2) *raconter* is to tell, but in the sense of narration, of telling a story. We know in English the word "a raconteur" (in fact, a French word) which means a story-teller. If I want to say "Tell me. ."a piece of information etc. I say *Dites-moi.* .

(3) *Conduire* (to drive) ; *je conduis ; tu conduis ; il conduit ; nous conduisons ; vous conduisez ; ils conduisent* [kondweez] past participle : *conduit.*

(4) *En quelque sorte* is a very useful expression meaning : in a certain way, in a manner of speaking.

(5) *construire* (to build) conjugated like *conduire.*

8 j'ai vendu (6) des glaces aux‿Esquimaux...
9 – Sans doute. Mais dans la haute-couture ?
10 – Vous tenez (7) absolument à le savoir ? -Bien sûr !
11 – Eh bien, quand j'étais en prison, j'ai repassé des chemises !

PRONONCIATION

8 . . .owzeskeemow
11 . .repassay

EXERCICES

1. Ils ont construit de nouveaux immeubles là-bas. – **2.** Qu'est-ce que vous faites actuellement ; ? – **3.** Etes-vous poète ? -En quelque sorte, j'écris des slogans [slowgohn]publicitaires. – **4.** Vous tenez absolument à y aller ? – **5.** Racontez-moi une histoire. – **6.** Il a fait beaucoup de métiers.

Fill in the blanks :

1 Qu'est .. - .. 'il . déjà .... ?

What has he done already ?

2 Il n'aime pas ... .

He doesn't like his present job.

8 I have sold ice-creams to Eskimos.
9 – Without doubt. But in (the) high fashion ?
10 – You insist absolutely on knowing ? -Of course!
11 – Well, when I was in prison, I ironed shirts !

NOTES (suite)

(6) *vendre* – past participle – *vendu*
rendre (to give back) – *rendu*, etc. .

(7) *tenir* : to hold. *Je tiens ; tu tiens ; il tient ; nous tenons ; vous tenez ; ils tiennent* [tyen] - past participle (irreg.) : *tenu.* This idiomatic construction (followed by *à)* means : to insist on, to hold on to,.
Il tient à le faire : he insists on doing it.
Elle y tient comme à la prunelle de ses yeux : she holds to it like the apple of her eye
Vous tenez à savoir ? : you really want to know ?

EXERCISES

1. They have built some new blocks of flats over there. – **2.** What are you doing at the moment ? – **3.** Are you (a) poet ? -In a manner of speaking. I write publicity slogans. – **4.** You really want to go there ? – **5.** Tell me a story. – **6.** He has done a lot of jobs.

3 Quand j' .... prison, j'ai repassé des ....

When I was in prison, I ironed shirts.

4 C'est très intéressant ....

It's undoubtedly very interesting.

5 Elle n' . ... de voiture.

She has never driven a car.

CINQUANTE-TROISIEME (53ème) LEÇON

Encore le passé !

1 — Regardez ce que j'ai trouvé ! Un billet de cent francs !
2 — Ça alors ! J'en ai justement perdu un !
3 — Est-ce que vous avez vu (1) le nouveau film de Godard ?
4 — Non, j'ai voulu **(2)** le voir mais je n'ai pas encore **(N-2)** eu le temps.
5 — Qu'est-ce qu'il y a ? Le cafard ? **(3)**
6 — Oui ; ce matin, j'ai reçu ma feuille d'impôts ;
7 hier, j'ai reçu deux factures, un relevé **(5)** d'électricité

PRONONCIATION

4 . .pazonkor yoo
5 . .kafar
6 . .foy dampoh
7 . .relevay

Fill in the blanks

1 - ce qu' - a - fait. — **2** - son emploi actuel. — **3** - étais en - chemises. — **4** - sans doute. — **5** - a jamais conduit -.

* * *

Second wave : Troisième Leçon

53rd LESSON

Again the past !

1 — Look what I've found ! A 100 F. note !
2 — There's a thing ! I've lost one !
3 — Have you seen the new film by (of) Godard ?
4 — No, I wanted to see it but I haven't yet had the time.
5 — What's the matter ? Down in the dumps ?
6 — Yes, this morning I received my tax-form ;
7 yesterday, I received two bills, an electricity bill

NOTES

(1) *Voir* (to see) — past participle *vu*
(2) *Vouloir* (to want) — past participle *voulu*
(3) *Un cafard* is literally a cockroach !
We suppose that if one has a surplus of them, one feels down in the dumps because that's what this idiom means !
Oh la la ; j'ai le cafard ! : Oh dear ! I feel down !
(4) *Recevoir* (to receive) — *je reçois, tu reçois, il reçoit, nous recevons, vous recevez, ils reçoivent* [reswahv] — past participle : *reçu.*
(5) *Une facture* or *une note* both mean bill or invoice (the latter is especially used for restaurant bills), *un relevé* is a word used for electricity, gas or phone bills — or, as in line 6, a bank statement.

8 et mon relevé de banque : je n'ai pas le sou **(6)**.

9 – Est-ce qu'ils‿ont fini leur repas ? Je veux débarrasser la table.

10 – Ils‿ont commencé il y a **(7)** deux heures à peu près

11 mais ils n'ont pas‿encore pris le dessert. **(8)**

PRONONCIATION

11 . .dayssair

EXERCICES

1. J'en ai perdu un il y a deux minutes. – **2.** Qu'est-ce qu'elle a ? -Elle a le cafard. – **3.** Est-ce que vous avez fini votre repas ? – **4.** Non, je n'ai pas encore pris le dessert. – **5.** Elle n'a pas encore eu le temps de le voir. – **6.** Ils ont débarrassé la table il y a un quart d'heure.

QU'EST-CE QU'IL
Y A ?
LE CAFARD
?

Fill in the blanks :

1 Il est fauché ; il . 'a ... . ! [foshay]

He is broke ; he hasn't got a bean !

8 and my bank-statement : I haven't got a bean.
9 – Have they finished their meal ? I want to clear the table.
10 – They began two hours ago, about
11 but they haven't yet had (taken the) dessert.

NOTES (suite)

(6) *Un sou* is a coin which no longer exists (it was worth 5 old centimes) ; the word, however, is used popularly to mean money.
Il est près de ses sous : he is close to his money (i.e.miserly)
Je n'ai pas le (or *un) sou :* I haven't a penny.
(7) We know *il y a* meaning "there is" or "there are". If we find it **before** a measure of time, it means "ago".
Je l'ai vu il y a cinq minutes : I saw it (him) 5 minutes ago.
Notice it must be placed **before** the noun.
(8) *Prendre* (take) – past participle *pris*

EXERCISES

1. I lost one (of them) 2 minutes ago. – **2.** What's the matter with her ? She's down in the dumps. – **3.** Have you finished your meal ? – **4.** No, I haven't yet had dessert. – **5.** She hasn't yet had time to see it/him. – **6.** They cleared the table a quarter of an hour ago.

2 C'est un ...... de 100 F. J' .. .. un.

Is that a 100 F. note ? I have lost one.

3 J'ai toujours ..... voir ce film.

I have always wanted to see that film.

4 Moi aussi ; je .. l' .. ... encore ..

Me too ; I haven't seen it yet.

5 Ce matin, . ' .. .... deux .... et mon

...... de banque.

This morning, I received two bills and my bank-statement.

CINQUANTE-QUATRIEME (54ème) LEÇON

Une mauvaise rencontre

1 Un jour, à Paris, Monsieur Le Clerc va faire des courses (1).
2 Au marché il rencontre un étranger (2) un grand (3) homme habillé en noir.
3 L'étranger lui dit : -Mais que faites-vous ici M. Le Clerc ?
4 – Qui êtes-vous ? répond notre homme -Je suis la Mort.
5 Terrifié (4), M. Le Clerc rentre à la maison, fait sa valise
6 et dit à sa femme : -J'ai rencontré la Mort.

PRONONCIATION

1 . .koorss
2 .etronzhay. .grontom abeeyay. .

Fill in the blanks

1 - n' - pas le/un sou. — **2** - billet - en ai perdu -. — **3** - voulu - **4**- ne ai pas - vu. — **5** - j'ai reçu - factures - relevé -

* * *

Second wave : Quatrième Leçon

54th LESSON

A bad encounter

1 One day in Paris, Mr. L.C. goes shopping.
2 At the market, he meets a stranger - a tall man dressed in black.
3 The stranger says to him : -But what are you doing here Mr. L.C. ?
4 — Who are you ? replies our man ; -I am Death
5 Terrified, Mr. L.C. goes back to his house, packs (does) his case
6 and says to his wife : -I have met Death

NOTES

(1) *Faire des courses :* to go shopping (usually in the market). You may also hear the expression : *faire du shopping* (no translation). *Une course* is also a race.
(2) *Un étranger* has two meanings : a stranger (someone you don't know) and a foreigner : rely on the context. *Etrange* (adj.) : strange, unusual.
à l'étranger also means abroad :
Il habite à l'étranger : he lives abroad
(3) *Grand* means big, but applied to a person, can also mean "tall". For a building, we would say *haut* [oh].
(4) The past participle is also used as an adjective, in which case it will of course, agree. If we were talking about Mme Le Clerc, we would write *terrifiée* (the pronunciation does not alter).

7 Je pars pour Toulouse. Adieu **(5)** chérie !
8 Mme Le Clerc est furieuse **(6)** : elle croit à **(7)** une mauvaise plaisanterie.
9 Alors elle va au marché et trouve le grand étranger.
10 – Alors, pourquoi vous‿avez effrayé mon mari ?
11 La Mort lui répond : -Bien, Madame, je suis surpris :
12 J'ai vu votre mari à Paris, mais j'ai rendez-vous avec lui
13 ce soir . . . à Toulouse.

PRONONCIATION

7 . .adyeu
8 . .krwa. .plezontree

EXERCICES

1. Elle a vu son mari au marché et elle est surprise. – **2.** Est-ce qu'il vient demain ? -Je crois. – **3.** Il rentre à la maison et fait sa valise. – **4.** J'ai rendez-vous avec lui à dix heures et demie. – **5.** C'est un grand homme habillé en noir.

Fill in the blanks :

1 Elle a . . . . la Mort et elle est . . . .

She has met Death and she is terrified.

7 I'm leaving for Toulouse. Goodbye darling !
8 Mme L.C. is furious ; she believes it is a bad joke.
9 So she goes to the market and finds the tall stranger.
10 – Well, why did you frighten my husband ?
11 Death replies : -Well, Mme I am surprised.
12 I saw your husband in Paris but I have [a] meeting with him
13 this evening . . .in Toulouse.

NOTES (suite)

(5) This way of saying goodbye has an air of finality i.e. the next time we see each other if will be with God *(Dieu)*. In some parts of France, it is colloquially used to replace the usual *Au revoir !*

(6) masc. : *furieux.*

(7) *Croire* (to believe) ; *je crois ; tu crois ; il croit ; nous croyons ; vous croyez ; ils croient* [krwah] - past participle : *cru*
croire en quelqu'un : to believe in someone i.e. to trust them have faith in them.
croire à quelque chose : to believe something to be true. French uses : *Je crois* where English says : I think so.

EXERCISES

1. She saw her husband at the market and she is surprised. – **2.** He is coming tomorrow ? -I think so. – **3.** He goes back to the house and packs his suitcase. – **4.** I have a meeting with him at 10.30. – **5.** He's a tall man dressed in black.

2 Est-ce que vous .... Dieu ?

Do you believe in God ?

3 Je .... dans cinq minutes pour ....

I'm leaving in five minutes to do the shopping.

4 Mais que ...... - .... ici ?

But what are you doing here ?

5 ..... histoire est un peu ....

This story is a little strange.

CINQUANTE-CINQUIEME (55ème) LEÇON

1 L'autre soir, M. Martin a assisté à un cocktail **(1)** au bureau.
2 Il a mangé quelques petits sandwichs **(1)** et des canapés
3 mais il a surtout bu **(2)** !
4 Il a bu quatre grands whiskys **(1)**
5 et ensuite il a vidé une bouteille de champagne !
6 A dix‿heures, il a décidé de rentrer chez lui.
7 Il a laissé sa voiture et il a pris un taxi.
8 Arrivé devant sa maison, il a réalisé qu'il n'avait **(3)** pas ses clefs **(4)**.

Il est important de faire votre étude **tous les jours** *(It is important to do your study every day).*

PRONONCIATION

1 . .koktel. .sondweesh. . .
3 . .byoo. .weeskee. .
5 . .veeday
8 . .navay. .klay

Fill in the blanks

1 - rencontré - terrifiée. — **2** - croyez en -. — **3** - pars - faire les courses. — **4** -faites-vous -. — **5** Cette - étrange.

* * *

Second wave : Cinquième Leçon

55th LESSON

1 The other evening, Mr M. attended (at) a cocktail [party] at the office.
2 He ate a few small sandwiches and some canapés.
3 but above all he drank !
4 He drank 4 big whiskies
5 and afterwards he emptied a bottle of champagne !
6 At 10.00 he decided to go back home.
7 He left his car and (he) took a taxi.
8 Arriving (arrived) in front of his house, he realized that he didn't have his keys.

NOTES

(1) In this lesson, we can see how French has adopted certain English words directly. There are in fact many and for several years, there has been a movement to prevent this phenomenon, called "Franglais". To pluralise these words, the French simply add a silent "s".

(2) *boire* (to drink) ; *je bois ; tu bois ; il boit ; nous buvons ; vous buvez ; ils boivent* [bwahv] - past participle : *bu ; une boisson* : a drink.

(3) We have already seen *j'étais, il était* (I/he was), *j'avais, il avait* (I/he had). This is the imperfect tense which we will study later. Note how these two forms are used in this text.

(4) *Une clef :* a key is sometimes written *une clé* (pl. *des clés) ;* this doesn't change the meaning.
fermer à clef : to lock. To unlock is simply *ouvrir.*

9 Alors il a voulu entrer par la fenêtre mais, étant **(N-3)** un peu ivre,
10 il n'a pas pu **(5)** : il a cassé un carreau.
11 Tout‿à coup, quelqu'un a ouvert la fenêtre en haut
12 et a crié : -Mais qu'est-ce que vous faites, nom de Dieu !
13 C'était son voisin. Ce n'était pas sa maison !

PRONONCIATION

9 . .eevr
10 . .pyoo. .karroh
11 . .on oh
13 .Setay. .

EXERCICES

1. Pouvez-vous assister à la réunion (*) ce soir ? – **2.** Ils ont bu trois bouteilles de champagne ! – **3.** Il n'avait pas ses clefs et il n'a pas pu entrer. – **4.** Etant un peu ivre, il a cassé un carreau. – **5.** Nous avons laissé notre voiture et nous allons prendre un taxi.
(*) la réunion : the meeting.

Fill in the blanks :

1 Ils ... . entrer ... la fenêtre.

They wanted to go in through the window.

2 Il a entendu une voix [vwa] ; . ' ..... son ......

He heard a voice ; it was his neighbour.

3 Il . ..... mais il a ....

He ate but, above all, he drank.

9 So he wanted to enter through (by) the window but, being a little drunk,
10 he couldn't : he broke a [window]-pane.
11 Suddenly, someone opened the window above (on high)
12 and shouted : -But what are you doing, for God's sake (in the name of God) !
13 It was his neighbour. It wasn't his house !

NOTES (suite)

(5) *pouvoir* (can, be able to) ; *je peux ; tu peux ; il peut ; nous pouvons ; vous pouvez ; ils peuvent* [perv] - past participle : *pu.* Any verb following it is in the infinitive.

EXERCISES

1. Can you attend the meeting, this evening ? – **2.** They drank three bottles of champagne ! – **3.** He didn't have his keys and he could not get (go) in. – **4.** Being a little drunk, he broke a [window] - pane.– **5.** We have left our car and we are going to take a taxi.

4 Elle . ... qu'elle n' ..... pas ... clefs.

She realized that she didn't have her keys.

5 Ils .... venir ..... ils veulent.

They can come when they like.

CINQUANTE-SIXIEME (56ème) LEÇON

REVISION ET NOTES

1. We know that *quel (quelle,* etc. .) means which but we can also use these words in exlamations :

Quel homme !	What a man !
Quelle ville !	What a town !
Quels élèves !	What pupils !

Notice that there is no indefinite article in French. Also, like any adjective, *quel* must agree with its noun. (This only makes a difference in pronunciation when the noun is plural and begins with a vowel, in which case we make the *"liaison"* : *Quels élèves* [kelzelev]. The exclamation "What ? !", indicating surprise or disbelief, is *Quoi* ?!

2. *Encore,* with a negative verb, means yet :
Je ne l'ai pas encore vu : I haven't seen it/him yet.
Elle n'a pas encore fini : She hasn't finished yet.
However, in the interrogative, the word disappears : whereas English says : Has she finished yet ?, French would say : *Est-ce qu'elle a fini ?*
Est-ce que vous l'avez vu ? : Have you seen it yet ?

To be more emphatic, in English, we use "still" instead of "yet" : She still hasn't finished (i.e. and she started

Fill in the blanks

1 - ont voulu - par - . — **2** C'était - - voisin. — **3** - a mangé - surtout bu. — **4** - a réalisé - avait - ses -. — **5** - peuvent - quand -.

* * *

Second Wave : Sixième leçon

56th LESSON

some time ago). French translates this idea with *toujours*
Elle n'a toujours pas fini ! : She still hasn't finished !
Il ne m'a toujours pas payé ! : He still hasn't paid me !
Notice that *encore* comes after *pas* and *toujours* before it. (to revise another use of *encore,* see Lesson 20).

3. *Le participe présent* is formed by taking the first person plural of the verb and replacing *-ons* by *-ant.*

Donner — donnons — donnant giving
finir — finissons — finissant finishing
vendre — vendons — vendant selling

It can be used as an adjective — in which case it must agree with the noun :
Quelle ville charmante ! : What a charming town !
or as part of a verb - then it is invariable.
Etant un peu ivre, elle a cassé . . : Being a little drunk, she broke . . .Often, we put *en* before it. This gives us the idea of "while" "on", etc. .
but is often left untranslated in English.
Elle descend la rue en mangeant : She goes down the road eating
Il se coupe en se rasant : he cuts himself (while) shaving
Be careful of the English construction :
I saw him going upstairs
The subject is **not** the person who is climbing the stairs : to avoid any possible ambiguity in French, we express

the second action by an infinitive :
Je l'ai vu monter les escaliers
We heard him singing : *nous l'avons entendu chanter*

Special note : verbs like to lie *(s'étendre),* to hang *(pendre)* and to sit *(s'asseoir) :* French uses the past participle where English uses the present.

Perhaps you have noticed that we have given you very few rules about writing French - especially why, when and where to put accents (however, you already know the difference, for example, between *à* -the preposition (to, at, etc. .) and *a* -the verb (has) or between the preposition *sur* (on) and the adjective *sûr*. This lack of rules

---

CINQUANTE-SEPTIEME (57ème) LEÇON

Deux bonnes réponses

1 Un homme est‿assis dans‿un bus, une pipe à la bouche.
2 Un contrôleur lui dit : -Vous ne pouvez pas fumer ici !
3 — Je ne fume pas, répond l'homme calmement.
4 — Mais vous‿avez une pipe à la bouche ! s'écrie le contrôleur.
5 — D'accord. J'ai aussi des chaussures aux pieds
6 mais je ne marche pas !

7 Visitant la Sorbonne **(1)**, un touriste

PRONONCIATION

4 . .saykree

is deliberate because firstly we want to stimulate your intuition and secondly because there are more important things to worry about ! We will come to writing in due time.

Meanwhile, work regularly and do the Second Wave. You should be able now to start generating sentences and start substituting different pronouns and verb forms, or different nouns. But don't try to run before you can walk !

* * *

Second Wave : Septième leçon

57th LESSON

Two good answers

1 A man is sitting in a bus, a pipe in his (the) mouth.
2 An inspector says [to] him : -You can't smoke here !
3 — I'm not smoking replies the man calmly.
4 — But you have a pipe in your (the) mouth ! cries the inspector.
5 — O.K. I also have shoes on my (the) feet
6 But I'm not walking !

7 Visiting the Sorbonne, a tourist sees an impres-

NOTES

(1) La Sorbonne, in the Latin Quarter, is one of the oldest and most prestigious universities in Europe.

voit une bibliothèque (2) impressionnante.
8 Au-dessus de la porte est marqué : "Bibliothèque Félix Fournier"
9 — Je ne connais pas cet‿auteur ; qu'est-ce qu'il a écrit ?
10 — Son guide sourit et lui répond : -Un gros chèque !

PRONONCIATION

8 . .fayleeks fourneeyay
9 . setohteur
10 . .groh shek

EXERCICES

1. Visitant la Sorbonne, ils ont vu un bâtiment impressionnant. — **2.** Si vous voulez acheter mon livre, allez dans une librairie. — **3.** Il a des chaussures aux pieds et un chapeau sur la tête. — **4.** Passez-moi un coup de fil demain. -D'accord. — **5.** L'affiche est au-dessus de la porte.

Fill in the blanks :

1 Vous ...... fumer si vous ......

You can (may) smoke if you want.

2 Je .. .. auteur ; qu'est-ce qu'il . ..... ?

I don't know this author ; what did he write ?

sive library

8 Above the door is marked "Library F.F."

9 – I don't know this author ; what did he write ?

10 – His guide smiles and replies (to him) : -A fat cheque !

NOTES (suite)

(2) *Une bibliothèque* : a library. In a house, it is a bookcase. A "false friend" : *une librairie :* a book-shop. *un libraire :* a book-shop owner. *un bouquin* [bookan] is a slang word for a book.
Have you noticed that, when telling stories, French prefers the present tense to the past ? This is called *"le présent historique"* and gives added force to the narrative, bringing incidents right up to the present moment. (it also makes our life simpler !).
Detective or adventure stories often use this device, though not newspapers.

EXERCISES

1. Visiting the Sorbonne, they saw an impressive building. – **2.** If you want to buy my book, go (in) to a book-shop. – **3.** He has shoes on his feet and a hat on his head. – **4.** -Give me a ring tomorrow. -O.K. – **5.** The poster is above the door.

IL A DES CHAUSSURES AUX PIEDS ET UN CHAPEAU SUR LA TÊTE.
CENSURÉ

3 Il ...... et ... . : -Un chèque.

He smiles and answers (him) : -A chèque.

4 Remettez le livre dans .. ..

Put the book back in my book-case.

5 Il .... , une pipe . .. bouche.

He was seated, a pipe in his mouth.

CINQUANTE-HUITIEME (58ème) LEÇON

Un peu de tourisme

1 St-Jean-le-Mont est‿un ravissant petit village qui se trouve
2 à cinquante kilomètres de Paris en pleine forêt **(1)**.
3 Vous sortez de l'autoroute et vous prenez la R N 6 **(2)** ;
4 ensuite vous prenez une petite route, bordée d'arbres

DE TOUTE FAÇON, J'AIME SEULEMENT LA MUSIQUE CLASSIQUE.

PRONONCIATION

1 .sahzhohn lemohn. .raveessohn. .veelazh
2 . .foray
3 . .air en seess
4 . .borday. .

Fill in the blanks

1 - pouvez - voulez. — **2** - ne connais pas cet - a écrit. — **3.** - sourit - lui répond : - . — **4** - ma bibliothèque. — **5** - était assis - à la - .

* * *

Second Wave : Septième Leçon
better see that one twice !

58th LESSON

A little tourism

1 St-Jean-le-M. is a ravishing little village which is situated (finds itself)
2 (at) 50 km from Paris in the middle of a (full) forest.
3 You get off the motorway and you take the RN 6 ;
4 next you take a tiny (a little) road lined [with] (of) trees

NOTES

(1) *plein* means full (empty : *vide)* but, used in expressions with *en,* it means "right in the middle of", etc. .
En plein désert : in the middle of the desert
En pleine rue : right out in the road (notice the agreement with a feminine noun).
En plein air : in the open air.

(2) French roads are designated by a number and an initial letter.
Une autoroute : a motorway e.g. A 6.
Next in importance, we have *la route nationale : e.g. la R.N 10* then comes *la départementale : e.g. la D 603.*
There are other, lower orders too.
une carte routière : a road map
Notice the difference between *la rue :* the street and *la route :* the road.

5 et vous entrez dans le village au bout de (3) trois kilomètres.
6 Vous passez d'abord devant un étang et tout de suite
7 vous arrivez devant la Mairie et la place du marché.
8 Il faut aller (N-1) d'abord au Syndicat d'Initiative (4)
9 pour savoir (5) ce qu'il y a à visiter.
10 Ensuite, une visite à l'église s'impose (6) ;
11 elle date du quatorzième siècle et elle est splendide.
12 Comme la plupart (7) des églises en France, elle est catholique.

à suivre

PRONONCIATION

5 . .oh boo. .
6 . .aytohn. .tootsweet. .sandeeka deeniseeateev
10 . .sampohz. .
12 . .plyoopar

UNE VISITE À L'ÉGLISE S'IMPOSE.

EXERCICES

1. Vous passez devant la Mairie et vous arrivez à la place du marché. – **2.** Il faut aller tout de suite au Syndicat d'Initiative, – **3.** pour savoir ce qu'il y a à visiter. – **4.** Une visite à l'église s'impose. – **5.** Il est assis en plein soleil.

5 and you enter (in) the village at the end of 3 km.
6 You pass first in front of a pond and straight away
7 you arrive in front of the Town Hall and the market place.
8 You must go first to the Information Office
9 to find out what there is to visit.
10 After, a visit to the church is called for :
11 it dates from the 14th century and it is splendid.
12 Like (the) most (of) churches in France, it is Catholic.

to be continued

NOTES (suite)

(3) *Le bout* [boo] : the end (meaning the final extremity, the tip; the end meaning the finish of a performance, or of a narrative, is *la fin).*
au bout de trois ans : after, at the end of 3 years
L'avion est au bout de la piste : the plane is at the end of the runway.
Aller au bout de la rue : go to the end of the street.
(4) *Le Syndicat d'Initiative* is an office, run by the town or city council, responsible for the promotion of that town (its tourist attractions, events, shows, etc. .)
(5) *savoir* (to know something) ; *je sais ; tu sais ; il sait ; nous savons ; vous savez ; ils savent ;* - past participle (irreg.) : *su*
pour savoir : to find out
(6) *imposer :* to impose ; *imposant :* imposing
The reflexive form, used to describe an object, means "is called for", "is necessary"
Le champagne s'impose ! : champagne is called for !
(7) *La plupart des gens :* most people
La plupart des gens dans la rue : most of the people in the street. Only English makes the distinction between definite and indefinite.

EXERCISES

1. You pass in front of the Town Hall and you arrive at the market place. – **2** You must go straight away to the Tourist Office, – **3** to find out what there is to visit. – **4**. A visit to the church is called for. – **5.** He is sitting right in the sun.

Fill in the blanks :

1 Allez .. .. la rue et tournez . ...

Go to the end of the road and turn left.

2 .. maison est ...... en ...... forêt.

His/her house is situated in the middle of the forest.

3 Je .... savoir .. .. ' .. . . à faire ici.

I want to know what there is to do here.

4 .. .. églises ici sont catholiques.

Most of the churches here are Catholic.

CINQUANTE-NEUVIEME (59ème) LEÇON

Un peu de tourisme (suite)

1 Nous sommes toujours dans notre joli village
2 et nous venons de visiter **(N-2)** l'église de Sainte-Marie **(1)**.
3 Nous‿allons maintenant faire un petit tour dehors
4 pour admirer les beaux jardins publics avec leurs pelouses,
5 leurs rosiers et leurs‿arbres en fleurs.

PRONONCIATION

3 . .de-or
5 . .rohzeeyay

5 . .   . . . .   visiter la cathédrale :   . . . .   est splendide.

You must visit the cathedral ; it is splendid.

Fill in the blanks

1 - au bout de - à gauche. — **2** Sa - située - pleine -. — **3** - veux - ce qu'il y a -. — **4** La plupart des - . — **5** Il faut - elle .

* * *

Second Wave : Huitième Leçon

59th LESSON

A little tourism (continued)

1 We are still in our pretty village
2 and we have just visited the church of St Mary.
3 We are now going to make a little tour outside
4 to admire the beautiful public gardens with their lawns,
5 their rose-bushes and their trees in bloom(s).

NOTES

(1) *Saint* is considered, before a name, as an adjective. So, it must agree : *Saint-Jean* [sahn zhon] but *Sainte Marie* [sant maree], abbreviated respectively to S^t. and S^{te}.

6 Maintenant, si ça vous dit **(2)**, on peut visiter le musée
7 où l'on **(3)** peut voir toute l'histoire de St-Jean-le-Mont. . .
8 Ah bon ? Vous n'êtes pas friands **(4)** de musées ?
9 Quoi alors ? Ah, ça y est **(5)** ; j'ai compris.
10 Nous continuons alors notre promenade, contournant la gendarmerie
11 et nous nous dirigeons vers la place du marché
12 et voici la fin de notre voyage : le "Restaurant de France".

PRONONCIATION

6 . .myoozay
8 . .freeohn
11 . .direezhon vair

EXERCICES

1. Ça y est ! Il a enfin compris !. – **2.** Je suis friand de poulet. – **3.** Nous allons faire un petit tour dehors, d'accord ? – **4.** Nous pouvons visiter le musée, est-ce que ça vous dit ? – **5.** Nous sommes toujours à la leçon cinquante-neuf.

6 Now, if you feel like it, we (one) can visit the museum
7 where we (one) can see all the history of St. -J. -le. -M.
8 Oh really ? You're not fond of museums ?
9 What then ? Ah, so that's it ; I've understood.
10 We continue, therefore, our walk, going around the police-station,
11 and we go (direct ourselves) towards the market place
12 and here is the end of our journey : (the) "Restaurant of France".

NOTES (suite)

(2) *Est-ce que cela (ça) vous dit ? :* does that tempt you ?
Mmm une glace ! Ça me dit ! : Mmm an ice-cream ! I'd love one !
Ça ne me dit rien du tout : that really doesn't tempt me (remember, idioms are impossible to translate : we attempt to give you the best equivalents).
(3) The I is only here for emphasis, to avoid the two vowels *ou on.* However, in spoken French, it would seem a little precious to put it in. Its use is a matter of style.
(4) *J'aime les musées :* I like museums
Je suis friand de musées : I'm found of museums
If a woman is speaking, she says : *je suis friande. . .*
(5) Another idiom, an exclamation uttered when something has been understood, realised, etc. .
Had Archimedes been French, *Ça y est !* would have been his Eureka !

EXERCISES

1. That's it ! He has understood at last ! – **2.** I'm fond of chicken. – **3.** We are going to make a little tour outside, OK ? – **4.** We can visit the museum, do you feel like it ? . – **5.** We're still at lesson 59

Fill in the blanks :

1 Sortir maintenant ? Ça .. .. du tout.

Go out now ? That really doesn't tempt me.

2 Nous .... la belle pelouse et le rosier.

We admired the beautiful lawn and the rose-bush.

3 .. . ... ! J'ai ...... la réponse !

That's it ! I've found the answer !

SOIXANTIEME (60ème) LEÇON

Le téléphone

1 "Une moitié de la France attend **(N-3)** le téléphone
2 et l'autre moitié attend la tonalité".
3 Cette boutade était vraie il y a quelques années,
4 mais aujourd'hui elle ne l'est plus,
5 parce que, depuis dix‿ans, le réseau s'est modernisé **(1)**

PRONONCIATION

1 . .mwateeyay. .
3 bootad
5 . .rayzoh

4 Je .... vous dire que ça ne m'intéresse pas.

I have just told you that it doesn't interest me.

5 .. .... visiter le jardin si .. ..

We can visit the garden if that interests you.

Fill in the blanks

1 -ne me dit rien -. — **2** - avons admiré. — **3** Ça y est - trouvé. — **4** - viens de - . — **5** On peut - ça vous dit.

* * *

Second Wave : Neuvième Leçon

60th LESSON

The telephone

1 One half of France [is] waiting [for] the telephone
2 and the other half [is] waiting [for] the dialling-tone.
3 This joke was true a few years ago
4 but today it is no longer [so]
5 because for ten years, the network has been modernised (modernised itself)

NOTES

(1) We have seen how most verbs form their past tense with *avoir* + past participle. But, for reflexive verbs (those with *se* in front of the infinitive), we must use *être* preceded by the relevant relative pronoun.
Je me suis coupé hier : I cut myself yesterday
Il s'est blessé : he injured himself
Vous vous êtes lavé ce matin : You (sing.) washed yourself this morning.

6 et maintenant il est l'un des meilleurs (2) du monde.
7 Si vous n'avez pas le téléphone (3) chez vous,
8 il vous suffit de trouver l'une (4) des nombreuses cabines publiques
9 ou bien, vous pouvez téléphoner à partir d'un café (5)
10 ou encore d'un bureau de poste.
11 Mais faites‿attention : à partir de certaines cabines,
12 vous ne pouvez téléphoner qu'à Paris. (6)

PRONONCIATION

6 . .mayeur
8 . .kabeen
12 . .kaparee

NOUS N'AVONS QUE VINGT FRANCS.

EXERCICES

1. Il s'est coupé le doigt il y a dix minutes. – **2.** Il vous suffit de téléphoner pour avoir un taxi. – **3.** Cette boutade n'est plus vraie. – **4.** Nous n'avons que vingt francs. – **5.** Vous ne pouvez pas m'appeler ; je n'ai pas le téléphone. – **6.** C'est l'un des meilleurs du monde.

6 and now it is one of the best in the world.
7 If you don't have a (the) telephone [at] your home
8 it is sufficient [for] you to find one of the numerous public cabins
9 or, you can telephone from a café
10 or again from a post-office.
11 But be careful : from certain cabins,
12 you can only phone in (to) Paris.

NOTES (suite)

(2) *Bon* : good ; *meilleur :* better *; le meilleur :* the best
Ce café est meilleur que l'autre : this coffee is better than the other.
Il est le meilleur [mayeur] *de la classe* : he is the best in the class (fem. : *la meilleure*).
Remember that *mieux,* which is the comparative of *bien,* is often used instead of the adjective *bon* and its comparative.
(3) *Je n'ai pas le téléphone* : I don't have a phone. The use of *le* is idiomatic.
(4) The *l',* like in lesson 59 line 7, is euphonic. The same comments apply.
(5) *Nous sommes ouverts à partir de dix heures :* We are open from ten o'clock (BUT :
Nous sommes ouverts de 9h à 12 h : we are open from 9h. to 12 h).
A partir de maintenant : from now on. . .
A partir de cette cabine, vous pouvez appeler l'étranger : From this cabin, you can call abroad.
(6) Here is another negation *ne. . . que :* only
Je n'ai que cinq minutes : I only have 5 minutes
Il ne parle qu'anglais : He only speaks English.
(an alternative construction is with *seulement*
J'ai seulement cinq minutes ; il parle seulement anglais)

EXERCISES

1. He cut his finger 10 minutes ago. — **2.** It is sufficient for you to telephone to have a taxi. — **3.** This joke is no longer true. — **4.** We have only 20 francs. — **5.** You can't call me ; I don't have a phone. — **6.** It/he is one of the best in the world.

Fill in the blanks :

1 Je .. .. ce matin.

I washed (myself) this morning.

2 Il .. comprend ... le français. -C'est dommage.

He only understands French. -That's a pity.

3 . ... maintenant, vous êtes seul.

From now on, you are alone.

4 Il est .... en mathématiques.

He is better than me at maths.

SOIXANTE-ET-UNIEME (61ème) LEÇON

Le téléphone (suite)

1 Pour téléphoner, il est préférable de connaître (1) le numéro de votre correspondant (2).
2 Si vous ne le connaissez pas, vous pouvez le chercher dans l'annuaire

PRONONCIATION

2 . .lannyooair. .

5 Qu'est- .. .. ' .. . . ? J' .... la tonalité.

What's the matter ? I'm waiting for the dialling tone.

Fill in the blanks

1 - me suis lavé -. —**2** - ne - que -. — **3** - à partir de -. — **4** - meilleur que moi - . — **5** - ce qu'il y a - attends -.

* * *

Second Wave : Dixième leçon

61st LESSON

The telephone (cont.)

1 To telephone, it is preferable to know the number of your correspondent.

2 If you don't know it, you can look [for] it in the phone-book

NOTES

(1) *Connaître* : to know ; *je connais ; tu connais ; il connait ; nous connaissons ; vous connaissez ; ils connaissent* -past participle *: connu*
Elle est connue : she is well-known

(2) Notice the difference in spelling with English. The sense is broader than in English, where "correspondent" means a person to whom one writes. In the metro, you will see signs : *correspondance ;* this means : transfer lines.

3 ou, plus simplement, faire **(3)** le douze et demander aux Renseignements **(4)**.
4 Ensuite, vous décrochez le combiné, mettez vos pièces
5 et faites le numéro au cadran. Simple, n'est-ce pas **(5)** ?
6 Zut ! Occupé ! Raccrochez et essayez plus tard.
7 – Pardon Madame, pouvez-vous m'aider s'il vous plaît ?
8 Je n'arrive pas **(6)** à obtenir ce numéro.
9 – Qu'est-ce que c'est comme numéro ? -Le 86.53.97
10 – Et c'est‿à Paris ? -Non, à Lyon
11 – Eh bien, vous devez faire le 16 pour la province **(7)**
12 et ensuite, l'indicatif pour Lyon et enfin votre numéro.

PRONONCIATION

3 . .ronsaynyemohn
4 . . kombeenay. .
5 . .kadrohn. Sampl ness-pa
6 Zyoot
9 . . .katrevanseess.sankontrwa.katrevandeesset
11 . .provanss

3 or, more simply, dial (the) 12 and ask (to the) Information
4 Next, you lift (unhook) the receiver, put [in] your coins
5 and dial the number (do the number on the dial). Simple, isn't it ?
6 Blast ! Engaged ! Hang up and try later.
7 – Pardon, Madam, Can you help me please ?
8 I can't get this number.
9 – What number is it ? -86.53.97
10 – And is it in Paris ? -No, in Lyon.
11 – Well, you must dial (do the) 16 for the provinces
12 and after, the code for Lyon and finally your number.

NOTES (suite)

(3) This verb has over thirty different uses (when preceded by the reflexive pronoun *se*, many of them correspond to the English use of "get") : here we see it in the sense of to dial a number (a dial : *un cadran ;* a sun-dial : *un cadran solaire).*

(4) One complication in English is our distinction between countable and uncountable nouns (for example, we cannot put the indefinite article in front of words like furniture, news etc. . .). This does not exist in French.
un renseignement : a (piece of) information
un meuble : a (piece of) furniture

(5) This invariable expression corresponds to the English "tag" questions "isn't it" ?, etc. .It is not nearly as frequently used as its English counterparts.
Il fait chaud, n'est-ce-pas ? : It is hot, isn't it ?
Vous habitez ici, n'est-ce pas ? : You live here, don't you ?
Vous l'avez vu, n'est-ce pas ? : You saw him, didn't you ?
Another simplification !

(6) *J'essaie, mais je n'arrive pas. . :* I try but I can't manage. . .
Il n'arrive pas à comprendre : he just can't understand.
The use of *ne pas arriver* gives us the idea of a repeated effort that fails.
Je ne peux pas le faire : I can't do it (but I've only tried once or twice)
Je n'arrive pas à le faire : I can't manage to do it (no matter how many times I try)

(7) *La province* [provanss] : the provinces -i.e. anything which is not Paris
Ils ‿ habitent en province means more that they don't live in Paris than that they live in the provinces ! *un(e) provincial(e) :* someone from the provinces. Do not confuse with *la Provence* [provonss], that beautiful region in the South East of France.

EXERCICES

1. Décrochez le combiné, mettez vos pièces et faites le numéro. – **2.** Je veux un renseignement, s'il vous plaît. – **3.** Il est plus simple de le chercher dans l'annuaire. – **4.** Le numéro que vous avez fait est occupé. – **5.** Je n'arrive pas à obtenir mon correspondant.

Fill in the blanks :

1 Cet homme est ..... ; Oui, c'est Alain Delon . ' n' ... - .. ... ?

This man is well-known ; Yes, it's Alain Delon, isn't it ?

2 Elle . ... plusieurs fois, mais elle n'y ....

She has tried several times but she can't manage it.

3 J'ai .. .. très important.

I have a very important piece of information.

SOIXANTE-DEUXIEME (62ème) LEÇON

Ne soyons (1) pas trop sérieux

PRONONCIATION

swayohn

EXERCISES

1. Lift the receiver, put [in] your coins and dial the number. — **2.** I want a piece of information, please. — **3.** It is simpler to look it up in the directory. — **4.** The number you have dialled is engaged. — **5.** I can't get through to my correspondent.

4 Je .... l' .... pour Lyon d'abord.

I must dial the code for Lyon first.

5 .. .. d'arriver ..... neuf heures

It is preferable to arrive before nine o'clock

Fill in the blanks

1 - connu - n'est-ce pas ? — **2** - a essayé - arrive pas. — **3** - un renseignement. — **4** - dois faire - indicatif. — **5** Il est préférable - avant -.

* * *

Second Wave : Onzième Leçon

62nd LESSON

Let's not be too serious

NOTES

(1) This is a subjunctive of *être* and it corresponds to the English imperative Let's be . . .(which, in fact, is itself a subjunctive). *Soyez heureux :* Be happy. We will look at the subjunctive in more detail later.

1 Un homme baratine **(2)** une jolie serveuse dans un restaurant :
2 — Ma chère, n'y a t-il pas trois petits mots que vous aimeriez entendre ?
3 — En effet répond la fille - et ils sont "Gardez la monnaie"

4 Un Breton fête la naissance de l'enfant de sa soeur.
5 — Patron, servez une tournée générale : c'est moi qui paie.
6 Ma soeur vient d'accoucher !
7 Le patron du bistrot **(3)** lui demande : - C'est un garçon ou une fille ?
8 Le Breton se tait **(4)** brusquement. -J'ai oublié de le demander ;
9 Je ne sais pas si je suis un oncle ou une tante **(5)**

10 Pendant un entretien **(6)** un journaliste ose demander à Brigitte Bardot :
11 — Qu'est-ce que vous vous mettez **(7)** la nuit ?
12 Réponse : —Du Chanel numéro cinq !

PRONONCIATION

1 . .barateen
2 . .neeyateelpa. . .emereeyay
4 . .fet. .nessonss
5 . .dakooshay
7 . .beestroh
8 . .se tay brooskemohn

1 A man [is] chatting up a pretty waitress in a restaurant :
2 – My dear, are there not three little words that you would like to hear ?
3 – In fact [there are] replies the girl -and they are "Keep the change"

4 A Breton [is] celebrating the birth of his sister's child.
5 – Landlord serve a round for everybody (a general round) : I am paying (it is me who pays)
6 My sister has just given birth !
7 The landlord of the café asks him -Is it a boy or a girl ?
8 The Breton suddenly shuts up : I forgot to ask. (it)
9 I don't know if I am an uncle or an aunt.
10 During an interview a journalist dared ask Brigitte Bardot :
11 – What do you put on at night ?
12 Reply : -Chanel number 5 !

NOTES (suite)

(2) *Baratiner* is a popular expression which means to chat up, to turn on the charm. People say : *Du baratin !* to dismiss the unctuous phrase, much as we say Rubbish ! or Baloney ! in English

(3) A slang word for *café* (or sometimes a small restaurant) the origin comes from the Russian officers who, at the turn of the century, shouted at the Parisien waiters the Russian words for "Quickly". . .*bistro !*

(4) *Se taire :* to shut up.
Je me tais, tu te tais, il se tait, nous nous taisons, vous vous taisez, ils se taisent. Past participle : *tu. Taisez-vous !* : Shut up !

(5) *Les parents* means both parents and relatives ; other relatives are : *un cousin* [koozan] (Fem. : *une cousine). Un grand-père* a grand father. *Une grand-mère* (notice that *grand* does not agree) a grand mother ; *(les grands-parents) -un beau-père* a father-in-law. *Une belle-mère* : a mother-in-law *(les beaux-parents) ;* more later.

(6) *"Franglais"* (See Lesson 55, note 1) prefers : *une interview* and the (hideous) verb *interviewer* [anterviouvay]. Notice that we say *un journaliste* or *une journaliste,* the noun remaining unchanged.

(7) *Se mettre* : to put on (clothes, etc...)

EXERCICES

1. L'homme a commencé à baratiner la jolie serveuse – **2.** qui lui a répondu "Taisez-vous !". – **3.** Vous avez des frères ou des soeurs ? -En effet. J'ai un frère et une soeur. – **4.** Patron, ce n'est pas moi qui paie.! – **5.** Qu'est-ce que vous vous mettez quand vous allez à l'Opéra ?

Fill in the blanks :

1 La ..... - .... et le ..... - .... sont les ..... - ....

The grand mother and the grand father are the grand parents

2 Ma .... ' avoir un enfant !

My cousin has just has a child !

3 N' . . . . ' .. pas quelque chose ... vous voulez entendre ?

Isn't there something you want to hear ?

4 Vous êtes Breton . ' ... - .. - ... ? En ..... .

You are Breton aren't you ? I am indeed

SOIXANTE-TROISIEME (63ème) LEÇON

REVISION ET NOTES

1 *Falloir* (to be necessary, to have to) is what is called

EXERCISES

1. The man began to chat up the pretty waitress. — **2.** who answered (to him) : -Shut up ! — **3.** Have you [any] brothers or sisters ? -Indeed. I have one brother and one sister. — **4.** Landlord, I'm not paying ! — **5.** What do you put on you when you go to the Opera ?

5 Jacques ! ..... sérieux s'il vous plaît !

Jacques ! Be serious, please !

Fill in the blanks

1 - grand-mère - grand-père - grands-parents. — **2** - cousine vient d'-. — **3** -y a t-il - que -. — **4** - n'est-ce pas ? - effet. — **5** -soyez.

* * *

Second Wave : Douzième Leçon

63rd LESSON

an "impersonal verb" and it takes a little time to master. First, in the present, it is only found in the third person singular form *il* (never *elle*) faut.
Quand on fait une omelette, il faut trois oeufs [euh]

When you (one) make(s) an omelet, you need (one needs) 3 eggs.
Il faut beaucoup de patience pour faire cela :
You need a lot of patience (or : a lot of patience is necessary) to do that. The problem here is that English dislikes impersonal forms like "one" and usually either attributes an imaginary "you" or constructs a passive form, making it difficult to convey the "impersonal" empirical feeling of *il faut. Je ne veux pas manger ça ! -Il faut manger ! :* I don't want to eat that !
-You must eat (i.e. it is necessary that you do so). *Pour aller en France, est-ce qu'il faut un passeport ? :* To go to France, is a passport necessary ?
Enough for now. We will look at more complex forms later.

2 "Have just done. ." is expressed in French by the idiomatic construction *venir de . . .* (please, don't translate it literally !) + infinitive :
Il vient de partir : he has just left
Nous venons de manger : we have just eaten
With reflexive verbs, it comes before the reflexive pronoun :

SOIXANTE-QUATRIEME (64ème) LEÇON

1 (Yannick, un jeune Canadien, est‿en vacances en France)
Chers parents,
2 Mon séjour à Paris se passe **(1)** très bien, -mais si vite !

PRONONCIATION

2 . .sayzhour

Elle vient de se lever : She has just got up
Je viens de me laver les mains : I have just washed my hands.
As in English, there is no real negative or interrogative.

3 *Ah, ces maudites prépositions !* (Ah, these cursed prepositions !)
which to use - or when not to use one ? It will make life easier if you remember the word : CAPERED - this stands for :

C*hercher* (to look for) – **A***ttendre* (to wait for)
P*ayer* (to pay for) – **E***couter* (to listen to)
R*egarder* (to look at) – **E***spérer* (to hope for)
D*emander* (to ask for)

None of these verbs is followed by a preposition in French (except for one or two special uses we will see later).

* * *

Second Wave : Treizième Leçon

64th LESSON

1 Yannick, a young Canadian, is on holiday in France. Dear Parents
2 My stay in Paris is going (happening) very well - but so quickly !

NOTES

(1) *Se passer :* to happen
Qu'est-ce qu'il s'est passé ? : What happened ?
Il se passe toujours quelque chose à Paris : Something is always happening in P. We also use the verb to describe the passing of time
Trois ans se sont passés . . . : 3 years went by. .
Mon cours se passe bien : My lesson is going well
(notice the "s" *on cours* : it is still singular).

3 Hier, je suis allé **(N-1)** à la Tour Eiffel. Que c'est impressionnant ! **(2)**
4 Je suis monté au deuxième étage, qui est déjà très haut :
5 quelque chose comme cent quinze mètres, je crois.
6 Alors, je suis descendu au bout de cinq minutes.
7 (Pierre est resté plus longtemps, au moins un quart d'heure)
8 Je sais que **(3)** c'est très sûr, mais j'ai quand même **(4)** eu peur.
9 La semaine dernière, paraît-il **(5)**, quelqu'un est tombé !
10 Pierre est redescendu enfin et nous sommes partis voir les fontaines du Trocadéro.
11 Nous sommes rentrés à la maison à sept heures du soir.
12 Que j'ai bien dormi !

PRONONCIATION

3 . .tour effel
7 . .kar deur
8 . .syoor
9 . .paray teel
10 . .fonten

EXERCICES

1. Il fait beau ! Que je suis contente ! – **2.** Elle a gagné quelque chose comme deux mille francs. – **3.** Nous sommes partis au bout de vingt minutes. – **4.** C'est votre fils ? Qu'il est grand ! – **5.** Il m'a appelé, paraît-il, mais je n'ai rien entendu. – **6.** Qu'est ce qui se passe ici ?

3 Yesterday, I went to the Eiffel Tower. How impressive it is !
4 I went up to the second floor, which is already very high :
5 something like 115 metres I think.
6 So I went down after 5 minutes
7 (P. stayed longer, at least a quarter of an hour)
8 I know that it is very safe, but all the same I was scared (had fear).
9 Last week, so it seems, someone fell !
10 P. came down finally and we left to see the T. fountains.
11 We went back (to) home at 7.00 in the evening
12 How well I slept !

NOTES (suite)

(2) Another exclamatory form, after *Que. . .!*
Que c'est joli ! : How pretty it is !
Qu'elle est belle ! : How pretty she is !
Que je suis content ! : How happy I am !
We can use it with verbs as in line 12 :
Que j'ai bien mangé ! : How well I have eaten ! (i.e. what a great meal !)

(3) We would tend to say in English : I know it is safe i.e. we suppress the relative "that". We must *never* do this in French: *qui + que* must always be included.

(4) *Quand même :* even so ; all the same
Je vais quand même essayer : I'll try all the same
Il est quand même venu : He came all the same.
Notice its position : between the auxiliary and the participle. *(eu* you will remember, is the past participle of *avoir)*

(5) *Paraître* : to appear (in the sense of : to seem) ; *je parais ; tu parais ; il paraît, nous paraissons ; vous paraissez ; ils paraissent*. past participle : *paru*
Paraît-il : so it seems, it is said to be (implies doubt)
Il est millionnaire, paraît-il : He is supposedly a millionaire.

EXERCISES

1. The weather is fine ! How happy I am ! – **2.** She won something like 2.000 F. – **3.** We left after 20 minutes. – **4.** Is this your son ? How big (tall) he is ! – **5.** Apparently he called me, but I heard nothing. – **6.** What's happening here ?

Fill in the blanks :

1 Je .... au deuxième étage

I went up to the second floor.

2 Il ... . au .... de dix minutes

He came down after ten minutes

3 Il ... . voir ses amis

He left to see his friends

4 Nous .... à la maison très tôt.

We went back home very early

5 Quelqu'un ... . du troisième étage

Someone fell from the third floor

SOIXANTE-CINQUIEME (65ème) LEÇON

La Tour Eiffel

1 Gustave Eiffel est né **(N-1)** en mil huit cent trente deux - 1832 - **(N-2)** à Dijon.
2 Il est devenu ingénieur très jeune.
3 Il a toujours voulu construire quelque chose d'extraordinaire **(1)**

PRONONCIATION
1 .Goostav effel. .nay. .meel weesohn vantrwa
2 . .anzhenyeur
3 . .konstrweer

6 Je .... deux fois en Bretagne

I went twice to Brittany

Fill in the blanks

1 - suis monté - – **2** - est descendu - bout. – **3** -est parti - – **4** -sommes rentrés – **5** - est tombé - – **6** - suis allé.

* * *

Seconde Wave : Quatorzième Leçon

65th LESSON

The Eiffel Tower

1 G.E. was born in Dijon
2 He became [an] engineer very young.
3 He always wanted to construct something (of) extraordinary

NOTES

(1) Notice the presence of the partitive article *de* in such expressions as *quelque chose de grand :* something big ; *quelque chose d'intéressant :* something interesting ; *Qu'est-ce que vous voulez boire ? -Quelque chose de chaud :* What do you want to drink ? -Something hot.

4 donc il est venu à Paris en mil huit cent quatre-vingt-six -1886-
5 pour la Grande Exposition, où sa tour a gagné le premier prix (2)
6 La construction a commencé en mil huit cent quatre - vingt - sept -1887- et a duré deux‿ans.
7 La tour est construite en fer et mesure trois cent vingt mètres de haut (3).
8 Il y a trois‿étages et une antenne de télévision tout‿en haut.
9 Heureusement, depuis mil neuf cent soixante-cinq -1965- il y a un ascenseur électrique.
10 Mais en mil neuf cent vingt -‿trois, -1923- un journaliste est descendu du troisième étage en bicyclette !
11 La tour a coûté six millions et demi de francs à construire
12 et elle appartient maintenant à la ville de Paris (4)
13 Gustave Eiffel est mort en mil neuf cent vingt-trois -1923-

PRONONCIATION

5 . .pree
7 . .fair
10 . .beeseeklet

EXERCICES

1. Si on va au cinéma, je veux voir quelque chose de drôle. – **2.** Sa tour a gagné le premier prix à l'exposition. – **3.** La boîte fait un mètre de haut et soixante-dix centimètres de large. – **4.** Il a toujours voulu être ingénieur. – **5.** Il y a une antenne de télévision tout en haut.

4 so he came to Paris in 1886 -
5 for the Great Exhibition, where his tower won the first prize.
6 The construction began in 1887 and lasted two years.
7 The tower is constructed of (in) iron and measures 320 m. in height.
8 There are 3 floors and a television aerial right at the top.
9 Fortunately, since 1965 there is an electric lift.
10 But in 1923, a journalist went down from the 3rd floor by bicycle !
11 The tower cost 6 and a half million francs to construct
12 and it now belongs to the city of Paris.
13 G.E. died in 1923.

NOTES (suite)

(2) *Un prix* [pree] (pl. *des prix)* means either : a price or a prize
gagner un prix : to win a prize
payer le prix : to pay the price
gagner also means : to earn money.
Combien est-ce qu'il gagne ? : How much does he earn ?
(3) *Six mètres de haut :* six meters high. Once again the (untranslated) partitive article.
deux mètres de large : two meters wide
vingt centimètres de long : 20 cm long
la hauteur [ohteur] : the height ; *la longueur :* the length
la largeur : the width ; *la profondeur :* the depth
(4) *Une ville* means both town and city.

EXERCISES

1. If we go to the cinema, I want to see something funny. — **2.** His tower won first prize in the Exhibition. — **3.** The box is (makes) I m. high and 70 cm wide. — **4.** He has always wanted to be an engineer. — **5.** There is a television aerial right at the top.

Fill in the blanks :

1 Il ... . professeur . l' ... .. vingt ans

He became a teacher at the age of 20.

2 Elle ..... quatre mille francs par mois.

She earns 4.000 francs a month.

3 Son père ... . il y a deux ans.

His father died two years ago.

4 Ce livre .... ma belle-mère.

This book belongs to my mother-in-law.

5 Le film . .... deux heures

The film lasted two hours.

SOIXANTE-SIXIEME (66ème) LEÇON

La promenade du dimanche

1 La famille Leclerc a bien déjeuné ce dimanche
2 et les‿enfants viennent de terminer la vaisselle
3 pendant que (1) les parents font‿une petite sieste ;

PRONONCIATION

2 . .vessel

Fill in the blanks

1 - est devenu - à - âge de- — **2** - gagne - — **3** - est mort - — **4** - appartient à - — **5** - a duré.

IL EST DEVENU INGÉNIEUR TRÈS JEUNE.

* * *

Second Wave : Quinzième Leçon

66 th LESSON

The Sunday walk

1 The Leclerc family has eaten well this Sunday
2 and the children have just finished the washing up
3 while the parents [are] taking (doing) a little nap ;

NOTES

(1) *pendant trois ans :* for 3 years ;
pendant la guerre : during the war.
pendant que : while. *Pendant que je lis :* While I am reading
Cependant : however

4 mais maintenant, ils vont se promener (2) dans les bois.
5 Ils s'apprêtent (3) à partir quand, tout‿à coup. . .
6 Valérie : -Oh, ça y est. Il pleut. Quel dommage !
7 Pierre : -Ça ne fait rien (4). Je vais chercher nos‿imperméables et nos bottes.
8 — Bon. A qui est (5) ce manteau ? Jean : -C'est le mien (N-3).
9 Pierre : -Voilà le tien, Valérie. Et tes bottes. A qui sont celles-là ?
10 Valérie : -Ce sont les miennes, je crois. Pierre : -D'accord ; et voilà les tiennes, Jean.
11 Tout le monde est prêt ? Bon. On y va. (6)
12 Le mien ; le vôtre ; la mienne ; la vôtre ; le/la nôtre.

PRONONCIATION

4 . .bwa
7 . .ampairmayabl
8 . . .myehn. .
9 . .tyehn
10 . .myenn. .tyenn
11 . .pray

EXERCICES

1. Il s'est promené dans les bois dimanche. – **2.** Pendant que les parents font une sieste, – **3.** les enfants terminent la vaisselle. – **4.** Je n'ai pas d'argent ! -Ça ne fait rien. C'est moi qui paie. – **5.** A qui sont ces bottes ? -A Jean. – **6.** Prêt ? Bon. On y va !

4 but now, they are going for a walk in the woods.
5 They [are] getting ready to leave when, suddenly. . .
6 V. -Oh, that's it. It [is] raining ! What a pity !
7 P. -That doesn't matter. I will (am going) fetch our raincoats and our boots.
8 – Good ; whose is this coat ? J. -It's mine
9 P. -Here is yours V. - And your boots. Whose are those (there) ?
10 V. -They are mine, I think. P. -O.K. and here are yours, J.
11 Everybody is ready ? Good. Let's go.
12 Mine (masc) ; yours (masc.) ; mine (fem.) ; yours (fem.) ours (masc +fem.)

NOTES (suite)

(2) *marcher :* to walk ; *se promener :* to go for a walk (for pleasure) *Il s'est promené* : he went for a walk ; *une promenade* : a (pleasure) walk *une marche :* a walk (as opposed to a drive, etc. .)
(3) *Vous êtes prêt ? :* Are you ready ?
s'apprêter à : to get ready
(4) This expression found its way into English as "san fairy ann !" It means it's not important, it doesn't matter.
Je suis en retard ! -Ça ne fait rien : I'm late -It doesn't matter.
(5) *A qui est ce manteau ? :* Whose is this coat ?
A qui appartient ce chapeau ? : To whom does this hat belong ?
A qui sont ces lunettes ? : Whose are these glasses ?
A moi : to me (mine) ; *A lui /elle :* to him/her.
(6) We have seen that *Allons* . . means Let's go. . if it is followed by another verb.
*Allons voir s'il est là :*Let's go and see if he is there.
But if we want to say : Let's go ! Let's be off !, we usually say *On y va !*

EXERCISES

1. He went for a walk in the woods (on) Sunday. – **2.** While the parents are having a nap, – **3.** the children are finishing the dishes. – **4.** I haven't got any money ! It doesn't matter. I'm paying. – **5.** Whose are these boots ? -John's – **6.** Ready ? Good. Let's go !

Fill in the blanks :

1 Je vais .... les imperméables ; il .....

I will fetch the raincoats ; it is raining

2 Les enfants .... terminer la leçon

The children have just finished the lesson

3 . ... ce stylo ? C'est .. ....

Whose is this pen ? It's mine.

4 . ... ces bottes ? Ce sont ... .

Whose are these boots ? They're yours (familiar form)

5 Où ... . ? Le .....

Where is mine ? (mas. sing.) Here it is.

SOIXANTE-SEPTIEME (67ème) LEÇON

L'optimiste et le pessimiste

1 La bouteille est‿à moitié pleine - La bouteille est‿à moitié vide !

2 (Au Nouvel‿An) Bonne année ! -Un

Fill in the blanks

1 - chercher - pleut. — **2** -viennent de -. — **3** -A qui est - le mien. — **4** A qui sont - les tiennes. — **5** - est le mien ? voilà.

You noticed that we have started to use the "familiar" pronoun "tu" : this is because members of the same family - and children, too - are addressing each other. It shouldn't present too many problems.

* * *

Second Wave : Seizième Leçon

67th LESSON

The optimist and the pessimist

1 The bottle is (at) half full -The bottle is (at) half empty !

2 (At the new year) Happy New Year (good

an de moins à vivre **(1)** !

3 "Après la pluie vient le beau temps "
-Quel temps de chien **(2)** !

4 Enfin les premiers beaux jours ! -Une hirondelle ne fait pas le printemps.

5 Ah ! Un mois de vacances au soleil ! -La rentrée **(3)** va être triste et dure.

6 Le vin va être très bon cette année ! - Les prix du vin vont ‿ augmenter.

7 Cette leçon est facile -Attendez demain !

8 Quelle différence y a-t-il entre un homme politique et un miroir ?

9 Les miroirs, eux **(4)**, réfléchissent **(5)** sans parler **(6)**,

PRONONCIATION

4 . .eerondel. .prahntohn
7 . .owgmontay
8 . .eeyateel
9 . .reflesheess. .

year) ! -One year less to live !

3 After the rain comes the fine weather. -What terrible weather !

4 At last the first fine days ! -One swallow doesn't make the spring

5 Ah ! One month of holidays in the sun ! - The return [is] going to be sad and hard.

6 The wine will be very good this year ! -The prices of wine [are] going to increase.

7 This lesson is easy -Wait for tomorrow !

8 What difference is there between a politician (political man) and a mirror ?

9 Mirrors (them) reflect without speaking,

NOTES

(1) We have already seen the difference between *un matin* and *une matinée.* Here we have a similar pair of words : *un an* and *une année.* It is easier to make the following generalisation : *une année* refers to the duration of the year whereas *un an* is a statistic (i.e.one year). We say :
Pendant l'année : during the year but *deux (trois. .) ans :* two (three etc.) years
Le Nouvel An : The New Year
Il a soixante-quinze ans : He is 75 years old.
Rather than try to give rules, we suggest you memorize a few examples

(2) An idiom meaning, literally : what a weather of dog (what terrible weather). You can also say : *Il tombe des cordes :* It's pouring down.

(3) A very French expression ! The majority of paid holidays are taken in the month of August (Paris, for example, is a ghost town). *La rentrée* (the return) is usually in September, when everyone comes back to work - usually at the same time. *La rentrée scolaire :* the new school year. *Rentrer* : to go back.

(4) Another idiomatic turn of phrase : we repeat the tonic pronoun to lend emphasis to the thing(s) or person(s) in question :
Marie est étudiante (Mary is a student) *mais Pierre, lui, est ingénieur* (but Peter, he's an engineer). In English. we achieve the same effect by repeating the noun. Line 9 Mirrors. .mirrors reflect without etc. .

(5) *réfléchir ; je réfléchis ; tu réfléchis ; il réfléchit ; nous réfléchissons ; vous réfléchissez ; ils réfléchissent* -past participle : *réfléchi*
Les verbes réfléchis : réflexive verbs. The verb means : to reflect (for mirrors or people).

(6) *sans parler :* without talking. The infinitive is always used after *sans.*

10 alors que (7) les hommes politiques parlent sans réfléchir.

EXERCICES

1. La salle était à moitié vide. – **2.** Le prix du vin a beaucoup augmenté. – **3.** Il a donné la réponse sans réfléchir. – **4.** Quelle différence y a-t-il entre un an et une année ? – **5.** Il a travaillé pendant trente ans. – **6.** Le vin va être très bon l'année prochaine.

Fill in the blanks :

1 Quel ..... de ..... ! - Attendez l' ....

What terrible weather ! Wait for next year

2 Pierre ne travaille pas, mais Marie, ... , travaille très ...

Peter doesn't work but Mary, she works very hard.

3 La tasse est . ...

The cup is half-full

4 Jeanne ne vient pas ! -Une personne .. ..

Jean isn't coming ! -One person less

10 whereas politicians speak without reflecting.

NOTES (suite)

(7) *alors :* well, so etc. *alors que :* whereas
(another expression with the same meaning is *tandis que* [tondeeke])

EXERCISES

1. The hall was half empty. – **2.** The price of wine has increased a lot. – **3.** He gave the answer without thinking. – **4.** What difference is there between "un an" and "une année" ? – **5.** He worked for 30 years. – **6.** The wine is going to be very good next year.

5 Ils .... toujours ....

They always talk without thinking (reflecting)

Fill in the blanks

1. temps-chien - année prochaine . – **2** - elle - dur -. – **3** - à moitié pleine. – **4** de moins. – **5** -parlent - sans réfléchir.

* * *

Second Wave : Dix-septième Leçon

SOIXANTE-HUITIEME (68ème) LEÇON

Le corps humain

1 Le corps de l'homme et de la femme est composé de trois parties :
2 la tête, le tronc et les membres.
3 La tête est d'habitude (1) couverte de cheveux (2), sinon on est chauve.
4 Les‿yeux (3), les sourcils, le nez, la bouche et le menton
5 forment le visage, beau ou laid !
6 Entre la tête et le tronc, il y a le cou.
7 Le tronc porte généralement deux bras et deux jambes.
8 Il y a d'autres‿usages pour ces mots que nous venons de voir :
9 Par exemple, on parle d'un tronc d'arbre ou des membres d'un gouvernement.

PRONONCIATION

kor yooma
2 . .trohn. .mombr
3 . .sheveu. .showv
4 .Layzyeu. .soorsee. .mohntohn
5 . . .lay

68th LESSON

The human body

1 The body of a (the) man and of a (the) woman is composed of 3 parts :
2 the head, the trunk and the limbs.
3 The head is usually covered with hair, if not you are (one is) bald.
4 The eyes, the eyebrows, the nose, the mouth and the chin.
5 form the face, beautiful or ugly !
6 Between the head and the trunk there is the neck.
7 The trunk usually has (carries) two arms and two legs.
8 There are other uses for these words which we have just seen :
9 For example, we talk (one talks) of a tree-trunk, or of the members of a government.

NOTES

(1) *Une habitude :* a habit ; *s'habituer à :* to get used to
Elle s'habitue à la vie en France : She is getting used to life in France
Avoir l'habitude : to be used to
J'ai l'habitude de conduire à droite : I am used to driving on the right
d'habitude : usually

(2) *Un cheveu :* a hair ; *des cheveux :* hair
Whereas English says : Your hair is long, the French more logically say : *vos cheveux sont longs. Couper les cheveux en quatre :* to split hairs (cut them in 4!)
La tête est couverte : Remember that the past participle is an adjective and, as such, must agree :
Les mains sont couvertes ; le corps est couvert.

(3) *un oeil* [oy] ; *des yeux* [yeu] is one of the few irregularly pronounced plurals in French. Three others are : *un oeuf ; des oeufs* [euh] : eggs
un boeuf ; des boeufs [beu] : ox(en) – *un os* [oss] *; des os* [oh] : bone

10 La Bible nous‿apprend : **(4)** oeil pour oeil, dent pour dent –
11 et si vous n'aimez pas ça, vous pouvez toujours faire la tête **(5)** !

PRONONCIATION

10 . .beebl. .oy. .dohn

EXERCICES

1. Il n'a pas envie d'y aller ; regardez sa tête ! – **2.** D'habitude, je bois du café le matin. – **3.** J'apprends ma leçon tous les soirs. – **4.** Il n'a pas l'habitude de cette machine. – **5.** Elle est grande, belle et elle a des cheveux blonds.

Fill in the blanks :

1 Le comité ... . de vingt ....

The committee is composed of twenty members

2 C'est notre professeur ; il .... l'histoire

He's our teacher ; he teaches us history.

3 Au Canada, .. parle .. français et . 'anglais.

In Canada, one speaks French and English.

4 . ' .... la tête est .... de ....

Usually the head is covered with hair.

10 The Bible teaches us : an eye for an eye and a tooth for a tooth.
11 and if you don't like that you can always pull (make the) a face !

NOTES (suite)

(4) There is a confusion in French between two verbs : to teach is *enseigner :*
Elle enseigne l'histoire : she teaches history
To learn is *apprendre ;* but often. French uses *apprendre* to mean both *Il apprend le français aux étrangers :* he teaches French to foreigners. Be on guard for this usage.
(5) *Il fait la tête ! :* He's pulling a face (i.e. he doesn't look happy)
Elle a une bonne tête : she looks honest, respectable, etc. .
tête is often used where English would use : face

EXERCISES

1. He doesn't want to go ; look at his face ! – **2.** Usually I drink coffee in the morning. – **3.** I learn my lesson every evening. – **4.** He is not used to this machine. – **5.** She is tall, beautiful and she has blond hair.

5 Il . . d' . . . . . . mots pour dire cela.

There are other words to say that.

Fill in the blanks

1 est composé - membres. – **2** - nous apprend - . – **3** on - le - l' - – **4** D'habitude - couverte - cheveux. – **5** - y a - autres -

* * *

Second Wave : Dix-huitième Leçon

SOIXANTE-NEUVIEME (69ème) LEÇON

Le corps humain (suite et fin)

1 Les bras se plient aux coudes et aux poignets.
2 Ils sont terminés par les mains, formées de cinq doigts dont **(N4)** le pouce
3 est un des plus utiles. Les doigts se terminent par les ongles.
4 Les jambes se plient aux genoux et aux chevilles.
5 D'habitude, on se tient debout **(1)** sur ses **(2)** pieds
6 et on dort couché **(3)** sur le dos.
7 Les gens peuvent être grands ou petits, gros ou maigres.
8 Nous espérons en tous cas que vous êtes en bonne santé.
9 Si vous avez faim et que vous êtes très pressé,

JE N'AI PAS LE TEMPS;
JE SUIS TRÈS PRESSÉ.
69

PRONONCIATION

1 . . .kood. .pwanyay
2 . .dwa. .pooss
4 . .plee. .zhenoo. .shevee
6 . .doh
7 . .groh. .megr
8 . .sontay

69th LESSON

The human body (continuation and end)

1 The arms bend (themselves) at the elbows and at the wrists.
2 They finish (themselves) by the hands, formed of 5 fingers of which the thumb
3 is one of the most useful. The fingers finish by the nails.
4 The legs bend at the knees and at the ankles.
5 Usually, one holds oneself up on one's feet
6 and one sleeps lying on one's back.
7 People can be large or small, fat or thin.
8 We hope, in any case, that you are in good health.
9 If you are hungry and (that) you are (very hurried) in a hurry

NOTES

(1) When in English, we say : she is standing over there, the word ' standing' is a supplementary piece of information - the main idea is that the person **is** over there. This is how we treat the situation in French:
Elle est là-bas
If we really wish to know if the person is sitting, standing, lying, etc. we must add the necessary adverb :
Elle est debout là-bas : she is over there, standing.
se mettre debout : to stand up
se tenir debout : to hold oneself up on one's feet
(2) *Il a mis ses chaussures là :* He put his shoes there.
On se tient debout sur ses pieds : One holds oneself up on one's feet
On a sa réputation : One has one's reputation.
Remember that *on* is much less formal than "one" in English and is often translated either by a passive construction or by an imaginary "you", "we".
(3) Remember that French considers *couché, assis, pendu* etc. as past participles (the initial action having been accomplished) whereas English treats them as present participles.
Il est assis en plein soleil : He is sitting right in the sun

10 vous pouvez manger sur le pouce (4) et si vous‿avez besoin d'aide
11 vous pouvez demander un coup (5) de main – et si on vous le refuse
12 on dit qu'on vous‿a tourné le dos.

PRONONCIATION

11 . .koo

EXERCICES

1. Elle est assise là-bas. – **2.** Nous espérons que vous êtes en bonne santé. – **3.** Je n'ai pas le temps ; je suis très pressé. – **4.** Vous avez cinq doigts dont un qui s'appelle "le pouce". – **5.** Donne-moi un coup de main, s'il te plaît. – **6.** Je lui ai demandé de l'argent et il m'a tourné le dos.

Fill in the blanks :

1 Trois personnes .... deux enfants étaient blessées

Three people, two of whom were children, were wounded

2 J'ai reçu six lettres .... trois de l' ....

I received 6 letters, three of them were from abroad.

3 C'est l'homme .... je vous .. ..

He's the man about whom I spoke to you.

4 Les mains .... par les doigts.

The hands end in fingers.

10 you can have a quick snack and if you need help
11 you can ask for a hand - and if one refuses you
12 we say that one has turned one's back [on] you.

NOTES (suite)

(4) An idiom : *manger sur le pouce :* to have a quick bite to eat. Where ? In *un snack* (a snack-bar), *un self* (a self-service restaurant) or *un fast-food* (!) Who says Anglo-Saxon cuisine has no influence ?

(5) One of the most common words to be found in French idiomatic expressions :
un coup literally means : a blow (we know, in English, a *"coup d'état")*
Donnez-moi un coup de main : give me a hand
We already know *un coup de fil :* a phone call
donner un coup de poing : to punch - *un coup de fusil :* a gun-shot and the famous *coup de foudre :* love at first sight.
We'll become good friends with *coup* during our studies !

EXERCISES

1. She is sitting over there. — **2.** We hope you are in good health. — **3.** I don't have time ; I'm in a hurry. — **4.** You have 5 fingers, one of which is called "the thumb". — **5.** Give me a hand, please (fam. form.). — **6.** I asked him for money and he turned his back on me. —

5 Elle dort .... sur .. dos.

She sleeps lying on her back.

Fill in the blanks

1 - dont - — **2** - dont - étranger. — **3** - dont - ai parlé. — **4** - sont terminées - — **5** - couchée - le - —

* * *

Second Wave : Dix-neuvième Leçon

SOIXANTE-DIXIEME (70ème) LEÇON

REVISION ET NOTES

1 The past tense with *être* : certain verbs form their past tense not with *avoir* + past participle, but with *être* + past participle (we already know that this is the case for reflexive verbs : *il s'est couché à huit heures :* he went to bed at 8.00).
Here is a list of the verbs which take *être* in the past. All except one concern movement.
Most denote a change in position and form opposite pairs :

aller (to go) ; *venir* (to come) ; *arriver* (to arrive) ; *partir* (to leave) ; *entrer* (to enter) ; *sortir* (to go out) ; *monter* (to go up) ; *descendre* (to go down) ; *retourner* (to return) ; *tomber* (to fall)
(and all compounds of these verbs beginning with *re - :* e.g. *revenir :* to come back ; *rentrer :* to go back in etc..
Three of them denote a change of state :
naître (to be born) ; *devenir* (to become) ; *mourir* (to die) and, just to be perverse : *rester* (to remain).
Read the following passage :
John came to the house at nine o'clock. He went to the front door. He went in and went up to the first floor. Nobody. He went downstairs and went out the back door. He returned and went back inside. His father was born in this house, he became famous and he died there : he fell from a window.
John stayed for ten minutes then he left.
Try and depict the situation. Now go back over it in your mind and read the translation:

John est venu à la maison à neuf heures. Il est allé à la porte principale. Il est entré et il est monté au premier étage. Personne. Il est descendu et il est sorti par la porte de derrière. Il est retourné et il est rentré. Son père est né dans cette maison ; il est devenu célèbre et il y est mort : il est tombé d'une fenêtre. Jean est resté dix minutes et puis il est parti.
A little far-fetched but it might help you to remember

70th LESSON

the verbs.

Since the past participle in these cases is an adjective, it must agree with its subject.
Elle est descendue : she went down ; *ils sont partis* : they (masc ;) left *elles sont sorties :* they went out (as always, if the subject includes both genders, we choose the masculine : *Jean et Marie sont restés :* John and Mary stayed.)
For the moment, this detail should not bother us too much since (a) it does not change the pronunciation and (b) we will return to written French later on.

2 *mille* . a thousand ; *un million :* a million
trois mille neuf cent vingt-deux : 3.922
un million neuf cent mille : 1.900.000
trois mille personnes : 3.000 people **but**
deux millions **de** *personnes* , **de** *francs,* etc. .
For dates, *mille* is often written *mil* (no difference in pronunciation) ; a date is treated simply as a number : 1625 : one thousand, six hundred and twenty five : *mil six cent vingt-cinq,* or *mille six cent vingt-cinq.* 1982 : one thousand nine hundred and eighty two : *mil neuf cent quatre-vingt-deux.* How do we say the following dates ? (answers at the end of the lesson)

1945 . 1863 . 1495 . 1787 . 1960 .

3 The possessive pronoun, like the possessive adjective *(mon, ma, mes,* etc. . .) agrees with the gender of the object possessed (not, as in English, with the possessor). Here are the pronouns :

le mien , la mienne, les miens, les miennes (mine)
le tien, la tienne, les tiens, les tiennes (your fam.)
le sien, la sienne, les siens, les siennes (his/hers)

le nôtre, la nôtre, les nôtres (ours)
*le vôtre, la vôtre, les vôtres (*yours -polite or plural)
le leur, la leur, les leurs (theirs)

This list might appear redoutable but a closer look will show you that in fact it is very regular and easy to remember.

4 *dont* is a very useful relative which expresses the English ideas of : "of whom" "of which" "whose" Look at these examples :
Les gens dont vous parlez : The people of whom you are speaking
La femme dont la voiture est dehors : The woman whose car is outside
La maison dont les fenêtres sont cassées : The house the windows of which are broken.

Do you notice that *dont* always follows the noun to which it relates ? Look again at the word order:
Le compositeur dont j'aime la musique : the composer whose music I like

We obviously do not expect you to learn all these rules

SOIXANTE ET ONZIEME (71ème) LEÇON

Une déception

1 – Anne, est-ce que c'est vrai que les Français aiment bien manger ?
2 – Mais oui. Cela fait partie **(1)** de nos qualités (ou de nos défauts !) ;
3 mais pourquoi tu me poses cette question ?
4 – Avant de venir en France, tout le monde m'a dit :

PRONONCIATION

2 . .kalitay. .dayfoh
3 . .powz

and tables by heart straight away. Look at the examples given in the texts and try, with this extra information, to extend your knowledge.

Answers to dates
1945 – *mil* (or *mille) neuf cent quarante-cinq*
1863 – *mil* (or *mille) huit cent soixante-trois*
1495 – *mil* (or *mille) quatre cent quatre-vingt-quinze*
1787 – *mil* (or *mille) sept cent quatre-vingt-sept*
1960 – *mil* (or *mille) neuf cent soixante.*

* * *

Second Wave : Vingtième Leçon

71st LESSON

A disappointment

1 – Anne, is it true that the French like to eat well ?
2 – But of course. That is part of our qualities (or of our faults !) ;
3 but why [do] you ask me this question ?
4 – Before coming (to come) to France, everybody told me :

NOTES

(1) *Cela (ça) fait partie de :* that is part of (one of) *une partie* a part ; *une partie de cartes :* a card-game (i.e. a session) ; a party : *une fête*
ça fait partie des traditions : that's one of the traditions.

5 "Ah, vous verrez (N1), en France, on mange bien ;
6 vous mangerez des spécialités, des produits frais,
7 vous goûterez à des "petits vins de pays" et tout et tout (2).
8 Mais ça fait trois jours que je suis ici (3)
9 et, aux Champs Elysées, par exemple, je n'ai vu que
10 des restaurants à hamburgers ou des pizzerias ... pas très typiques !
11 — Oui, mais le prix du mètre carré (4) est tellement élevé (5) là
12 que seuls les restaurants "industriels" sont rentables.
13 Mais ne t'en fais pas (6), mon touriste affamé.
14 Demain, je t'emmènerai dans un vrai restaurant français.

PRONONCIATION

5 . .veray
6 . .monzheray. .prodwee fray
7 . .gooteray. .payee aytooaytoo
10 . .omboorgair. .peetzeria
11 . .elevay
14 . . .tomeneray

EXERCICES

1. La cravate fait partie de l'uniforme. — **2.** En France, on mange bien. — **3.** Ça fait deux semaines que je travaille très dur. — **4.** Les prix en Suisse sont très élevés, mais les salaires sont élevés aussi. — **5.** Il n'a vu que des restaurants industriels.

5 "Ah you will see, in France, they eat well ;
6 you will eat specialities, fresh produce,
7 you will taste (at) "little country wines" and so on –
8 But I have been here for three days
9 and on (at) the CE for example, I have only seen
10 hamburger restaurants or pizzerias. . not very typical !
11 – Yes but the price of a (the) square metre is so high there
12 that only "industrial"restaurants are profitable.
13 But don't worry, my starving tourist.
14 Tomorrow I will take you to a real French restaurant.

NOTES (suite)

(2) We can say *et cetera (etc)* [etseterah] or *et ainsi de suite :* for; and so on, and so forth. *et tout et tout :* at the end of a phrase, is a more familiar way of expressing the same idea.

(3) An idiomatic construction :
Ça fait deux ans qu'il est mort : He has been dead for two years
ça fait trois mois qu'il étudie le français : he has been studying French for 3 months.
Notice this use of the present tense, which we will see in greater detail when we look at "for" + "since".

(4) *un carré* : a square shape ; *un rond* [rohn] : a round shape
une racine carrée : a square root ; *un bâtiment rond :* a round building

(5) We say *haut* (high) for a building, etc. .but *élevé* (lit. raised) for prices : *un prix bas* : a low price ; *un niveau élevé :* a high level.

(6) *S'inquiéter :* to worry (oneself) ;
Ne vous inquiétez pas : Don't worry
Je m'inquiète : I am worried
Ne vous en faites pas (fam. *Ne t'en fais pas)* is a colloquial way of saying the same thing.

EXERCISES

1. The tie is part of the uniform. – **2.** In France, they eat well – **3.** I have been working hard for two weeks. – **4.** The prices in Switzerland are very high, but the salaries are high too – **5.** He only saw industrial restaurants.

Fill in the blanks :

1 Ne vous .. .. ; ce n'est pas dur.

Don't worry, it's not difficult.

2 Nous .... à Paris et nous . ' avons vu ... des touristes

We went to Paris and we only saw tourists.

3 Ça .... ses défauts, tu sais.

It's one of his faults, you know.

4 ..... les restaurants industriels sont ....

Only industrial restaurants are profitable.

SOIXANTE-DOUZIEME (72ème) LEÇON

Le lendemain, au grand (1) restaurant

1 — Cette carte ! (2) Quelle merveille ! Je n'ai jamais vu une chose pareille ! (3)

PRONONCIATION

1 . .mairvay. .paray

5 Ça .... deux semaines qu'il essaye de le faire.

He has been trying to do it for two weeks.

LA CRAVATE
FAIT PARTIE
DE
L'UNIFORME !

Fill in the blanks

1 - en faites pas - — **2** - sommes allés - n' - que - — **3** - fait partie de — **4** Seuls - rentables. — **5** - fait -

* * *

Second Wave : Vingt et unième Leçon

72nd LESSON

The next day at the top-class restaurant

1 — This menu ! What [a] marvel ! I have never seen anything like it !

NOTES

(1) *grand* has a much wider meaning than just big or large
La grande majorité des gens : the great majority of people
Un grand vent : a high wind ; *un grand vin :* a great wine
Un grand restaurant : a top-class restaurant
Also, retain the expression *grand-chose*
Ça ne vaut pas grand-chose : it's not worth much
Je n'ai pas vu grand-chose : I didn't see much.
As you can see, it has many of the same uses as *beaucoup*

2 – Oui, c'est ‿ impressionnant ... et ce cadre **(4)**. Quel luxe !
3 – Dis-moi, Anne, qu'est-ce que c'est que ce machin-là **(5)** ?
4 "Cardinal de l'océan avec son accompagnement de diamants du Périgord" ?
5 – Je suppose que c'est tout simplement un homard avec des truffes.
6 – Ah bon ... ? Heu, dis-moi Anne : tu es bien une fille moderne ?
7 Tu me dis toujours que tu vis avec ton‿époque **(6)**, n'est-ce pas ?
8 – Mais oui, et j'en suis fière ; mais où veux-tu en venir **(7)** ?

PRONONCIATION

2 . . .lyooks
4 . .lowsayohn. .deeamohn. .pereegor
5 . .omar. .tryoof
8 . .fyair

2 – Yes, it's impressive. . .and the surroundings. What luxury !
3 – Tell me, Anne, what the hell's this thing :
4 "Cardinal of the ocean with its accompaniment of diamonds of the P." ?
5 – I suppose it's quite simply a lobster with truffles.
6 – Oh really ? Emm, tell me A. you are really a modern girl ?
7 You always tell me that you live with your age (epoch), don't you ?
8 – Of course, and I am proud of it ; but what are you getting at ?

NOTES (suite)

(2) *Une carte de France :* a map of France ; *une carte de visite :* a visiting card. In a restaurant, , *le menu* means a fixed price menu (which we call, in English (!) table d'hôte) ; *la carte* is the menu - the list of dishes and their prices ; *manger à la carte* is to choose from the menu rather than take the fixed-price three course meal.

(3) *C'est toujours la même chose = C'est toujours pareil :* it's always the same. *pareil* (fem. *pareille)* is both an adjective and an adverb. As an adjective it is used like *même*
Elle en a une pareille : she has one the same.
or like *comme ça*
Je n'ai jamais vu une chose comme ça : I have never seen anything like that ; *je n'ai jamais entendu une chose pareille :* I have never heard anything like that
avec un temps comme ça - avec un temps pareil : with weather like that - (with such weather)
as an adverb
Ils s'habillent pareil : they dress alike

(4) *un cadre luxueux :* luxurious surroudings, or décor *un cadre* is also a person in middle management or an executive - the word is widely used in this context.
la C.G.C. - La Confédération Générale des Cadres is the trade-union for executives and workers who are neither technicians nor manual workers. *Le cadre d'un tableau :* a picture frame.

(5) See Lesson 48 note 2

(6) Although *époque* is feminine, we use *ton* instead of *ta* to avoid having two vowels together (in the same way as we say *mon amie)*
ta voiture but *ton amie*

(7) Another idiom : *Je ne sais pas où il veut en venir :* I don't know what he's getting at, what he's leading up to.
Où voulez-vous (veux-tu) en venir ? : What are you getting at ? i.e. Get to the point.

9 – Heu, voilà ... je propose que chacun (8) paye sa part de l'addition. D'accord ?
10 – Mais bien sûr ! Maintenant, tu pourras manger tranquillement !

PRONONCIATION

10 . .poora. .tronkeelmohn

EXERCICES

1. Je ne vois pas où vous voulez en venir. – **2.** Ton amie est très belle ! -La tienne aussi ! – **3.** Chacun sait que ce n'est pas vrai. – **4.** Je n'ai jamais entendu une chose pareille. – **5.** C'est une fille moderne et elle en est fière. – **6.** Tu prends le menu ou tu manges à la carte ?

Fill in the blanks :

1 Ta bague est jolie ; j' .. ai une ....

Your ring is pretty ; I have one the same.

2 ...... paye sa part, d' ...... ?

Each one pays his part, O.K. ?

3 Elle ... . à l'Opéra mais elle n'a pas .. ..
- .....

She went to the Opéra but she didn't see much.

4 Demain, c'est ..... ; tu .... aller à la banque.

Tomorrow is Monday ; you will be able to go to the bank.

9 — Emm, well . . I propose that each one pays his part of the bill, O.K. ?
10 — But of course ! Now you will be able to eat in peace!

NOTES (suite)

(8) *Chacun* (fem. *chacune*) means : each one
Chacun des deux est cher : each of the two is expensive
Chacune des soeurs est belle : each one of the sisters is beautiful
Ils m'ont donné chacun dix francs : Each one gave me 10 F.
or **everyone** *: comme chacun sait :* as everyone knows
chacun son tour : everyone in turn - and the famous phrase :
Chacun pour soi et Dieu pour tous ! : Everyone for himself and God for us all !

EXERCISES

1. I don't see what you are getting at . — **2.** Your friend is very beautiful ! — Yours too ! — **3.** Everyone knows that it isn't true. — **4.** I have never heard anything like it. — **5.** She is a modern girl and she is proud of it. — **6.** Are you taking the "table d'hôte" or are you choosing from the menu ?

5 Qu' . . . - . . que c'est . . . ce . . . . . . -là ?

What the hell is that thing there ?

Fill in the blanks

1 - en - pareille - — **2** Chacun - accord - — **3** - est allée - vu grand-chose. — **4** - lundi - pourras - — **5** -est-ce - que - machin.

* * *

Second Wave : Vingt-deuxième Leçon

SOIXANTE-TREIZIEME (73ème) LEÇON

Les souvenirs

1 — C'était comment la France avant la guerre, grand-père ?
2 — Ah tu sais, c'était bien différent de maintenant !
3 — Nous n'étions pas aussi riches et nous n'avions pas autant de **(1)** belles choses,
4 mais je pense que nous vivions **(N-2)** mieux qu'aujourd'hui.
5 Mon père avait un grand jardin et il cultivait **(2)** tous nos légumes
6 et moi et mes copains **(3)** travaillions pour un fermier
7 qui nous donnait des oeufs frais et du lait qui était encore tiède **(4)**.
8 On ne mangeait pas beaucoup de viande à cette époque.
9 Mais il y avait autre chose : les gens étaient plus aimables.

PRONONCIATION

1 .Setay. .gair grohnpair
2 . .deefairohn
3 . .netiohn owtohn
4 . .veeviohn
5 . .avay. .koolteevay
6 . .kopan traveyiohn. .fairmeeyay
7 . .dayzeu. .tyed
8 . .mohnzhay

73rd LESSON

Memories

1 — How was France before the war, grand-father ?
2 — Ah, you know, it was really different than now!
3 — We weren't as rich and we didn't have as many beautiful things
4 but I think that we used to live better than today.
5 My father had a big garden and he used to grow all our vegetables
6 and me and my mates used to work for a farmer
7 who [would] give us us fresh eggs and milk which was still lukewarm.
8 We didn't use to eat much meat at that time.
9 But there was something else : people were more likeable.

NOTES

(1) *Autant de :* as much /many *que :* as
Il n'y a pas autant de neige que l'année dernière : there is not as much snow as last year
Il a autant de vêtements que moi : He has as many clothes as me
If we omit the noun, we also drop the *de*
Il en a autant que moi : he has as much/many (of them) as me
J'en ai autant que lui : I have as much/many as him

(2) *Un homme cultivé :* a cultured man
cultiver des légumes, etc. . . . : to grow vegetables, etc. .
The verb *grandir* is intransitive
Son fils a grandi : his son has grown

(3) A very common slang word for friend. The feminine is *une copine.*

(4) *Tiède :* lukewarm ; *frais* can mean either fresh or cool
une boisson fraîche : a cool drink
des oeufs frais : fresh eggs
(incidentally, be careful of taps in France : C. stands, not for Cold, but for *Chaud* — the opposite ! F : *froid)*

10 Ils se parlaient **(5)**, ils se connaissaient tous et nous demandaient toujours des nouvelles.

11 Puis, il y a eu la guerre et les‿hommes sont partis **(6)**

12 Et les‿enfants étaient mieux‿élevés que de nos jours !

13 Ils ne s'endormaient pas pendant que leur grand-père leur parlait ! **(7)**

PRONONCIATION

10 . . . .tooss
13 . .sondormay

MES COPAINS ET MOI POUVONS
VOUS DONNER UN COUP DE MAIN...

EXERCICES

1. Nous étions plus heureux mais nous n'avions pas grand-chose. – **2.** Nous vivions mieux qu'aujourd'hui. – **3.** Je crois qu'ils se connaissent bien. – **4.** Mes copains et moi pouvons vous donner un coup de main. – **5.** Cet enfant est très bien élevé. – **6.** La bière en Angleterre est tiède!

Fill in the blanks :

1 . . . . père . . . . a dit de prendre . . . . . affaires

Their father told them to take their things

10 They used to speak [to] each other, they used to know each other and used to ask us always for news. .

11 Then, there was the war and the men left.

12 And children were better brought up than today !

13 They didn't use to fall asleep when their grandfather talked to them !

NOTES (suite)

(5) This is what we call a "reciprocal verb"
Il se regarde dans le miroir : he looks at himself in the mirror *but Il se regardent :* they look at each other (or one another). *Elle se connait :* she knows herself (i.e. qualities and faults) but
elles se connaissent : they know each other
Vous vous connaissez n'est-ce pas ? . . . . You know each other don't you ?

(6) Notice the change in tense in this sentence. All the other, imperfect verbs describe habitual actions in the past but the arrival of the war and the departure of the men were two specific incidents, thus we use the past tense.
Il parlait au téléphone quand nous sommes arrivés : He was speaking on the phone when we arrived.

(7) *Leur grand-père. . .leur,* here, is the possessive adjective - *leur parlait* : spoke to them is a personal pronoun. No difference in either spelling or pronunciation ; but only the possessive can take an "s".
Pierre et Jean ont pris leurs affaires -Peter and John took their things

EXERCISES

1. We were happier but we didn't have very much. — **2.** We used to live better than today. — **3.** I think they know each other well. — **4.** My mates and me can give you a hand. — **5.** This child is very well brought up (i.e. well-mannered) — **6.** The beer in England is lukewarm !

2 Il .... des légumes mais il ne .... pas de viande

He used to grow vegetables but he didn't eat meat.

3 Ils .. .... regardés pendant dix minutes avant de .. reconnaître

They looked at each other for ten minutes before recognising each other

4 Quand je .... , il lisait un livre

When I entered, he was reading a book

SOIXANTE-QUATORZIEME (74ème) LEÇON

1 — Madame, mademoiselle, monsieur bonsoir et bienvenue à "Mardi-Cinéma"
2 Aujourd'hui, nous‿avons le plaisir d'accueillir l'acteur Jean Belmont. (1)
3 — Merci d'être venu (2) Jean. Alors vous‿avez eu une vie fabuleuse, n'est-ce pas ?
4 — Oui, en effet. Très variée. Mais j'ai toujours été très‿apprécié.

PRONONCIATION

_2 . .akeuyeer

5 Il y ..... autre chose, les gens .... plus aimables.

There was something else ; people were more likeable.

Fill in the blanks

1 Leur - leur - leurs - — **2** - cultivait - mangeait - — **3** - se sont - se— **4** - suis entré - — **5** - avait - étaient.

* * *

Second Wave : Vingt-troisième Leçon

74th LESSON

1 — Ladies, and gentlemen, good evening and welcome to "Tuesday-Cinema".
2 Today, we have the pleasure to welcome the actor J.B.
3 — Thank you for coming, J. Well, you have had a fabulous life, haven't you ?
4 — Yes, indeed. Very varied. But I have always been very appreciated.

NOTES

(1) *Accueillir quelqu'un :* to welcome somebody.
Bienvenue ! (or *Soyez le bienvenu !) :* Welcome !
Je vous en prie : You're welcome (U.S.) - Don't mention it (G.B.)
(2) *Merci d'avoir pensé à moi :* thank you for thinking of me.
Merci de l'avoir acheté : Thank you for buying it.
Merci d'ëtre venu : Thank you for coming
(remember our verbs conjugated with *être,* Lesson 70 ?)

5 Quand j étais à l'école, tout le monde m'aimait énormément.
6 Il faut dire que j'étais très doué **(3)** et j'avais la cote avec **(4)** les filles.
7 Puis, à l'armée, les autres gars **(5)** me respectaient.
8 J'ai quitté l'armée après la guerre – ils m'ont demandé de rester –
9 et là, j'ai rencontré Brigitte Charlot, qui a commencé ma brillante carrière.
10 J'étais d'abord cascadeur, mais ensuite, comme je suis si beau
11 Jules Bassin m'a sorti des figurants et —me voilà aujourd'hui.
12 – Et quelle est la qualité que vous préférez chez **(7)** les gens ?
13 – La modestie.

PRONONCIATION

6 . .dooay. .kot
7 . . .ga
9 . .breeyont

EXERCICES

1. Vous avez eu une carrière très intéressante, n'est-ce pas ? – **2.** Elle a sorti toutes les vieilles lettres. – **3.** Jean est un pianiste très doué. – **4.** Il a toujours été comme ça. – **5.** Quelle qualité aimez-vous chez votre mari ? – **6.** Il faut dire que ce n'était pas à moi.

5 When I was at school, everybody liked me enormously
6 It must be said that I was very clever and I was popular with girls.
7 Then, in the army, the other guys respected me.
8 I left the army after the war - they asked me to stay-
9 and then (there) I met B.C. who began my brilliant carreer.
10 I was first a stunt man but afterwards, as I am so handsome
11 J.B. took me out of the extras and -here I am today.
12 — And what is the quality that you prefer in people ?
13 — Modesty.

NOTES (suite)

(3) *Un don :* a gift (either material or talent)
doué (douée) : literally means gifted, but is often used simply to mean clever.
Il est doué pour ça : he's good at that.
Qu'est-ce qu'elle est douée ! : She's really bright !
(4) *Il a la cote :* he is very successful (with people) (slang)
Un diplôme très coté : a prized diploma.
(5) A slang word for guy, bloke. You may also hear *un type* or *un mec* which have the same meaning but are more popular.
(6) *Il est sorti :* he went out, but if *sortir* is used transitively (i.e. with a direct object), it is conjugated with *avoir*
Elle a sorti un mouchoir de sa poche : she took a handkerchief from her pocket
Elle est descendue : she came down
Il a descendu les valises : he brought down the suitcases.
(7) *Ce que j'aime chez lui, c'est son honnêteté :* what I like in him is his honesty.
Ce qui me plaît chez eux, c'est leur humour [youmour]: what pleases me in them is their humour.

EXERCISES

1. You have had a very interesting career, haven't you ? — **2.** She took out all the old letters. — **3.** John is a very gifted pianist. — **4.** He has always been like that. — **5.** What quality do you like in your husband ? — **6.** It must be said that it wasn't mine.

Fill in the blanks :

1 Merci d' .... ; je veux vous parler

Thank you for staying ; I want to talk to you.

2 Nous .... les trois boîtes ....

We brought down the three boxes yesterday.

3 Nous .... une journée ....

We have had a marvellous day.

SOIXANTE-QUINZIEME (75ème) LEÇON

Une consultation efficace

1 Le docteur Leblond est non seulement médecin, mais un peu psychiâtre (1) aussi.
2 Un jour, un homme entre dans son cabinet
3 en se plaignant de maux (2) de tête affreux.

PRONONCIATION

1 . . .pseekeeatr
2 . . .kabeenay
3 . .playniohn. .mow

4 Il . ' . ... de ......

He asked me to leave.

5 Les autres .... me .... énormément.

The other guys respected me enormously.

Fill in the blanks

1 - être resté - — **2** - avons descendu - hier. — **3** - avons eu - merveilleuse. — **4** - m'a demandé - partir. — **5** - gars - respectaient.

* * *

Second Wave : Vingt-quatrième Leçon

75th LESSON

An efficient consultation

1 Docteur L. is not only [a] doctor, but a little [of a] psychiatrist, too.
2 One day a man comes into his surgery
3 complaining of awful headaches.

NOTES

(1) Be careful of the pronunciation of all those words which come from Greek and which begin *ps* - or *pn* - : the "p" is sounded
la pneumonie [peuneumoany] : pneumonia
un psychologue [pesseekolog] : a psychologist
(in fact the "p" is not quite as strong as our figurative pronunciation suggests. Listen to the recording.)

(2) *Un mal de tête :* a headache *(des maux de tête)*
J'ai mal à la tête : my head hurts
Est-ce que vous avez mal ? : Does it hurt ?
Faire mal is to hurt someone
Le dentiste m'a fait mal : the dentist hurt me.

4 — Alors, dit le docteur, ça dure depuis combien de temps ? **(3)**
5 — Oh, depuis que je suis au monde. Enfin, depuis quelques années.
6 — Et vous avez mal maintenant ? -Oh que **(4)** oui, docteur.
7 J'ai bigrement **(5)** mal depuis . . oh, depuis dix minutes.
8 — Qu'est-ce que vous faites comme travail ? -Je suis guitariste de rock.
9 — Et où habitez-vous ?
10 — J'habite à côté de l'aéroport d'Orly depuis cinq ou six ans.
11 Le docteur a compris depuis longtemps **(6)** Il se lève
12 et va à un placard d'où il sort une énorme scie.
13 — Bon, on va examiner votre cerveau, pour voir. .

QU'EST CE QUE VOUS FAITES COMME TRAVAIL ?

PRONONCIATION

7 . . .beegremohn. . .
9 . .abeetay. . .eye-ropor
12 . . .see
13 . .servoh

4 — Well, says the doctor, how long has this being going on ?
5 — Oh, since I have been in the world. Well, for several years.
6 — And does it hurt now ? -Yes, and how, doctor !
7 It has been hurting like mad for . .oh, for ten minutes.
8 — What is your job ? -I'm a rock guitarist.
9 — And where do you live ?
10 — I have been living next to the Airport of Orly for 5 or 6 years
11 The doctor understood a long time ago. He gets up
12 and goes to a cupboard from which (where) he takes out an enormous saw.
13 — Good. We are going to examine your brain to see. . .

NOTES (suite)

(3) Another great simplification : the present perfect continuous tense (have + been + doing) is translated by the present tense, with both "for" and "since" being translated by *depuis.*
Je suis ici depuis dix minutes : I have been here for ten minutes
Elle vit à Paris depuis août : she has been living in Paris since August.
Je vous aime depuis mon enfance : I have loved you since my childhood (we can't say "have been loving" in English).
(4) The *que* merely adds emphasis : Oh, yes really !
Oh que non ! : Not at all !
(5) English has a whole battery of familiar adjectives to replace "very" ranging from "really" to bloody". French has very few ; *bigrement* is one. Another, which you will hear (but we advise you not to use), is *vachement.*
Il joue vachement bien : he plays bloody well !
Elle parle bigrement bien l'anglais ! : she speaks pretty amazing English !
(6) *Il est parti depuis dix minutes :* (literally - he has been left for ten minutes) can only be translated in English by : He left 10 minutes ago.
Il l'a perdu depuis deux semaines : he lost it two weeks ago
In this case (i.e. with the verb in the past tense, not the present) *depuis* can be replaced by *il y a*
Il l'a perdu il y a deux semaines.

14 — Ce n'est pas la peine, docteur, je me sens mieux **(7)** depuis deux minutes. Au revoir !

EXERCICES

1. Qu'est-ce que vous faites comme travail ? – **2.** Vous sentez-vous mieux ? -Oui, depuis hier, merci. – **3.** Il aime ça depuis qu'il est au monde. – **4.** Vous avez mal maintenant ? -Oh que oui ! – **5.** Il est non seulement psychiâtre mais aussi psychologue.

Fill in the blanks :

1 Je .... chez Michelin ...... deux ans.

I have been working at Michelin for 2 years.

2 L'appartement ... vide ...... le mois dernier.

The flat has been empty since last month.

3 Elle . ..... son chien ...... quatre jours.

She lost her dog 4 days ago.

SOIXANTE-SEIZIEME (76ème) LEÇON

1 Après un concert donné par l'orchestre de Paris, un spectateur -

2 — sans doute pas très futé **(1)** - passe un petit mot au chef d'orchestre :

PRONONCIATION

2 . .fyootay

14 — It's not worth it doctor. I have been feeling much better for 2 minutes. Goodbye !

NOTES (suite)

(7) *Se sentir :* to feel (i.e. one's physical condition)
Elle se sent malade : she feels ill
Je me sens mieux : I feel better

EXERCISES

1. What is your job ? — **2.** Do you feel better ? -Yes, since yesterday, thank you.— **3.** He has liked that since he has been in the world (since he was born). — **4.** Does it hurt now ? Yes, and how ! — **5.** He is not only a psychiatrist but a psychologist, too.

4 Ça .... depuis .... de ..... ?

How long has this been going on ?

5 Il ... . se plaignant de .... de tête.

He came in complaining of headaches.

Fill in the blanks

1 - travaille - depuis - — **2** - est - depuis - — **3** - a perdu - depuis - — **4** - dure combien - temps. — **5** - est entré en - maux -

* * *

Second Wave : Vingt-cinquième Leçon

76th LESSON

1 After a concert given by the orchestra of P. a spectator -

2 — no doubt not very bright - passes a little note to the conductor (orchestra chief)

NOTES

(1) *futé* means sharp, bright, smart. *Futé comme un renard* : As cunning as a fox.

3 – "Je ne veux pas paraître rapporteur, cher monsieur,
4 mais je crois utile de vous signaler que l'homme qui joue de la grosse caisse (2)
5 ne frappe que lorsque (3) vous le regardez".

6 – Ma femme voulait une nouvelle voiture pour Noël
7 alors je lui ai offert (4) un collier de perles.
8 Je sais ce que tu vas dire, mais tu comprends
9 on ne fabrique pas‿encore de fausses Citroën (5).

10 Jean-Michel Dupont était‿arriviste à tel point que
11 lorsqu'il entrait derrière vous dans‿une porte à tambour
12 il réussissait (6) quand même à en sortir le premier !

13 – Méfie-toi de ce dragueur (7) ! C'est‿un vrai nouveau riche
14 et je te préviens qu'il est beaucoup plus nouveau que riche !

PRONONCIATION

4 . .growss kess
5 . .lorske
7 . .offair. .koleeyay. .pairl
9 . .fowss
11 . . .tomboor
12 . .rayoosseessay

3 – "I don't want to appear [a] tell-tale, dear sir,
4 but I think it useful to point out [to] you that the man who plays (of) the bass drum
5 only hits when you look at him."

6 – My wife wanted a new car for Christmas
7 so I gave her a pearl necklace.
8 I know what you [are] going to say, but you understand
9 they don't yet make false Citroëns

10 J.M.D. was a social climber to such an extent that
11 when he went in behind you in a revolving door
12 he succeeded all the same in coming out (of it) the first !

13 – Beware of that wolf ! He's a real nouveau-riche,
14 and I warn you that he is much more new than rich !

NOTES (suite)

(2) *Une caisse* is either a packing-case or a cash-desk
Payez à la caisse : pay at the cash-desk
La grosse caisse : the bass drum.
(3) *Lorsque* means the same as *quand* (when).
(4) *offrir ; j'offre ; tu offres ; il offre ; nous offrons ; vous offrez ; ils offrent* - past participle : *offert*
means to offer but is also used to mean : to give a present :
Il lui a offert une belle bague : he gave her (him) a beautiful ring.
(5) Remember that names usually do not take an "s" in the plural :
Les Dupont : the Duponts
Les Renault : Renaults, etc. . .
(6) *réussir ; je réussis ; tu réussis ; il réussit ; nous réussissons ; vous réussissez ; ils réussissent* - past participle - *réussi*
to succeed in
J'ai réussi à le trouver : I succeeded in finding it/him.
Réussir un examen : to pass an exam
Une réussite : a success
(7) A prime slang word : *draguer* (lit. to dredge !) means to chase the opposite sex ; to chat up ; *un dragueur :* a "wolf"

EXERCICES

1. Il ne frappe que lorsque vous le regardez. – **2.** Je lui ai offert un beau cadeau. – **3.** Il en sort toujours le dernier. – **4.** Méfiez-vous de cet homme ! C'est un dragueur !– **5** Je vous préviens que c'est très difficile.

Fill in the blanks :

1 Je sais .. ... tu ... . , mais c'est faux.

I know what you are going to say, but it's false.

2 Il n'est .... pas très ....

He is undoubtedly not very bright.

3 Ils n' ... pas .... l'ouvrir.

They didn't succeed in opening it.

4 Il est riche . ... 'il a quatre maisons.

He is rich to such an extent that he has four houses.

5 Ils sont beaucoup .... nouveaux ... riches.

They are much more new than rich.

SOIXANTE-DIX-SEPTIEME (77ème) LEÇON

REVISION ET NOTES

1 The future tense : as well as expressing a future idea by using *aller* + infinitive (*je vais voir etc. .),* we can use

EXERCISES

1. He only hits when you look at him. — **2.** I gave him/her a beautiful present. — **3.** He always comes out of it last. — **4.** Beware of that man ! He's a wolf ! — **5.** I warn you that it's very difficult

Fill in the blanks

1 - ce que - vas dire - — **2** - sans doute - futé - — **3** - ont réussi - — **4** à tel point qu - — **5** - plus - que - .

* * *

Second Wave : Vingt-sixième Leçon

77th LESSON

the future tense.
This is formed by simply adding the verb-endings of the present tense of avoir : *-ai -as - a -ons -ez -ont* to the infinitive of the verb : *donner - je donnerai ; il donnera ; ils donneront*

finir - tu finiras ; vous finirez ; nous finirons
for verbs like *vendre* we drop the final "e"
Thus : *je vendrai ; tu vendras ; il vendra ; nous vendrons ; vous vendrez ; ils vendront.*
It is as simple as that ! All verbs take these endings ; however, a few irregular verbs change their stems. Remember the following which are the most common :

aller : *j'irai* etc. . . ; *avoir :* *j'aurai,* etc. . .
être : *je serai* etc. . . ; *pouvoir :* *je pourrai* etc. . .
faire : *je ferai* etc. . . ;

Here are some examples :

Ils finiront dans dix minutes : they will finish in ten minutes
Elle vendra sa voiture la semaine prochaine : she will sell her car next week
Je vous le donnerai demain : I'll give it to you tomorrow
Il sera si content de vous voir : he will be so happy to see you
Vous n'aurez pas de problème : you won't have any problems
Nous serons là à partir de dix heures : we will be there from 10.00

As you can see, this use is almost exactly the same as in English.
Remember that :
Will you follow me ? is *Voulez-vous me suivre ?* etc. .

2 The imperfect tense : whereas the past tense describes completed actions in the past (he went, I saw, we bought, etc. .), the imperfect tense describes a constant state or continuous action in the past.
Look at these examples:
Nous cultivions nos légumes : we used to grow our vegetables
Ils travaillaient pour un fermier : They used to work for a farmer

Elle allait à la messe toutes les semaines :
She would go to mass every week . . .
quand elle était jeune . . : when she was young.
We form this tense by replacing the *-ons* of the first person plural of the present by *-ais -ais -ait -ions -iez -aient :*
cultiver — cultivons — cultivions

(*être* is an exception, but notice that the endings are still the same : *j'étais ; tu étais ; il était ; nous étions ; vous étiez ; ils étaient).*
Il était heureux : He was happy
Le soleil brillait et les oiseaux chantaient dans les arbres : The sun was shining and the birds were singing in the trees.

You can see that the translation of the imperfect depends on whether we are talking about a state, a continuous action or an habitual action in the past. A single tense conveys all three ideas.
For the time being, just get the feel of the imperfect as it is used in the texts.

Have you noticed how much simpler French verb-tenses are than their English counterparts ?
Just to demonstrate what we mean, look at this table of equivalents :

Le PRESENT *(je fume)*	présent simple (I smoke) present continuous (I am smoking) present emphatic (I do smoke) present perfect continuous (I have been smoking)
LE PASSE COMPOSÉ *(j'ai fumé)*	past simple (I smoked) present perfect (I have smoked)

L'IMPARFAIT (*je fumais*)	past continuous (I was smoking) past frequentative (I used to smoke)
LE FUTUR	future simple (I will smoke)

SOIXANTE-DIX-HUITIEME (78ème) LEÇON

La femme est la patronne

1 Jean et Mireille font l'inventaire de leur magasin de vêtements :
2 – *M. :* Bon, ici, j'ai vingt-deux jupes gris clair **(1)**, taille trente-trois. . .
3 – *J. :* Oui, mais attends. Michelle en **(2)** a commandé une, n'est-ce pas ?
4 – *M. :* Je la lui ai donnée **(N-1)** la semaine dernière. On peut continuer ?
5 – *J. :* D'accord. *M. :* Après, nous avons dix chemisiers en soie, dix écharpes. .
6 – *J. :* Stop ! **(3)** Dix ? J'en ai douze. Où sont les deux autres ?

PRONONCIATION

1 . . .meeray
2 . .zhyoop. . .tie
5 . .swa. .deezaysharp

(je fumerai) future continuous (I will be smoking)

* * *

Second Wave : Vingt-septième Leçon

78th LESSON

The woman is the boss

1 – J and M. are doing the inventory of their clothes-shop :

2 – *M. :* Good ; here, I have 22 light-grey skirts, size 33 . .

3 – *J. :* Yes, but wait. M. ordered one, didn't she ?

4 – *M. :* I gave it to her last week. Can we continue ?

5 – *J. :* O.K. *M. :* After we have ten (in) silk blouses, ten scarves. .

6 – *J. :* Stop ! Ten ? I have 12. Where are the two others ?

NOTES

(1) Composite adjectives of colour remain invariable after nouns:
un chapeau bleu ciel : a sky-blue hat
deux écharpes bleu marine : two navy-blue scarves
Remember : *clair :* light ; *foncé* : dark (for çolours)

(2) Notice the use of *en* in this text. It is added to the sentence to replace the noun just referred to (it is not necessary to translate it). Try and see how it fits in to balance the sentence.

(3) We know *arrêter* for to stop. But there is also a French verb *stopper* (which is taken from English) and means to stop abruptly. It is most commonly found in the exclamation *Stop !*
Faire de l'auto-stop : to hitch-hike
un auto-stoppeur : a hitch-hiker.

7 — *M. :* Mais tu ne te souviens de rien ! Les deux Japonais ! Je leur en‿ai vendu deux hier !

8 — *J. :* Ça va alors. Ensuite il y a quarante paires de bas **(4)** et. .

9 — *M. :* Qu'est-ce qu'il y a ? *J. :* Je ne trouve pas mon crayon.

10 — *M. :* Mais je te l'ai passé tout‿à l'heure. **(5)**. Le voilà, sous l'escabeau **(6)**.

11 — *J. :* Tu sais je suis‿un peu fatigué ; on peut s'arrêter deux minutes, s'il te plaît ?

12 — *M.:* Je te l'ai déjà dit : on s'arrêtera quand on‿aura **(N-2)** fini - et pas‿avant

13 — *J. :* Qu'est-ce que tu es dure comme patronne alors ! **(7)**

PRONONCIATION

8 . . .ba
10 . .eskaboh

EXERCICES

1. Qu'est-ce que vous êtes gentil, alors ! – **2.** L'échelle ? Je la lui ai prêtée hier. – **3.** Mais tu ne te souviens de rien ! – **4.** Stop ! Il y a une voiture qui vient ! – **5.** Il en a commandé un avant-hier. – **6** Zut alors !

7 – *M. :* But you don't remember anything ! The two Japanese ! I sold them two yesterday !
8 – *J. :* That's alright then. Next, there are 40 pairs of stockings and. . .
9 – *M. :* What's the matter ? *J . :* I can't (don't) find my pencil.
10 – *M. :* But I passed it to you earlier. There it is, under the step-ladder.
11 – *J. :* You know, I'm a little tired ; can we stop (ourselves) two minutes, please ?
12 – *M. :* I already told you we will stop (ourselves) when we (will) have finished and not before.
13 – *J. :* What a hard boss you are !

NOTES (suite)

(4) Don't confuse the adjective *bas* (fem. *basse)* and the noun : *un bas :* a stocking (We would obviously avoid any such expression as : low stockings. . .)
une paire de gants : a pair of gloves.

(5) *Je l'ai vu tout à l'heure :* I saw him a little while ago
Je le verrai tout à l'heure : I will see him soon.
The meaning depends on whether the verb in the phrase is past or future.
A tout à l'heure (as a parting salutation) means : See you later.

(6) *Un escabeau :* a step-ladder ; *une échelle :* a ladder
Ladders are often used by *les pompiers :* the firemen.

(7) *alors !* is often added to exclamations to make them more emphatic :
Qu'est-ce que je suis content, alors ! : I'm really happy !
Zut alors ! : Bloody hell !
Chic alors ! : Great ! Wonderful !

Exercises

1. How kind you are ! – **2.** The ladder ? I lent it to him yesterday. – **3.** But you don't remember anything ! – **4.** Stop ! There is a car coming ! – **5.** He ordered one yesterday. – **6.** Bloody hell !

Fill in the blanks :

1 On s' .... quand on ....

We will stop when we have finished

2 Une écharpe ? Je ... . vendu une hier

A scarf ? I sold her one yesterday

3 Ton crayon ? Je .. . ' .. passé .... . l' .....

Your pencil ? I passed it to you a little while ago.

SOIXANTE-DIX-NEUVIEME (79ème) LEÇON

La politique

1 La semaine prochaine, les Français voteront pour élire un nouveau président.
2 Ces‿élections présidentielles ont lieu **(1)** tous les sept ans **(2)**.
3 Tous ceux qui ont plus de dix-huit‿ans ont le droit de voter.

PRONONCIATION

2 . . .lyeu
3 . .drwa

4 J' .. .. douze. Où sont les deux ...... ?

I have twelve (of them). Where are the two others ?

5 Quand il me .... je vous le .....

When he phones me, I will tell you.

Fill in the blanks

1 -arrêtera - aura fini. — **2** - lui en ai - — **3** - te l'ai - tout à - heure. — **4** - en ai - autres — **5** - téléphonera - dirai.

* * *

Second Wave : Vingt-huitième Leçon

79th LESSON

Politics

1 Next week, the French will vote to elect a new president.
2 These presidential elections take place every seven years.
3 All those who are older (have more) than 18 have the right to vote.

NOTES

(1) *La réunion aura lieu mardi prochain :* the meeting will take place next Tuesday.
Elle a eu lieu il y a dix jours : It took place ten days ago.
(Prenez place means : take a seat ; sit down)

(2) *Toutes les dix minutes :* every ten minutes *(minute* is feminine)
Tous les jours : every day
à toute heure : at any time
un sur deux : one in two.

4 L'élection se passe en deux temps **(3)** ou "tours", comme on les appelle.

5 Au premier tour il y a souvent une dizaine **(4)** de candidats

6 mais ce sont les deux qui ont obtenu le plus de voix **(5)**

7 qui peuvent se présenter au deuxième tour.

8 Donc il y a deux semaines, les candidats se sont présentés

9 et les électeurs leur ont donné leurs voix.

10 Maintenant il ne reste qu'un candidat de droite et un de gauche.

11 Lequel va être choisi ? Nous n'en savons rien **(6)**,

12 mais nous vous rappelons **(N-3)** ce dicton, qui dit :

13 "Le capitalisme est l'exploitation de l'homme par l'homme

14 alors que le socialisme, c'est le contraire" !

PRONONCIATION

5 . . .kondeedah
6 . .plyooss. .vwa
12 . .deektoh

EXERCICES

1. C'est lui qui a le plus de succès. – **2.** Ceux qui ont plus de soixante ans ne doivent pas travailler. – **3.** Le débat a eu lieu à dix heures et demie. – **4.** Je leur ai donné mon opinion. – **5.** Nous vous rappelons qu'il est interdit de fumer.

4 The election happens in two phases or "rounds" as they are called.
5 At the first round, there are often about ten candidates
6 but it is (these are) the two who have obtained the most votes
7 who can present themselves at the second round.
8 So, two weeks ago, the candidates presented themelves
9 and the voters gave them their votes.
10 Now, there remains only one candidate of [the] right and one of [the] left.
11 Which one is going to be chosen ? We have no idea,
12 but we remind you [of] this saying which says :
13 "Capitalism is the exploitation of man by man
14 whereas socialism (it) is the opposite" !

NOTES (suite)

(3) *en deux (trois. . .) temps :* in two (three. .) phases, steps
dans un premier temps : in the first stage

(4) *dix :* ten ; *une dizaine :* about ten
vingt : twenty ; *une vingtaine* : about twenty
(and thus for all multiples of ten)
L'homme avait la quarantaine : the man was about forty years old.
Be careful of *une douzaine :* a dozen ; *une quinzaine :* a fortnight.

(5) *Une voix (pl. des voix) :* a voice
une voix grave : a deep voice ; *une voix aiguë :* a high voice
une voix also means a vote

(6) *Je n'en sais rien* is a synonym for : *je n'en ai aucune idée*
Both mean : I have no idea
Je lui ai demandé mais il n'en savait rien : I asked him but he had no idea.

EXERCISES

1. It is he who has the most success. – **2.** Those who are older than sixty do not have to work. – **3.** The debate took place at 10.30 – **4.** I gave them my opinion. – **5.** We remind you that it is forbidden to smoke.

Fill in the blanks :

1 .... veux-tu ? Je n' .. ..

Which ones do you want ? I have no idea.

2 L'exposition . .... tous ... ...

The exhibition takes place every six years.

3 ..... qui obtient .. .. voix gagne.

The one who obtains the most votes wins.

4 Une .... candidats .. ..

About ten candidates presented themselves.

5 ... article est cher .... celui-ci est bon marché.

This article is expensive, whereas this one is cheap.

QUATRE-VINGTIEME (80ème) LEÇON

Les sondages

1 Pendant la période des‿élections, il y a beaucoup de sondages

2 qui donnent parfois des résultats curieux . . .

3 — Pardon, Monsieur, voulez-vous répondre à quelques questions, s'il vous plaît ?

Fill in the blanks

1 Lesquels - ' en sais rien. — **2** - a lieu - les six ans — **3** Celui - le plus de - — **4** - dizaine de - se sont présentés. — **5** Cet - alors que- .

LA SEMAINE PROCHAINE, LES FRANÇAIS VOTERONT POUR ÉLIRE UN NOUVEAU PRÉSIDENT.

* * *

Second Wave : Vingt-neuvième Leçon

80th LESSON

Opinion polls

1 During the period of the elections, there are many opinion-polls
2 which sometimes give curious results. .
3 — Excuse me, sir, will you answer (to) a few questions, please ?

PRONONCIATION sondazh
2 . .rayzootah

4 Pour qui avez-vous l'intention de voter ? -Aucune (1) idée.

5 — Y a-t-il un candidat dont vous avez entendu parler (2) davantage (3) ? -Non.

6 — A qui (4) pensez-vous quand on vous dit "Président" ? -A personne.

7 — De quoi (4) parlez-vous avec vos amis ? -Je n'en ai pas.

8 — Y a-t-il un meeting auquel (N-4) vous avez l'intention d'assister ? -Aucun

9 — Bon. Je dois noter que vous n'avez aucune opinion politique. Au revoir,

10 dit le sondeur, qui écrit sur ses papiers et s'en va.

11 Derrière lui, il entend la voix de l'homme qui marmonne :

PRONONCIATION

4 . .ohkyoon
8 . .ohkel. .ohkeun

4 For whom (have) do you intend to vote ? -No idea
5 – Is there one candidate of whom you have heard (speak) more ? -No,
6 – Of (to) whom do you think when someone says "President" ? -(to) Nobody.
7 – Of what do you talk with your friends ? -I haven't any.
8 – Is there a meeting which you intend to attend ? -None.
9 – Good. I must note that you have no political opinion at all. Good bye,
10 says the pollster who writes on his papers and goes away.
11 Behind him, he hears the voice of the man who mutters :

NOTES

(1) *aucun (aucune)* is more absolute than *pas de*
Vous n'avez pas d'opinion : you have no opinion
Vous n'avez aucune opinion : you have no opinion at all.
Aucune idée (i.e. *Je n'ai aucune idée) :* I haven't the slightest idea.
Je n'ai aucun ami : I have no friends whatsoever.

(2) *Entendre parler :* to hear of (i.e. reputation)
Est-ce que vous avez entendu parler de ce livre ? : Have you heard of this book ?
J'en ai entendu parler : I have heard of it/him/her (depending on what precedes the sentence)

(3) More than is *plus que :*
Je l'aime plus que l'autre : I like it/him/her more than the other.
But : *Je l'aime davantage :* I like it/him/her more.
davantage is used if there is no comparison and is usually found at the end of a clause.

(4) *A qui ; à quoi ; de qui ; de quoi ;* etc. .
We know the rules for *qui* and *que*
The preposition must **always** accompany the relative. Modern English has a tendency to push the preposition to the end of the sentence.
The man (that) I talk **to**. In French, we must say :
L'homme à qui je parle. It is not at all as formal as its literal translation in English. It is the only way to express the idea. Remember : preposition and relative together.

12 – Qu'est-ce qu'ils sont bêtes (5), ces sondages !

EXERCICES

1. Est-ce que tu as des idées ? -Aucune ! – **2.** Ils me donnent les résultats demain. – **3.** A qui pensez-vous ? -A mon ami Georges. – **4.** C'est une chose à laquelle je ne pense jamais. – **5.** Qu'est-ce que vous êtes bête ! – **6.** Y a-t-il quelque chose que vous voulez ?

Fill in the blanks

1 .... allez-vous voter ? - ...... idée.

For whom are you going to vote ? -No idea at all.

2 .. .... parlez-vous avec ... amis ?

What do you talk about with your friends ?

3 Ce sont des idées .... j'ai ....

Those are ideas which I have heard (of)

QUATRE-VINGT-UNIEME (81ème) LEÇON

L'argot

1 – Ah ! la ! la! Que c'est dur de trouver un appartement !

2 Je fais les petites‿annonces depuis un mois et je n'ai rien trouvé

12 — How stupid these opinion-polls are !

(5) *Qu'est-ce qu'il fait chaud !* (How hot it is !) — *Qu'est-ce que j'ai soif !* (How thirsty I am !) : although this use of "*qu'est-ce que . . .*" as an exclamatory phrase is grammatically incorrect, it is very common.

EXERCISES

1. Do you have any ideas ? -None at all ! — **2.** They will give me the results tomorrow. — **3.** Who are you thinking about ? -About my friend Georges : — **4.** It's a thing which I never think about. — **5.** How daft you are ! — **6.** Is there anything you want ?

4 C'est le genre de réunion à .... je n' .... jamais.

It is the type of meeting which I never attend.

5 Est-ce que vous .... l' .... d'y aller ?

Do you intend to go there ?

Fill in the blanks

1 Pour qui - -Aucune - — **2** De quoi - vos - — **3** - dont - entendu parler. — **4** - laquelle - assiste - — **5** - avez - intention -

* * *

Second Wave : Trentième Leçon

81st LESSON

Slang

1 — Oh dear, how hard it is to find an apartment !
2 I have been looking at (I do) the small ads. for a month and I haven't found anything

3 jusqu'à **(1)** présent. C'est désolant, non ?
4 – Qu'est-ce que tu cherches ? -Oh, un grand studio ou un truc **(2)** comme ça
5 mais tout‿est vachement cher **(3)**. Bon, tu as ton loyer **(4)**
6 mettons **(5)** deux mille balles **(6)** mais en plus, il faut payer une caution
7 et si tu passes par une agence, il faut compter les frais **(7)** d'agence en plus !
8 J'en‿ai vu un qui était chouette **(8)** mais je n'avais pas le fric **(9)**

J'EN AI MARRE
D'ÉCOUTER LA
MÊME CHANSON !

PRONONCIATION

4 . . .tryook
5 . .vashmohn. . .lwayay
6 . .kohseeyohn
7 . .azhonss. .fray
8 . .shwet

3 up to now. It's disheartening, isn't it ? (no?)
4 – What[are]you looking for ? -Oh, a large studio or a thing like that ;
5 but everything's so bloody expensive. Right. you have your rent
6 let's say 2.000 francs ; but on top you have to pay a deposit
7 and if you go through (by) an agency, you have to count the agency charges on top !
8 I saw one which was lovely, but I didn't have the cash.

NOTES

(1) *Jusqu'à* (until) can also be used for distance as well as time
jusqu'à dix heures : until 10.00
jusqu'au bout de la rue : to the end of the road

(2) We have already seen *un truc* : a thingamy. In this lesson we hear two young people talking and we hear their vocabulary, a lot of which is *argot* - slang.
In an (unconscious) attempt to combat the formalism of their language, the French replace many words by slang equivalents which do not have the same connotations as their "literal" translations in English.
We prefer you to recognize them and you will, after contact with French people, get to know when to use them (and when to avoid them). This you can't learn from a book. So read our notes, and keep your ears open (we will put an asterisk before slang words).

(3) **vachement* an adjective which amplifies (like *très)*
vachement dur : bloody hard, etc. . .

(4) *Un loyer :* a rent ; *louer* : to rent
un locataire : a tenant
une voiture de location : a rental car

(5) *mettons : disons :* let's say. .used when giving an estimate or an example.

(6) **balle* a slang word for a *franc* *une balle* is literally a small ball :
un ballon : a (foot-ball sized) ball.

(7) *des frais :* charges, expenses.
frais scolaires : school fees (always plural).

(8) **chouette* (lit. an owl !) : great ! wonderful ! lovely ! etc. . .

(9) **le fric :* money, bread, cash, etc. . .

9 — En plus ce n'est pas le bon **(10)** moment. Il vaut mieux attendre
10 les grandes vacances, quand tout le monde s'en va ;
11 et là, avec un peu de veine, **(11)** tu trouveras quelque chose.
12 — Oh et puis j'en‿ai marre **(12)** ! Allez, on va boire un pot **(13)** et parler d'autre chose.

PRONONCIATION

11 . . . .ven
12 . . .poh

EXERCICES

1. Il n'a jamais de fric, celui-là ! — **2.** Son appartement est chouette mais il est vachement cher. — **3.** J'en ai marre d'écouter la même chanson ! — **4.** Ça coûte, mettons, mille balles, mais il y a la caution en plus. — **5.** Il n'est pas là pour le moment. Il est allé boire un pot avec Jean.

Fill in the blanks :

1 Il .... les frais d'agence .. .... !

The agency fees have to be counted on top !

2 Vous n'avez pas une autre clef ? ..... - là n'est pas la .....

Do you have another key ? This one is not the right one.

9 – What's more, it's not the right moment. It is better to wait [for]
10 the big holidays when everyone goes away ;
11 and there, with a bit of luck, you'll find something.
12 – Oh and anyway, I'm fed up ! Come on, we'll go for a drink and talk of other things.

NOTES (suite)

(10) *bon* also means right :
Vous n'avez pas le bon numéro : you don't have the right number.
Cette pièce n'est pas la bonne : This part is not the right [one].

(11) *avoir de la veine :* to be lucky
* *un veinard :* a lucky devil
* *Pas de veine ! :* Out of luck !

(12) * *en avoir marre (de) :* to be fed up(with).
Il en a marre de son travail : He is fed up with his job.

(13) * *boire ou prendre un pot :* to go for a glass, for a drink.

All the above "argot" words are extremely common especially in the speech of the young.

EXERCICES

1. He's never got any cash, that one ! – **2.** His/her appartment is lovely but it's bloody expensive. – **3.** I'm fed up with listening to the same song ! – **4.** It costs, let's say, a thousand francs but there's the deposit on top. – **5.** He's not here for the moment. He's gone for a drink with John.

3 Nous .... cet exercice ...... un .....

d'heure.

We have been doing this exercise for a quarter of an hour.

4 Il .... attendre demain pour être sûr.

It's better to wait for tomorrow to be sure.

5 .... s' .. .. en vacances.

Everybody is going away on holiday.

QUATRE-VINGT-DEUXIEME (82ème) LEÇON

Un voyage à Beaune

1 — Je veux partir ce week-end - dit un jour Mme Martin à son mari.
2 N'importe où **(1)**, mais je veux partir ! J'en‿ai marre de Paris !
3 — Tiens ! On peut aller à Beaune. Comme ça, les enfants verront **(2)** les‿Hospices,
4 et nous pourrons acheter du vin pour notre cave. Qu'en penses-tu ?
5 — Superbe ! Je veux partir maintenant ! Tout de suite !
6 — Ne sois **(3)** pas bête ! Tu sais bien qu'entre huit‿heures et neuf‿heures, c'est l'heure de pointe,
7 et les routes sont bloquées. Prépare-nous un pique-nique

PRONONCIATION

bown
2 . . .namportoo . .layzosspeess
4 . . .kahv. .konponstyoo
6 . .swa. . .pwant

Fill in the blanks

1. - faut compter - en plus ! — **2** Celle- - bonne.— **3** - faisons - depuis - quart - — **4** - vaut mieux - — **5** Tout le monde - en va.

* * *

Second Wave : Trente et unième Leçon

82nd LESSON

A trip to Beaune

1 — I want to leave this week-end -said one day Mme M. to her husband.
2 Anywhere, but I want to leave ! I'm fed up with Paris !
3 — Hold on ! We can go to B. Like that, the children will see the almshouses
4 and we will be able to buy some wine for our cellar. What do you think ?
5 — Superb ! I want to leave now ! Straight away !
6 — Don't be stupid. You know [very] well that between 8.00 and 9.00 it's the rush-hour
7 and the roads are blocked. Prepare us a picnic

NOTES

(1) *n'importe où* : anywhere. . .
n'importe quand : at any time . .
n'importe comment : in any way . . . .
n'importe qui : anybody . . . .
N'importe quel jour : Any day (i.e. no restrictions)
N'importe qui peut venir : Anybody can come.
Choisissez une carte, n'importe laquelle : Choose a card, any one.
Prenez un cigare, n'importe lequel : Take a cigar, any one.

(2) *voir* (to see) in the future is : *je verrai ; tu verras,il verra ; nous verrons ; vous verrez ; ils verront .*
On peut y aller ? - On verra : Can we go ? -We'll see.

(3) This is the *tu* form of *soyez,* the subjunctive of *être,* that we use as an imperative.

8 et on partira vers onze‿heures. Comme ça on évitera les‿embouteillages.

9 – Où est-ce qu'on va coucher ? (4) Tes‿amis sont toujours là-bas ?

10 – Non, mais on choisira un hôtel dans le guide Michelin (5)

11 N'importe lequel (6) -ils sont tous bons.
Et si on ne trouve rien à Beaune même

12 on‿ira ailleurs (7). Allez ! Appelle les‿enfants et on‿y va !

PRONONCIATION

8 . . .ombootayazh
10 . .shwazeera. . .meeshlan

EXERCICE

1. Ne sois pas si pressé ! – **2.** Tu sais bien que c'est l'heure de pointe. – **3.** On pourra éviter les embouteillages si on part maintenant. – **4.** Je veux lire un journal. N'importe lequel. – **5.** Si on ne trouve rien on ira ailleurs.

Fill in the blanks :

1 N' .... a le ..... d'entrer.

Anybody has the right to go in.

8 and we will leave around 11.00. Like that, we'll avoid the traffic-jams.

9 – Where are we going to sleep ? Your friends are still there ?

10 – No, but we'll choose a hotel from (in) the G.M..

11 Any one - they are all good. And if we don't find anything in B. itself

12 we will go elsewhere. Come on ! Call the children and we're off !

NOTES (suite)

(4) *dormir* is the physical act of sleeping, *coucher* is to go to bed. *Une chambre à coucher :* a bedroom.

(5) *Le guide Michelin :* a very popular tourist guide which lists and recommends places of interest, hotels, and restaurants.

(6) *n'importe lequel :* any one, **but**
n'importe qui : anyone, anybody (person)

(7) *ailleurs :* elsewhere. *D'ailleurs. . .*(at the beginning of a sentence) : moreover.

EXERCISES

1. Don't be in such a hurry ! – **2.** You know very well that it's the rush-hour. – **3.** We will be able to avoid the traffic jams if we leave now. – **4.** I want to read a newspaper.Any one. – **5.** If we don't find anything, we will go elsewhere.

2 Il en ..... marre de Paris donc il ... parti ....

He was fed up with Paris so he left for somewhere else.

3 Nous .... les parents et les enfants .... jouer.

We will see the parents and the children will be able to play.

4 Je veux vous voir. Dites-moi un jour. N' ....

I want to see you. Tell me a day. At any time.

5 Qu' . . .. - . . ? -Ne .... pas bête !

What do you think (of it) ? -Don't be stupid !

QUATRE-VINGT-TROISIEME (83ème) LEÇON

Voyage à Beaune (II)

1 A onze‿heures, la voiture chargée (1) d'enfants, de nourriture et d'essence (2),
2 les Martin s'en vont pour Beaune. A la Porte d'Orléans (3)
3 ils prennent l'autoroute du Sud. Il n'y a pas trop de monde.
4 Il fait un temps magnifique et tout le monde est‿heureux.
5 Ils ne s'arrêtent pas mais ils mangent les sandwichs, que Mme Martin a préparés, dans la voiture.
6 Bientôt, ils‿arrivent en Bourgogne.
7 C'est facile à reconnaître à cause des vignobles qui couvrent toutes les collines.

PRONONCIATION

6 . .boorgoyn

Fill in the blanks

1 N'importe qui - droit. —**2** - avait - est ailleurs. — **3** - verrons-pourront - — **4** - 'importe quand - - **5** 'en penses-tu - sois - —

* * *

Second Wave : Trente-deuxième Leçon

83rd LESSON

Trip to Beaune (II)

1 At 11.00, the car laden with children, food and petrol,
2 the Martins leave for B. At the Porte d'Orléans
3 they take the Southern motorway. There are not too many people.
4 The weather is magnificent and everybody is happy.
5 They don't stop but they eat the sandwiches which Mme Martin has prepared, in the car.
6 Soon, they arrive in Burgundy.
7 It is easy to recognize because of the vineyards which cover all the hills.

NOTES

(1) We saw in Lesson 81 that *les frais* meant : charges.
Here is another" false friend" *charger :* to load
Ce fusil est chargé : this gun is loaded
Ils ont chargé le camion : they loaded the lorry.

(2) Be careful at petrol-stations in France !
L'essence (m.) : petrol
gazole or *gas-oil* [gazwal !] is diesel oil.
le pétrole : is mineral oil
l'huile : oil (for cars, for cooking, etc. . .)
Faites le plein : Fill it up.

(3) There are 22 entrances into Paris, called *portes* (gates). They all lead off from a circular expressway which is called *le boulevard périphérique.*

8 Ils prennent la sortie de Beaune et M. Martin s'arrête au péage **(4)**.

9 Ils passent quelques minutes à chercher des pièces dans leurs poches

10 et, les‿ayant trouvées **(5)**, M. Martin paie.

11 La famille continue son chemin **(6)** vers le centre ville.

PRONONCIATION

9 . . .fooyay

IL EST TRÈS FACILE À RECONNAÎTRE.

EXERCICES

1. Ayant fait un peu de chemin, il s'est arrêté. – **2.** Elle s'en va demain pour la Bourgogne. – **3.** Il est très facile à reconnaître. – **4.** On a passé dix minutes à chercher la sortie. – **5.** Il n'y a jamais trop de monde à cette heure. – **6.** Faites le plein s'il vous plaît.

Fill in the blanks :

1 Ils . . . . les sandwichs qu'elle . . . .

They ate the sandwiches she prepared.

2 Nous nous . . . . avant d' . . . .

We will stop before arriving.

8 They take the exit for (of) B. and Mr. M. stops at the toll-booth.
9 They spend several minutes looking for coins in their pockets
10 and, having found them, Mr. M. pays.
11 The family continues its way towards the town centre.

NOTES (suite)

(4) *Un péage :* is both a toll and a toll-booth.
Un pont à péage : a toll-bridge
payer un péage : to pay a toll
All motorways in France are toll-roads.

(5) *ayant* is the present participle of *avoir.*
And is used either as part of a verbal phrase :
Ayant un peu d'argent, il est allé au restaurant : Having a little money, he went to a restaurant.
or as an auxiliary :
Ayant demandé à un policier, il a continué son chemin : Having asked a policeman, he continued on his way.
(For a brief explanation of the "agreement" of the past participle, see Lesson 84).

(6) *Un chemin* : a way or a road.
Je vais lui demander le chemin : I am going to ask him/her the way.
Ce chemin mène à la gare : this road leads to the station.
Nous sommes sur le bon chemin : we are on the right road.
Le chemin de fer : the railway.
Le chemin des‿écoliers : (the shoolboy's road) : the longest possible way round !

EXERCISES

1. Having gone a little way, he stopped. — **2.** She is leaving tomorrow for Burgundy. — **3.** He is very easy to recognize. — **4.** We spent ten minutes looking for the exit. — **5.** There are never too many people at this time. — **6.** Fill it up, please.

3 J'ai ..... dix ans à .... pour lui.

I spent ten years working for him.

4 ...... - .... m'indiquer le ...... pour le ......

..... ?

Can you show me the way to the town centre ?

5 Ils ont cherché des .... Les ....

ils ont payé.

They looked for coins. Having found them, they paid.

QUATRE-VINGT-QUATRIEME (84ème) LEÇON

REVISION ET NOTES

1. Pronoun order : We have already a good notion of the order of pronouns before verbs. We know that personal pronouns come before the verb (*il me parle ; je lui donne, etc. .*)unless we are using the imperative mood *(Donnez-moi, téléphonez-moi, etc.).* But what happens when we have a more complex sentence with several pronouns ?

SUBJECT	INDIRECT OBJECT	DIRECT OBJECT	INDIRECT OBJECT	
je	*me*			
tu	*te*	*le*	*lui*	*verb*
il/elle	*se*	*la*		*or*
nous	*nous*			
vous	*vous*	*les*	*leur*	*auxiliary*
ils/elles				

It's not as bad as it looks !
If you memorise this, you will always know in what order the pronouns come.
For example, "I gave it to him". We need subject + direct object + indirect object + auxiliary which gives us : - *Je le lui ai donné.*

Fill in the blanks

1 - ont mangé - a préparés. — **2** - arrêterons - arriver. — **3** - passé - travailler. — **4** Pouvez-vous - chemin - centre-ville. — **5** - pièces ayant trouvées.

* * *

Second Wave : Trente-troisième Leçon

84th LESSON

She told me it : *Elle me l'a dit.*
Will you send them to us ? : *Voulez-vous nous les envoyer ?*
Check back to the list and verify the order.
These "mental gymnastics" take a little time to master but if you fix the order in your mind, you will find that, very soon, you will be able to form sentences automatically - and correctly !
(We can expand this table by adding *y* and *en* to it. We will see this in Lesson 88).

You have probably noticed that, in the past tense, the past participle changes form depending on what is in front of it. The basic rule that governs this is :
(a) verbs conjugated with *être* agree with their subject
(b) verbs conjugated with *avoir* agree with the nearest preceding direct object.
For the time being, we ask you simply to remember the rule. We do not intend to expand on it yet ; and since the pronunciation of the past participle does not change, it is something that need not worry us for the moment.

2. *Quand il viendra je vous le dirai :* when he comes, I will tell you. In such a sentence, French puts **both**

verbs into the future tense (which is logical since neither action has yet taken place !) in a future sentence. So, after *quand (lorsque) :* when : and *dès que (aussitôt que),* the following verb is in the future tense.
Dès que le courrier arrivera je vous l'apporterai : As soon as the mail arrives, I will bring it to you.
(Notice the order of the pronouns too).
So, when English uses the present perfect (when he **has** finished. . .), the French puts the auxiliary in the future : *dès qu'il* **aura** *fini.*
Quand vous l'aurez lu donnez-le moi : when you have read it, give it to me.

Being able to manipulate such constructions automatically is a question of reflex - which means practice. Memorise one or two of the model sentences and try and invent new, short ones based on them. You will be surprised how easily it becomes second nature.

3. French uses reflexive verbs (e.g. *se laver)* more extensively than English. Some verbs change their meaning depending on whether they are reflexive or not. Here are six very common ones. To help memorise them think of the word ABROAD :

Aller : to go ; *s'en aller :* to go away ; to leave.
Battre : to beat ; *se battre :* to fight.
Rappeler : to remind ; *se rappeler :* to remember.
Occuper : to occupy ; *s'occuper (de) :* to look after.
Attendre : to wait for ; *s'attendre à :* to expect.
Demander : to ask ; *se demander :* to wonder.

Here are a few examples :
Il est allé en Espagne hier : He went to Spain yesterday.

Ils s'en vont en vacances : They are going on holidays.
La France a battu la Suisse : France beat Switzerland.
Les supporters se sont battus : The supporters fought.
Rappelez-moi votre nom : Remind me of your name.
Elle ne se rappelle pas cette histoire. She does not remember this story.
Of course there are others - but we don't want to do everything at once.

4. We know how to use *quel; quelle ;* etc. . .
Now, look at these "compound relatives " (i. e. preposition + a relative pronoun).

Lequel laquelle (lesquels ; lesquelles)
Lequel de ces deux livres ? : Which of these two books ?
Lesquelles de ces cartes . . .? : Which of these cards (i.e. you can have more than one)
We can also use the above relatives in the affirmative form :

Un homme avec lequel je travaille : A man with whom I work.
Une société dans laquelle il a des actions : A company in which he has shares.

If the verb we are using takes the preposition *à* (e.g. *penser à)*, we use :

auquel à laquelle (auxquels ; auxquelles)
C'est une solution à laquelle j'ai déjà pensé : It' s a solution I have already thought of.

We sometimes find *duquel ; de laquelle (desquels ; desquelles)*
- of which, of whom - but *dont* is more common ; or *de qui* if there is a preposition before the preceding

noun :

C'est un homme duquel on dit du bien :) He is a
C'est un homme dont on dit du bien :) man who is
C'est un homme de qui on dit du bien :) well spoken of.

By giving you the above information, we don't wish to flood you with details but to show you how, from one simple rule you have already mastered, other more

QUATRE-VINGT-CINQUIEME (85ème) LEÇON

Une visite à Beaune (fin)

1 Les Martin sont‿arrivés à Beaune à trois‿heures dix,
2 et ils se sont précipités (1) pour voir les‿Hospices,
3 ces bâtiments, aux toits polychromes (2) datent du quinzième siècle ;
4 ils sont toujours habités (3) mais aujourd'hui il n'y a ni malades ni mendiants (4)

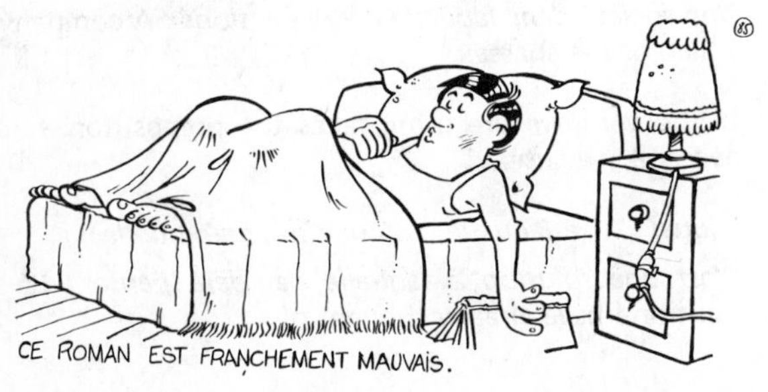
CE ROMAN EST FRANCHEMENT MAUVAIS.

PRONONCIATION

3 . .twa poleekrom dat

complex forms can be assembled. Remember that there is an enormous difference between "complex" and " complicated".

* * *

Second Wave : Trente-quatrième Leçon

85th LESSON

A visit to Beaune (end)

1 The Martins arrived at B. at 3.10.
2 and they rushed to see the Almhouses.
3 These buildings, with their polychromatic roofs, date from the 15th century,
4 they are still inhabited but today there are neither sick (people) nor beggars

NOTES

(1) *Je suis pressé :* I am in a hurry
Dépêchez-vous : Hurry up !
se précipiter : to rush
Elle s'est précipitée dans ses bras : she rushed into his arms. (Notice the "agreement" of the past participle, which takes an "s" with the plural subject *ils).*

(2) *La fille aux cheveux blonds :* the girl with blond hair.
au ; à la indicates a physical property (polychromatic is the adjective applied to a certain style of roofing found in Burgundy which used red, gold and green tiles).

(3) Be careful of this "false friend" : *habiter :* to live in
une maison habitée : an inhabited house
une maison inhabitée : an **un**inhabited house
un habitant : an inhabitant.

(4) *Je n'ai ni argent, ni amis :* I have neither money nor friends. Don't forget that the verb must be negative as well
Il ne veut ni manger ni boire : he wants neither to eat nor drink.
Vous pouvez prendre soit du cuir soit du plastique : you can take either leather or platic.
Je peux vous voir soit aujourd'hui, soit après-demain : I can see you either today or the day after tomorrow.
(another form of either. .or is *ou. . . ou* instead of *soit . . . soit)* **ou** *du cuir* **ou** *du plastique.*

5 mais des personnes du troisième âge (5).
6 Une fois la visite finie ils se sont rendus dans‿une cave
7 pour déguster du vin et pour en‿acheter.
8 — Qu'est-ce que tu penses de celui-ci ? -Il est franchement mauvais.
9 — Et celui-là n'est pas fameux (6) non plus. -Et ce Côtes du Rhône (7) ?
10 — Beurk ! C'est le pire de tous ! -Moi même (N1), je trouve qu'il n'est pas mauvais.
11 — D'accord. Commande-le et moi, comme d'habitude, je le paierai (8)
12 Après cet‿épisode hautement culturel, M. Martin a décidé
13 de chercher un petit‿hôtel sympathique pour y coucher.
14 Mais, n'ayant rien trouvé ni à Beaune, ni dans les‿environs,
15 ils sont repartis pour Paris à huit‿heures.

IL N'A PAS FAIT UN
BON VOYAGE,
IL ÉTAIT
MALADE.

PRONONCIATION

6 . .fronshmohn
10 . .peer. . .tooss
13 . .sampateek

5 but "senior citizens"
6 Once the visit[was]finished they went (rendered themselves) (in) to a cellar.
7 to taste wine and to buy some.
8 – What do you think of this one ? -It's frankly bad.
9 – And this one isn't wonderful either. -and this C. du R. ?
10 – Yuk ! It's the worst of all ! -Myself, I find that it isn't bad.
11 – O.K. order it and (me), as usual, I will pay[for] it.
12 After this highly cultural episode, Mr. M. decided.
13 to look [for] a little, nice hotel to sleep in (there)
14 But, having found nothing either in B. or in the surroundings.
15 they left again for P. at 8.00

NOTES (suite)

(5) *Le troisième âge* is an euphemism for old people *(les vieux)* like, in English, we transformed "old age pensioners" into "senior citizens".

(6) famous is *célèbre ; fameux* is a familiar way of saying "first-rate" "great".
Il est fameux, ton vin ! : Your wine is really great !
pas fameux : not up to much, or for a person, not good at
Je ne suis pas fameux en maths : I'm not good at maths.

(7) *La côte* : the coast.
La Côte d'Ivoire : the Ivory Coast
The word is often found in wine-names, indicating which region the wine comes from * :
Le Côte de Nuits, le Côte de Beaune, etc. .
* but the gender changes since *"le vin"* is masculine.

(8) *payer quelque chose :* to pay **for** something
payer quelqu'un : to pay someone
We can write either *je paie, tu paies, il paie, ils paient,*
or *je paye, tu payes, il paye, ils payent.*
(nous payons and *vous payez* are the only possible forms with these pronouns).
This is true for other verbs ending in *-ayer* like *bégayer* - to stammer, *rayer* - to cross out.

EXERCICES

1. J'habite à Paris -Paris même ou les environs ? – **2.** C'est un Bourgogne ou un Bordeaux ? -Ni l'un ni l'autre. – **3.** Ce roman * est franchement mauvais. -Celui-ci est pire. – **4.** Regarde ! là-bas, c'est le Président lui-même ! – **5.** Une fois le repas fini, il est reparti chez lui. – **6.** Beurk ! Pas fameux, ton vin !

* un roman [roamoh] : a novel

Fill in the blanks :

1 .. ma femme .. moi .. pourrons venir.

Neither my wife nor I can come.

2 Il les .... d' .... avec deux mois de retard.

He pays them, as usual, two months late.

3 Elle s' ... . pour le voir.

She rushed to see him.

QUATRE-VINGT SIXIEME (86ème) LEÇON

A l'école primaire

1 L'institutrice (1) s'adresse à ses élèves à la fin de la leçon :

NOTES

(1) *Un professeur :* a teacher works in *un lycée :* a secondary school

EXERCISES

1. I live in Paris. -Paris itself or the surroundings ? — **2.** Is it a Burgundy or a Bordeaux ? Neither one nor the other. — **3.** This novel is frankly bad. -This one is worse. — **4.** Look ! over there. It's the President himself ! — **5.** Once the meal was finished, he left again for his house. — **6.** Yuk ! Your wine isn't up to much !

4 Les Hospices accueillaient .... des mendiants .... des ....

The Almhouses welcomed either beggars or sick people.

5 Ils .... . ' ont dit ... - .....

They told us it themselves.

Fill in the blanks

1 Ni - ni - ne — **2** -paie/paye - comme - habitude - — **3** - est précipitée - — **4** - soit - soit - malades. — **5** - nous - l' - eux-mêmes.

* * *

Second Wave : Trente-cinquième Leçon

86th LESSON

At the primary school

1 The teacher addresses (herself to) her pupils at the end of the lesson :

NOTES (suite)

Un instituteur (une institutrice) works in *une école primaire :* a primary school
un élève : a pupil ;
un lycéen (-éenne) : a high school pupil

2 — Allons, mes petits, je vous‿ai appris les temps (2) de tous les verbes.
3 Vous connaissez le présent, le passé, le futur et l'imparfait.
4 J'espère que vous‿avez bien compris ? Voyons voir. . .
5 Yvon, si je te dis (3) "Je me suis lavé, tu t'es lavé, il s'est lavé
6 nous nous sommes lavés, vous vous‿êtes lavés, ils se sont lavés ; qu'est-ce que c'est ?
7 — Ben, Mademoiselle, c'est dimanche !

8 — Passons‿à autre chose. Laurence, nous‿avons parlé de sens (4) civique :
9 alors, qu'est-ce qu'on fait d'une voiture qui est trop vieille
10 qui est rouillée et dont on ne veut plus ?
11 — On la vend à mon père, Mademoiselle ! (5)

12 — Aïe ! Qu'est-ce que j'ai mal au genou ! dit le cancre
13 — Ah, un peu de migraine, répond son professeur.

PRONONCIATION

2 . .too
8 . .sohnss
10 . .rooyay
13 . .meegren

2 – Well my little [ones], I have taught you the tenses of all the verbs.
3 You know the present, the past, the future, and the imperfect.
4 I hope you have really (well) understood ? Let's see. .
5 Y. , if I say to you : I have washed, you have washed, he has washed,
6 we have w. you have w., they have washed -what is it ?
7 – Ehm, Miss, it's Sunday !

8 – Let's go on (pass) to other things. L., we have spoken of civic pride (sense)
9 so what do people (one) do with a car which is too old
10 which is rusty and (of) which one wants no longer ?
11 – They sell it to my father, miss.

12 – Ouch ! (How) my knee hurts ! says the dunce.
13 – Ah, a slight (little of) migraine -replies his teacher.

NOTES (suite)

(2) *un temps* in a grammatical sense, is a verb tense
(3) Primary school teachers use the *tu* form when addressing their pupils, who reply with the *vous* form. Note that *Yvon* is a boy's name (the male form of *Yvonne)* and that *Laurence* (line 8) is a girl's name ; the female form of *Laurent.*
(4) *le sens* [sohnss] : the sense, the feeling of
il n'a pas le sens de l'humour : he has no sense of humour
The word can also mean "direction" and we find it in the expression
une rue en sens unique : (lit. : one direction) one-way street.
(5) Notice how we translate *on* in this exchange.
The pronoun here refers to people in general, a habit or custom shared, and we translate it accordingly. *On* is very widely used in modern French.

EXERCICES

1. Passons à autre chose, si vous voulez bien. – **2.** Quel jour sommes-nous ? -C'est mardi. – **3.** Qu'est-ce que j'ai mal à la tête ! – **4.** Je me suis adressé au bureau de renseignements. – **5.** Qu'est-ce qu'on fait de ce vieux meuble ?

Fill in the blanks :

1 Qu'est-ce qu' .. dit .. français quand .. est malheureux ?

What do you say in French when you're unhappy ?

2 Elle .. . ' . expliqué, mais je n'ai pas ....

compris.

She explained it to me but I didn't really understand.

3 Une voiture qui est vieille et .... .. ne veut ....

A car which is old and which one no longer wants.

4 Il .... . ' a appris la semaine dernière

He taught it to us last week.

QUATRE-VINGT-SEPTIEME (87ème) LEÇON

Faites attention à "faire"

1 Voici quelques‿exemples de l'emploi du verbe "faire"

EXERCISES

1. Let's go on to something else, if you please.– **2.** What day is it ? -It's Tuesday. – **3.** I've got a terrible headache ! – **4.** I asked at the information desk – **5.** What do we do with this old piece of furniture ?

QU'EST CE QUE
J'AI MAL À LA
TÊTE !

5 Nous en .... l'année prochaine

We will talk about it next year.

Fill in the blanks

1 - on - en - on - – **2** - me l'a - bien - – **3** - dont - on - plus. – **4** - nous l' - – **5** - parlerons - .

* * *

Second Wave : Trente-sixième Leçon

87th LESSON

Be careful with "to do/to make"

1 Here are a few examples of the use of the verb "to do/to make".

2 — Il fait bon ici. Il ne fait ni trop chaud, ni trop froid.
3 Je crois que je vais faire une petite promenade.
4 — Excusez-moi de vous faire attendre.
5 Si je rentre trop tard, mon mari va faire des‿histoires.
6 — Ne fais pas l'idiot ! Tu m'as fait peur avec tes bêtises. (1)
7 Le fromage n'était pas‿assez "fait" ; en revanche (2), le poisson l'était trop.
8 J'ai fait une gaffe monumentale ! Je croyais que c'était sa femme !
9 Ce tableau faisait deux cents francs au marché. Je l'ai payé cent francs. -On vous‿a refait ! (3)
10 Si tu leur téléphones maintenant, tu feras d'une pierre deux coups.
11 L'habit ne fait pas le moine.
12 Il a gagné au loto mais il a perdu son ticket ! Faut le faire ! (4)

PRONONCIATION

7 . .revonsh
10 . .koo
11 . .labee. . .mwan

EXERCICES

1. Il a fait d'une pierre deux coups. — **2.** Elle est partie faire une petite promenade. — **3.** Excuse-nous de te faire attendre. — **4.** Quelle gaffe ! Tu ne fais que des bêtises ! — **5.** Combien fait ce tableau ? — **6.** On t'a eu, mon pauvre ami.

2 – It's nice here. It is neither too hot nor too cold.
3 I think that I will go for a little walk.
4 – Excuse me for making you wait.
5 If I go back too late, my husband will make a fuss.
6 – Don't be an idiot ! You frightened me with your idiocies.
7 The cheese wasn't ripe ("done") enough ; on the other hand, the fish was too (much)
8 I made a monumental blunder ! I thought she was his wife !
9 This painting was 200 francs in the market. I paid 100 francs[for]it. -You were done !
10 If you phone them, you will kill two birds with one stone (make of one stone two blows).
11 The clothes don't make the monk (i.e. appearances are not everything)
12 He won (at) the Loto but lost his ticket ! That takes some doing ! (it is necessary to do it !)

NOTES

(1) We know *bête* which means stupid
une bêtise is a stupid action
Cet enfant ne fait que des bêtises : this child is always doing stupid things.

(2) *en revanche :* on the other hand ; to make up for it
Il n'est pas très beau, mais en revanche, il est très intelligent : He's not very handsome, but, to make up for it, he's very intelligent.
Nous ne sommes pas pour l'idée, mais en revanche, nous ne la critiquons pas : We are not for the idea, but, on the other hand, we don't criticize it.

(3) The idiom is very similar to the English. So is the alternative *On vous a eu ! :* you have been had !

(4) This is an exclamation of astonishment, either pejorative - as here - or complimentary.
Elle parle quatre langues couramment. Faut le faire ! : She speaks four languages fluently. That takes some doing !

EXERCISES

1. He killed two birds with one stone. – **2.** She has left to go for a little walk. – **3.** Excuse us for making you wait. – **4.** What a blunder ! You're always doing stupid things ! – **5.** How much is this painting ? – **6.** You were had, my poor friend.

Fill in the blanks :

1 Il .... très chaud en Inde.

It was very hot in India

2 Il .. ' . .... peur !

He frightened me !

3 On .. .. une petite ....

We are going to go for a little walk

4 Ils ... . quatre fois. .... !

They won four times. That takes some doing !

QUATRE-VINGT-HUITIEME (88ème) LEÇON

La Télévision

1 Le "petit‿écran" devient de plus‿en plus (1) répandu (2)

5 Ils . ' ont ....

They made me wait

6 Ce n'est pas très grand mais .. .. c'est très fort.

It's not very big but, to make up for it, it's very strong.

Fill in the blanks

1 - faisait - 2 - m'a fait - — 3 - va faire - promenade — 4 - ont gagné - Faut le faire ! — 5 - m'- fait attendre — 6 - en revanche -

* * *

Second Wave : Trente-septième Leçon

88th LESSON

The Television

1 The "little screen" [is] becoming more and more widespread

NOTES

(1) The pronunciation of *plus* depends on its function : if it is part of the negation *ne . .plus,* it is pronounced [plyoo] if it means more, it is pronounced [plyooss]. In the expression *de plus en plus* (more and more), we make the liaison to form [plyoozon plyoo] *de moins en moins :* less and less.

(2) *répandre* conjugates like *vendre* and means to spread, diffuse, pour out. *J'ai répandu du sel sur la tache de vin :* I spread salt on the wine-stain. *répandu* as an adjective means widespread, common.

2 presque tous les foyers en possèdent au moins un **(N-2)**
3 Très souvent, on l'allume et on y passe **(3)** des heures
4 sans vraiment regarder ni y faire attention.
5 La télévision en France est un monopole d'état.
6 Il y a trois chaines **(4)** dont deux passent de la publicité.
7 (Les trois chaines sont en couleur)
8 "La télé" -comme on dit - est financée par la publicité
9 et une partie de l'argent versé **(5)** pour les redevances.
10 Mais il y en a qui **(6)** ne sont pas très "chauds" pour la télévision,
11 entre autres les instituteurs et les producteurs de cinéma.
12 Et aussi cet acteur célèbre qui a dit : -Je hais **(7)** la télévision ;
13 je la hais autant que les cacahuètes -
14 mais je ne peux pas m'empêcher de manger des cacahuètes !

PRONONCIATION

2 . .fwayay. .
6 . .shen. . .
12 . .ay
13 . .kakawet

2 almost all homes possess at least one (of them).
3 Very often, it is turned on (one lights it) and people spend hours there
4 without really watching nor paying attention [to it]
5 The television in France is a state monopoly
6 There are three channels of which two show publicity.
7 (All three channels are in colour).
8 "The telly" - as we say - is financed by publicity,
9 and a part of the money paid for T.V. licences
10 But there are [those] who are not very enthusiastic (warm) about (for) television
11 among others, primary-school teachers and cinema producers.
12 And also this famous actor who said : -I hate television ;
13 I hate it as much as peanuts ;
14 but I can't stop eating (prevent myself to eat) peanuts !

NOTES (suite)

(3) Let's remind ourselves of the uses of *passer*
Il a passé deux semaines dans le Midi : he spent two weeks in the South
Nous avons passé une annonce dans le journal : we put an advertisement in the paper.
Passez-moi le poivre : Pass me the pepper
Passons à autre chose : let's go on to something else.

(4) *Une chaîne de magasins, de montagnes* . .a chain of shops, of mountains
Une chaîne de télévision : a T.V. channel.

(5) *verser :* literally means to pour.
Versez-nous un verre de vin : Pour us a glass of wine.
but it is also used instead of "to pay" when we are talking about official payments - taxes, deposits, interest, etc. .
Il pleut à verse : it's pouring with rain

(6) *il y en a (ceux) qui :* there are those who . .
the *ceux* if often omitted when the group referred to is vague or general.

(7) *haïr* [eye-ear] to hate
Beware of the pronunciation of this verb *je hais* [ay], *tu hais ; il hait ; nous haïssons* [eye-ee-sohn], *vous haïssez* [eye-ee-say]
The past participle is *haï* [eye-ee]

EXERCICES

1. Est-ce que vous le haïssez vraiment ? – **2.** Les gens deviennent de plus en plus paresseux*. – **3.** La télévision - ou "la télé" - comme on dit - est un monopole d'état. – **4.** Il y a trois journaux dont deux sont à moi. – **5.** Je l'aime autant que j'aime les impôts. – **6.** Allumez la radio, s'il vous plaît.

*paresseux (-euse) : lazy

Fill in the blanks :

1 J' .. .. entendu parler, il paraît qu' .. . mange très bien.

I have heard of it ; apparently one eats very well there.

2 Ce n'est pas bon mais .. . .. . qui ...... ça.

It's not good but there are those who like it.

3 Je suis .. .. chaud pour cette idée

I am less and less enthusiastic about that idea.

QUATRE-VINGT-NEUVIEME (89ème) LEÇON

Le Tour de France

1 Cette course cycliste célèbre a beaucoup changé depuis sa création en mil neuf cent trois.

2 A cette époque,le Tour ne comptait que six‿étapes

EXERCISES

1. Do you really hate him ? — **2.** People are becoming more and more lazy. — **3.** The television or "the telly" - as they say - is a state monopoly. — **4.** There are three papers, two of which are mine. — **5.** I like him/her as much as I like taxes. — **6.** Turn on the radio, please.

4 Il . ..... deux semaines à attendre puis il . .....

une annonce.

He spent two weeks waiting, then he ran an advertisement.

5 .... tous les foyers .. possèdent .. ..

un(e)

Almost all homes own at least one (of them)

Fill in the blanks

1 - 'en ai - on y - — **2** - il y en a - aiment. — **3** - de moins en moins - — **4** - a passé - a passé - — **5** Presque - en - au moins.

* * *

Second Wave : Trente-huitième Leçon

89th LESSON

The Tour of France

1 This famous cycle race has changed a lot since its creation in 1903.
2 At that time, the Tour included (counted) only six stages.

PRONONCIATION

1 . . .krayaseeohn
2 . . .seezaytap

3 tandis qu'aujourd'hui, il en compte plus de vingt.
4 Aussi, à son‿origine, le Tour ne quittait pas la France alors que,
5 de nos jours, les coureurs se rendent en Espagne, en Belgique et aux Pays-Bas **(1)**
6 L'année dernière, cent cinquante participants venus de partout **(2)** ont couru.
7 Le Belge, Robet, a porté le maillot jaune **(3)** pendant dix jours de suite,
8 et le Français Moutet l'a porté pendant quinze jours **(4)**
9 il ne l'a perdu qu'une fois, lors d'**(5)** une étape contre la montre.
10 La dernière étape - l'entrée triomphale dans Paris, était très‿excitante :
11 Le Français et le Belge se sont disputé **(6)** la première place pendant douze kilomètres

PRONONCIATION

3 .tondee
5 . . .payee ba

3 whereas today it includes (counts) more than 20

4 Also, at its beginning (origin), the Tour did not leave France, whereas

5 nowadays (of our days) the racers go to Spain, to Belgium and to the Netherlands.

6 Last year, 150 participants (come) from all over raced.

7 The Belgian, R., wore the yellow jersey for ten consecutive days

8 and the Frenchman M. wore it for two weeks.

9 he only lost it once, during a stage against the clock (watch).

10 The last stage - the triumphal entry into Paris, was very exciting :

11 The Frenchman and the Belgian were neck and neck for 12 km.

NOTES

(1) We say **en** *Italie,* **en** *Pologne* (to Poland) etc. .but
aux Pays-bas (to the Netherlands) **aux** *Etas-Unis* etc. . because these latter are plural groups (like **The** Seychelles **Les** *Seychelles;* The Carribean **Les** *Caraïbes,* etc.)

(2) *partout :* everywhere, all over
Il y a des affiches partout : there are posters everywhere
Des musiciens venus de partout : musicians from all over.
Nulle part : nowhere anywhere : (negative).
Je n'en‿ai trouvé nulle part : I couldn't find any anywhere.

(3) *un maillot de bain :* a swimming costume
un maillot de corps : a (man's) vest
Le maillot jaune (the yellow jersey) is the singlet worn by the leading cyclist at each stage of the Tour de France.

(4) The French say *quinze jours* where the English would say "two weeks"
une quinzaine : a fortnight

(5) *lors de : pendant :* during
Lors d'un séjour aux Etats-Unis : Pendant un séjour aux Etats-Unis : During a stay in the U.S.
Lors de is more of a written form.

(6) *se disputer :* to argue
Les deux chauffeurs se sont disputés : the two drivers argued
Ils se sont disputé la première place : they were neck and neck.
une dispute : an argument (a heated exchange)
un argument : an argument (a series of reasons).

12 quand le Français à crevé (7) et a dû s'arrêter.
13 Ainsi, le Tour de France a été gagné par un Belge.

PRONONCIATION

7 . .maïyoh
9 . .lor

EXERCICES

1. Il vient de rentrer d'un séjour aux Pays-Bas et il est crevé. – **2.** Ils ont dû vendre leur voiture. – **3.** Il a porté le maillot jaune pendant quinze jours de suite. – **4.** Ne nous disputons pas ; ça n'en vaut pas la peine. – **5.** Lors d'un séjour en Europe, il s'est rendu deux fois en Espagne. – **6.** Il l'a perdu en mil neuf cent neuf.

Fill in the blanks :

1 Ils .... de .... pour courir.

They came from all over to race.

2 Nous avons ..... trois fois .. ..

We won three times running.

3 Elle a beaucoup changé ...... la dernière fois ... je l' .. vue.

She has changed a lot since the last time I saw her.

4 Il a gagné l'étape ; il .... le maillot jaune demain.

He has won the stage ; he will wear the yellow jersey tomorrow.

12 when the Frenchman had a puncture and had to stop.
13 Thus the Tour of France was won by a Belgian.

NOTES (suite)

(7) *un pneu* [peneuh] *crevé* : a punctured tire
Il a crevé sur l'autoroute : he had a puncture on the motorway.
We also find the word used in a very frequent idiom :
Je suis crevé ! : I'm worn out !

EXERCISES

1. He has just returned from a stay in the Netherlands and he is worn out. — **2.** They had to sell their car. — **3.** He wore the yellow jersey for 2 weeks running. — **4.** Let's not argue ; it s not worth it. — **5.** During a stay in Europe, he went to Spain twice. — **6.** He lost it in 1909.

5 Ils l'ont cherché mais ils .. . ' ... trouvé .....
....
They looked for it but they couldn't find it anywhere.

Fill in the blanks

1 - sont venus - partout - **2** - gagné - de suite — **3** - depuis - que - ai — **4** - portera - **5** - ne l'ont - nulle part.

* * *

Second Wave : Trente-neuvième Leçon

89ème LEÇON

QUATRE-VINGT-DIXIEME (90ème) LEÇON

Avez-vous bien lu ?

1 Quand le Tour de France, a-t-il été créé ? **(1)**
2 Combien y avait-il d'étapes à l'origine ?
3 Combien y en‿(2)a-t-il aujourd'hui ?
4 Dans quels pays les coureurs se rendent-‿ils **(3)** ?
5 Pendant combien de temps le Français a-t-il porté le maillot jaune ?
6 Quand l'a-t-il perdu ? Comment s'appelait‿-il ?
7 Pourquoi le Français s'est‿-il arrêté ?

8 — Ma chère, je suis‿en train de lire un bouquin **(4)** passionnant !
9 Il y a un tel suspense ! On ne sait pas s'il va finir bien
10 ou en catastrophe !
11 — J'espère que vous me le prêterez quand vous l'aurez fini.
12 Je suppose que c'est‿un roman policier ?
13 — Pas du tout. C'est‿un livre de cuisine !

PRONONCIATION

1 . .krayay
4 . .rondeteel
6 . . .sapelayteel
8 . . .bookan
9 . .syoosspenss
10 . .katastroff
12 . . .poleeseeyay

90th LESSON

Have you read carefully (well) ?

1 When was the T.d.F. created ?
2 How many stages were there at the beginning ?
3 How many (of them) are there today ?
4 To (in) which countries do the racers go ?
5 For how long did the Frenchman wear the yellow jersey ?
6 When did he lose it ? -What was the Frenchman's name ?
7 Why did the Frenchman stop ?

8 – My dear, I am in the middle of reading a fascinating book !
9 There is (a) such suspense ! One doesn't know if it's going to finish well
10 or in catastrophe !
11 – I hope that you will lend it to me when you (will) have finished.
12 I suppose that it's a police novel ?
13 – Not at all. It's a cookery (kitchen) book !

NOTES

(1) A difficult verb to pronounce *créer* [kray-ay]
Je crée [kray] *tu crées ; il crée ; nous créons ; vous créez* [kray-ay] *; ils créent*
past participle *: créé*
un créateur : a creator
We are now studying the more elegant - and correct - question form, where we replace *est-ce que* by an inversion.
(2) The *en* replaces the noun *étapes* we saw in line 2.
(3) Here, and in lines 4 and 6 *(rendent-ils ; s'appelait-il)* we do not need to add a euphonic "t" ; we simply pronounce the "t" at the end of the verb, making the liaison with the following vowel.
(4) We have seen that *un bouquin* is a familiar word for a book. In the centre of Paris, the sides of the River Seine are lined with tiny kiosks where people sell books, documents, maps, etc. .
We call these merchants *les bouquinistes.*

EXERCICES

1. Je vous le prêterai dès que je l'aurai fini. – **2.** L'année dernière, il y avait trois employés*, aujourd'hui il y en a vingt. – **3.** Ce bouquin est vraiment passionnant. – **4.** Qu'est-ce que vous êtes en train de lire là ? – **5.** Comment s'appelait ton ami allemand ?

**un(e) employé(e) :* an employee

Write the questions which correspond to the following answers :

1 *Le Tour de France a été créé en 1903*

Quand le Tour de France . - . - .. été .... ?

2 *Il y avait vingt étapes.*

Combien y ..... - .. d'étapes ?

3 *Il 'a porté pendant deux jours.*

Pendant .... de temps . ' . . - .. porté ?

4 *Il l'a perdu lors d'une étape contre la montre.*

Quand l' . - . - .. perdu ?

QUATRE-VINGT-ONZIEME (91ème) LEÇON

REVISION ET NOTES

1. *moi-même :* myself

nous-mêmes : ourselves

toi même : yourself

vous-même(s) : yourself, yourselves

EXERCISES

1. I will lend it to you as soon as I have finished it. – **2.** Last year, there were three employees, today there are 20. – **3.** This book is really fascinating. – **4.** What are you busy reading there ? – **5.** What was your German friend's name ?

CE BOUQUIN
EST VRAIMENT
PASSIONNANT.

5 *Le Français s'est arrêté parce qu'il a crevé .*

Pourquoi le Français s' ... - .. .. ?

Write the questions

1 - a-t-il - créé. – **2** -avait-il - – **3** combien - l'a-t-il - – **4** - 'a-t-il - **5** - 'est-il arrêté ?

* * *

Second Wave : Quarantième Leçon

91st LESSON

lui/elle-même : him/herself

eux-mêmes :
elles-mêmes : themselves

As in English, these disjunctive pronouns add emphasis to a verb.
Je le ferai : I will do it.

Je le ferai moi-même : I will do it myself
Compostez votre billet vous-même : Punch your own ticket (your ticket yourself)
"by yourself" is *seul(e)*
Faites-le seul : Do it by yourself, alone.
soi-même is used when the subject is an indefinite pronoun like *on ;*
tout le monde ; personne, etc. .
On composte son billet soi-même : One punches one's own ticket (one's ticket oneself)
-même can also be added to a proper noun :
Paris même : Paris itself ; *la ville même :* the town itself.

2. In Lesson 84, we saw a list of pronouns and their order before a verb. We can add *en + y* to this list but, so as not to make life too hard, let's remove the subject pronouns *(je, tu, il,* etc. .), taking it for granted that they always come first. This then gives us :

me				
te				
	le			
se		*lui*		
	la		*y*	*en*
nous		*leur*		
	les			
vous				

which is a football team with five forwards, 3 halves, two backs, goalkeeper and a referee !
Let's put this into practice : I will speak to him about it
je + lui + en + verb *(parlerai)*
He will answer it tomorrow : *il y répondra demain.*
He will drive you there : *il vous y conduira.*

If you retain this (playing) order, you will have no problem to place the pronouns correctly.
en + y are a little elusive : basically both replace a noun (or a pronoun) in a sentence much as English uses one + ones : (I want a cigarette. -I haven't got one). -to avoid repeating the object noun.
Let's look at some examples :

Vous allez à Paris ? Oui, j'y vais : Are you going to Paris ? : *Yes, I am (going there)*
Je dois y rester: I must stay here (there)
Est-ce qu'il va à l'école ? : Does he go to school ?
Oui, il y va tous les jours : Yes, he goes every day.
And some idiomatic uses :
On y va ! : Let's go !
Vous y êtes ? : Do you follow (an explanation) ?
Pensez-y : Think it over
Ça y est ! : That's it !

en expresses quantity but only the expression of quantity itself is translated (i.e. number, weight, etc. .)
J'en connais plusieurs : I know several
Combien de cigarettes fumez-vous ? J'en fume dix par jour . : How many cigarettes do you smoke ? I smoke 10 a day.
En voulez-vous deux ou trois ? : Do you want two or three ?
Il ne manque qu'un : Only one is missing.

In fact, it is easier for us to learn to place *en* than it is for a French person to learn whether or not to translate it.

When we use a numeral pronoun (i.e. One of them, several, etc. .)
we do not use *en :*
Quatre d'entre eux parlent le français : Four of them speak French
Deux d'entre nous sont fatigués : Two of us are tired.
Plusieurs ont acheté des actions : Several bought shares.

Just a couple of examples of the agreement of the past participle in the past tense. We know that in verbs conjugated with *être,* the participle agrees with the subject ; and with *avoir,* it agrees with the nearest preceding direct object - if there is one.
J'ai acheté des pommes (no preceding direct object) but :
Les pommes que j'ai achetées.
Il a trouvé les livres but *les livres qu'il a trouvés.*

Je l'ai vu : I saw him/it (masculine object)
Je l'ai vue : I saw her/it (feminine object)
There is **no** agreement when the preceding object is indirect (**to** them, etc. .)
Elle leur a donné un cadeau : She gave them (ind.) a present.

Don't worry unduly about this rule. For the time being

QUATRE-VINGT-DOUZIEME (92ème) LEÇON

1 Voilà que nous‿arrivons à la dernière semaine de notre étude ;
2 bien sûr, en quatre-vingt-dix-neuf leçons vous ne pouvez pas connaître à fond (1) une langue
3 ce serait (N-1) trop demander ! Mais ce qu'on peut faire,
4 c'est‿apprendre à manier la langue et se familiariser avec ses mécanismes ;
5 apprendre ses particularités (2) et ses‿idiotismes à travers des conversations réelles.
6 (Si vous‿écoutiez deux - ou plusieurs - Français parler maintenant

---

Faites-vous toujours la deuxième vague ? *Do you always do the "second wave" ?*

PRONONCIATION

4 . . .maneeyay
5 . ,a travair

we are less worried about writing correct French than speaking it.

* * *

Second Wave : Quarante-et-unième Leçon

92nd LESSON

1 Here we arrive at the last week of our study ;
2 of course, in 99 lessons, you cannot know in depth (to end) a language.
3 that would be too much to ask ! But what we can do
4 is to learn to manipulate the language and to familiarise ourselves with its mechanisms ;
5 learn its peculiarities and its idioms through real conversations.
6 (If you listened to two - or more - French (people) talking now

NOTES

(1) *Le fond :* the bottom ; *au fond du jardin :* at the bottom of the garden.
ça vient du fond de mon coeur [kur] : It comes from the bottom of my heart
connaître à fond : to know completely, thoroughly.
(2) *particulier :* particular - or special, unusual :
Ce plat a un goût particulier : This dish has an unusual taste.
Je n'ai rien de particulier à vous dire : I have nothing particular to tell you.
une particularité : a peculiarity, a characteristic.
un particulier : is also commonly used to mean a private individual as opposed to a company, organisation etc. . . If you wish to rent or buy property without going through a real estate agency, you can buy a publication called *"De particulier à particulier" :* From one private individual to another.

7 vous n'auriez pas trop de mal à les comprendre).

8 Et surtout, essayez de comprendre l'esprit des gens qui parlent la langue.

9 Par exemple, ces deux dames d'un certain âge **(3)** qui, pour la première fois,

10 vont‿à Longchamp **(4)** pour savoir ce qu'est une course de chevaux.

11 N'ayant jamais parié, elles misent sur des chevaux tocards

12 et perdent leur argent ; mais elles sont contentes de l'expérience.

13 Après, dans le taxi qui les ramène chez‿elles, l'une dit à l'autre :

14 – C'est bien de ne pas‿avoir **(5)** gagné.

15 Qu'est-ce que nous ferions d'un cheval ?

PRONONCIATION

10 . .longshahn
11 . . .pareeyay. . . .meez. .tokar

EXERCICES

1. Si vous l'écoutiez, vous ne seriez jamais riche ! – **2.** Ils ne devraient pas avoir trop de mal à trouver du travail. – **3.** Je veux savoir ce qu'est un "particulier". – **4.** Ce que j'aime le plus, c'est de ne pas me lever le matin. – **5.** Qu'est-ce que vous feriez d'un chien si vous en aviez un ?

Fill in the blanks :

1 Pouvez-vous me dire . . . . ' . . . un idiotisme ?

Can you tell me what an idiom is ?

7 you would not have too much difficulty (bad) in (to) understanding them).
8 And above all, try to understand the minds of the people who speak the language.
9 For example these two elderly ladies who, for the first time,
10 go to L. to find out what a horse race is
11 Never having betted, they put their money on outsiders (horses)
12 and lose their money ; but they are happy with (of) the experience
13 After, in the taxi which takes them back home, (the) one says to the other :
14 — It's good not to have won.
15 What would we do with (of) a horse ?

NOTES (suite)

(3) *Il est d'un certain âge* is an euphemism for "elderly".
(4) *Longchamp* is the famous race track in le Bois de Boulogne, just outside Paris, where most of the major racing meets are held.
(5) *C'est dur de ne pas fumer ! :* It's hard not to smoke !
To negate the infinitive, we must place both *ne* and *pas* together before it. If the infinitive has an auxiliary, *ne pas* is placed before that : *C'est triste de ne pas avoir gagné :* It's sad not to have won.
Ils regrettent de ne pas être venus : They regret not having come.
Do you remember your verbs which are conjugated with *"être"* in the past ?

EXERCISES

1. If you listened to him you would never be rich ! — **2.** They wouldn't have too much difficulty to find work. — **3.** I want to know what a "private person" is. — **4.** What I like the most is not to get up in the morning. — **5.** What would you do with a dog if you had one ?

2 Je m'excuse de .. .. venu plus tôt.

I'm sorry not to have come earlier.

3 Si vous l' .... vous ...... du mal à comprendre.

If you listened to him, you would have difficulty understanding.

4 On ne peut pas le/la connaître . .... ; mais .. .. ' .. .... faire, . ' ... essayer.

You can't know it thoroughly but what you can do is to try.

5 Qu'est-ce que vous .... vos vieux vêtements ?

What will you do with your old clothes ?

QUATRE-VINGT-TREIZIEME (93ème) LEÇON

Le Savoir-faire

1 Dans son compartiment de chemin de fer, M. Cachan attend le départ.

2 Dès que **(1)** le train démarre, il sort un cigare et il l'allume.

PRONONCIATION

2 ..dayke

CE QUE J'AIME LE PLUS, C'EST DE NE PAS ME LEVER LE MATIN.

Fill in the blanks

1 - ce qu'est - — **2** - ne pas être - — **3** - écoutiez - auriez - — **4** - à fond - ce qu'on peut - c'est- — **5** -ferez de - .

* * *

Second Wave : Quarante-deuxième Leçon

93rd LESSON

Know-how

1 In his railway compartment, Mr C. [is] waiting [for] the departure.

2 As soon as the train starts, he takes out a cigar and he lights it.

NOTES

(1) Or - *aussitôt que :* Both expressions mean : as soon as. Remember that in a sentence like : I will tell you as soon as I receive it, we must put the second verb into the future : *Je vous le dirai quand je le recevrai*

3 Un des passagers dans le compartiment lui dit : – Je vous prie **(2)** d'éteindre **(3)** ce cigare.

4 Vous ‿ êtes dans ‿ un compartiment non-fumeurs. Sinon, j'appellerai le contrôleur.

5 – Appelez qui vous voudrez **(4)** répond Mr Cachan. Fâché, l'homme part à la recherche du contrôleur.

6 Il le trouve, et les deux reviennent dans le compartiment.

7 Le contrôleur est sur le point de parler, quand Mr Cachan lui coupe la parole **(5)**

8 – Je vous prie de demander son billet à Monsieur.

9 Le voyageur tend **(6)** son billet et le contrôleur s'exclame :

10 – Mais vous voyagez en première classe avec un billet de seconde **(7)** !

MA VOITURE NE DÉMARRE PAS
QUAND IL FAIT FROID.

PRONONCIATION

3 . .aytandr
9 . .tohn
10 . .segond

3 One of the passengers in the compartment says [to] him : Please, put out that cigar.

4 You are in a non-smoking compartment. If not, I'll call the inspector.

5 – Call whom you like, replies Mr C. Angry, the man leaves in search of the inspector.

6 He finds him, and the two come back to the compartment.

7 The inspector is on the point of speaking (to speak) when Mr C. butts in (cuts his word).

8 – Please, ask the gentleman for his ticket (ask the ticket to sir).

9 The traveller holds out his ticket and the inspector exclaims :

10 – But you [are] travelling (in) first class with a second-[class] ticket !

NOTES (suite)

(2) *Je vous prie de . .* (see also line 8) is a formal, polite way of introducing a request. In everyday language, we would simply say : *Eteignez ce cigare, s'il vous plaît (Je vous‿en prie :* Don't mention it).

(3) *éteindre :* to put out : *j'éteins, tu éteins, il éteint nous‿ éteignons, vous éteignez, ils‿éteignent.* Participe passé : *éteint.* An awkward conjugation. The only other commonly-used verb that is so conjugated is *peindre* : to paint.

(4) *Venez quand vous voudrez* (lit. come when you will like) is a more elegant way of saying : *Venez quand vous voulez. Allez où vous voudrez :* go where you like.

(5) There are two ways of saying "a word" in French : *un mot* and *une parole.* The first is used for the grammatical unit, the second for what is behind the word itself :
J'ai donné ma parole : I gave my word
Les paroles de cette chanson sont de Prévert : the words of this song are by Prévert.
Mr C. a pris la parole : Mr C. took the floor (i.e. began to speak).

(6) *tendre :* to hold out, to stretch conjugates like *vendre.*
La main tendue : hand outstretched.
détendre : to relax ; *Détendez-vous ! :* Relax !
La détente , of which we hear so much in international politics means : 'relaxation' (and, ironically, the trigger of a gun) !
(tendre as an adjective means : tender)

(7) There are two words for "second". If we talk of the second of two things, we use *le (la) second(e)* (notice the "c" is pronounced as a "g") If we are talking about the second of several, we use *le (la) deuxième.*

11 Venez avec moi. Vous aurez une amende !

12 Quand ils sont partis, un autre passager demande à Mr C. :

13 – Dites-moi, comment avez-vous su que l'autre n'était pas en règle ? **(8)**

14 – C'était facile. Son billet dépassait de sa poche

15 et j'ai vu qu'il avait la même couleur que le mien !

EXERCICES

1. Dès qu'il sera parti, j'éteindrai la lumière. – **2.** Ma voiture ne démarre pas quand il fait froid. – **3.** Venez quand vous voudrez ; nous vous attendrons. – **4.** Il m'a tendu la main et m'a dit : Bonjour ! – **5.** Quand l'avez-vous su ? -Hier soir.

Fill in the blanks :

1 Les deux femmes .... le salon

The two women came back into the living-room.

2 Il ... . à la .... contrôleur

He left in search of the inspector

3 Elle lui ..... toujours .. ..

She always interrupts him (butts in)

4 Dépêche-toi ! Nous sommes ... . partir

Hurry up ! We're on the point of leaving

11 Come with me. You will be fined (have a fine) !
12 When they have (are) left, another passenger asks Mr C. :
13 — Tell me : how did you know that the other was not "legal" ?
14 — It was easy. His ticket was sticking out of his pocket
15 and I saw that it was (had) the same colour as mine !

(8) *Une règle :* a rule
Votre passeport n'est pas‿en règle : your passport is not in order.
A fine phrase of officialese, to be heard when doing something wrong !
régler means to put in order, to adjust
régler des comptes : to settle accounts
un règlement : a payment.
The use of the present tense - the historic present - is the usual way of telling stories. English would use the simple past.

EXERCISES

1. As soon as he leaves I will turn out the light. — **2.** My car doesn't start when it's cold. — **3.** Come when you like ; we will wait for you. — **4.** He held out his hand to me and said (to me) Good morning ! — **5.** When did you know ? -Yesterday evening.

5 Nous vous ...... d' .... vos cigarettes

We would ask you to put out your cigarettes.

Fill in the blanks

1 - sont revenues dans - — **2** - est parti - recherche du - — **3** - coupe - la parole. **4** - sur le point de - — **5** -prions - éteindre -

* * *

Second Wave : Quarante-troisième Leçon

93ème LEÇON

QUATRE-VINGT-QUATORZIEME (94ème) LEÇON

1 Les Français – selon eux – sont des gens débrouillards **(1)**, indisciplinés, cultivés.
2 Les‿Anglais sont "fair-play" **(2)**, un peu froids et pragmatiques.
3 Les‿Allemands sont disciplinés, mélomanes, martiaux –
4 Ce sont là des stéréotypes qui influencent notre façon de penser –
5 mais‿aussi notre façon de parler. Nous disons, par exemple
6 "filer à l'anglaise" **(3)** pour "partir discrètement" ;
7 Quelqu'un qui a trop bu est "saoul comme un Polonais"
8 Une personne que l'on‿attaque systématiquement est "une tête de Turc"! **(4)**
9 Si l'on ne gagne pas beaucoup d'argent on dit "ce n'est pas le Pérou" ! **(5)**

PRONONCIATION

1 .daybrooyar. .andeeseepleenay
3 . .marseeoh
6 . .feelay
7 . .soo

94th LESSON

1 The F. -according to them - are resourceful, undiciplined, [and] cultured people.
2 The E. are fair-play, a little cold and pragmatic.
3 The Germans are disciplined, music-lovers, martial
4 These are (here) all stereotypes which influence our way (fashion) of thinking
5 but also our way (fashion) of talking -We say for example
6 "to split in the English manner" for "to leave discreetly"
7 Someone who has drunk too much is [as] "drunk as a Pole" !
8 A person whom one attacks systematically is a "Turk's head"
9 If one doesn't earn much money, one says : "It isn't Peru"!

NOTES

(1) *Le brouillard* [brooyar] : fog
se débrouiller : (lit. to get out of the fog) means to get by
Il se débrouille bien en français : He gets by well in French.
Un débrouillard (a high compliment in French) is a canny, resourceful person who gets out of difficulties with ease.

(2) Yes ! That's how you say "fair-play" in French.
An attempt was made to introduce le *"franc-jeu"* but *le fair-play* (*-il est très fair-play)* has resisted all attempts to dislodge it. (Being a foreign word there is no agreement of the adjective).

(3) It is interesting how countries who have a long mutual history attribute different vices and virtues to each other : *filer à l'anglaise is . .* to take French leave !

(4) This was the name of a "test-your-strength" machine at funfairs and by transference refers to anyone who is pushed around or bullied.

(5) Peru was always the fabled land of gold and wealth.
C'est pas le Pérou (the *ne* is dropped in familiar speech) : I won't get rich this way !

10 Et si l'on parle mal le Français – ce qui n'est point (6) votre cas –
11 on dit qu'on parle comme une "vache espagnole" (7)

12 "L'Allemagne est faite pour y voyager ; l'Italie pour y séjourner,
13 L'Angleterre pour y penser –
14 et la France pour y vivre" (D'Alembert)

EXERCICES

1. Elle se débrouille en quatre langues : l'italien, l'allemand, l'anglais et le polonais. – **2.** Il a beaucoup trop bu. – **3.** Ce n'est point intéressant comme film. – **4.** Il a été beaucoup influencé par son père. – **5.** Vous gagneriez deux fois plus si vous preniez cet emploi. – **6.** C'est pas le Pérou !

Fill in the blanks :

1 Ce . ' ... . difficile à apprendre. Il faut essayer

It's not at all difficult to learn. You must try.

2 .... - vous l'Italie ? J' . .. séjourné.

Do you know Italy ? I have stayed there.

3 J'aime beaucoup sa ....

I like his way of speaking very much.

4 Ils .... très discrètement ; ils ... . à . ' .... !

They left very discreetly ; they "took French leave" !

10 And if one speaks French badly - which is not at all your case
11 one says that he speaks like "a Spanish cow" !

12 Germany is (made) to travel in, Italy to stay in,
13 England to think in
14 and France to live in (D'Alembert).

NOTES (suite)

(6) *ne. . .point* is simply an emphatic *ne. .pas*
Je n'aime point cet homme : I really don't like that man. The only way to render it in English is to add"really" or "at all" to the negative.
(7) The origin of this picturesque expression has in fact nothing to do with cows. The original expression was : *parler le français comme un Basque espagnol :* Years of use have tranformed *Basque* to *vache* and popular wisdom has left it that way.

EXERCISES

1. She gets by in four languages : Italian, German, English and Polish – **2.** He has drunk far too much. – **3.** The film is not at all interesting. – **4.** He was very much influenced by his father. – **5.** You would earn twice as much if you took that job. – **6.** I won't get rich like that !

5 .... , c'est un compositeur ....

According to them, he's a Polish composer.

Fill in the blanks

1 -n'est point - – **2** - Connaissez - y ai - – **3** - façon de parler - – **4** - sont partis - ont filé - l'anglaise. – **5** - Selon eux - polonais.

* * *

Second Wave : Quarante-quatrième Leçon

QUATRE-VINGT-QUINZIEME (95ème) LEÇON

Joindre l'utile à l'agréable

1 Aujourd'hui et demain nous verrons des‿expressions pratiques (1) qui vous‿aideront en voyage.
2 D'abord, des‿expressions de politesse (dont vous connaissez déjà un bon nombre)
3 – Excusez-moi de vous déranger ... Pouvez-vous me dire .. ?
4 Je voudrais savoir ... Pourriez-vous m'aider ... ?
5 C'est très gentil ... Vous‿êtes bien aimable ...
6 – Merci beaucoup – Je vous en prie (ou – De rien)
7 – Est-ce que cette place est prise ? Est-ce que ça vous gêne si ... ?
8 Allez‿-‿y. Ça ne fait rien. C'est sans‿importance. Ce n'est pas grave.
9 Je ne l'ai pas fait exprès (2). Je suis désolé. Excusez-moi.
10 Bon‿appétit ! Ça a l'air très bon. C'était délicieux.

C'EST TRÈS GENTIL ... VOUS ÊTES BIEN AIMABLE.
500

PRONONCIATION

9 . .ekspray

95th LESSON

To mix business with pleasure
(join the useful to the agreeable)

1 Today and tomorrow we will see some practical expressions which will help you when travelling (in travel).
2 First, polite expressions (of which you know already a good number).
3 — Excuse me for disturbing you. . .Can you tell me. .?
4 I would like to know.. .Could you help me. .?
5 It's very kind. .You're very kind. .
6 — Thank you very much. Don't mention it.
7 — Is this seat taken ? Does it disturb you if. .?
8 Go ahead. It doesn't matter. It's not (without) important. It doesn't matter/isn't serious.
9 I didn't do it on purpose. I'm [very] sorry. Excuse me.
10 Bon appétit ! [have a good meal] ! This looks very good. It was delicious.

NOTES

(1) *pratique :* practical. Notice the spelling.
pratiquer : means to practise a religion, rules, etc. .
C'est un catholique pratiquant : He's a practising Catholic. or for a sport where English would use "do" or" play" :
Elle pratique la natation : she goes swimming (regularly).
There are several ways of saying "to practise" (i.e. to rehearse) :
Elle essaye son français : She is practising her French
That exercise is good practice : *Cet exercice est un bon entraînement* Also *"La Pratique du français"* : Using French is the companion volume to this one.

(2) *exprès :* on purpose should not be confused with *express* :
un train express : an express train
Garçon ! Deux express ! : Waiter ! Two expressos ! (coffees)
Elle est venue exprès pour me voir : She came especially to see me.

11 Pardon ? Voulez-vous répéter s'il vous plaît(3) ? Je n'ai pas‿entendu.
12 Mes‿amitiés à votre femme / votre mari. Au revoir. Bon retour.

13 On ne peut pas‿être poli tout le temps cependant ...
14 Allez-vous‿en ! Fichez-moi la paix ! Taisez-vous !

PRONONCIATION

14 . .feeshay mwa. .tezay

EXERCICES

1. Parlez plus fort, s'il vous plaît. Je ne vous entends pas. – **2.** Est-ce que ça vous dérange si j'ouvre la fenêtre ? -Allez-y. – **3.** Pourriez-vous m'aider à traduire le menu ? – **4.** Au revoir et bon retour. -Au revoir et mes amitiés à votre femme. – **5.** Pouvez-vous me dire où se trouve la rue Cambon ? – **6.** -Désolé, je ne sais pas. -Ce n'est pas grave.

Fill in the blanks :

1 Je ...... si ça m' ....

I will see if it will help me.

2 Des expressions .... vous .... un ...

.....

Some expressions of which you know a good number.

11 Pardon ? Would you repeat please ? I didn't hear.
12 My regards to your wife/your husband. Goodbye. Get home safely.
13 One cannot be polite all the time however. .
14 Go away ! Get lost ! Shut up !

NOTES (suite)

(3) Remember that using such a sentence will probably cause the person to whom you are speaking to do just that : repeat without making any effort to slow down or use different words. A phrase like : *Dites-le autrement :* Say it in another way is rather unconventional, but very useful. Other "survival expressions" are : *Parlez plus lentement :* Speak more slowly ; *Parlez plus fort :* Speak louder.Also when you are hesitant in a foreign language, your voice tends to become a hoarse whisper ! Say what you want to say out loud (as you have been practising with this method). At least this way, if you make mistakes, people can hear you and correct you.

EXERCISES

1. Speak louder, please. I can't hear you. – **2.** Would it disturb if I open the window ? Go ahead. – **3.** Could you help me to translate the menu ? – **4.** -Goodbye and get home safely. -Goodbye and my regards to your wife – **5.** Can you tell me where the rue C. is ? – **6.** I'm very sorry, I don't know. -It doesn't matter.

3 Mangez- .. ; je l'ai acheté ...... pour vous.

Eat some ; I bought it specially for you.

4 .... - .... me dire l'heure s'il vous plaît ?

Could you tell me the time, please ?

5 Nous .... savoir combien ça coûte.

We would like to know how much that costs.

QUATRE-VINGT-SEIZIÈME (96ème) LEÇON

Dans un bureau de poste

1 — Je voudrais un timbre pour l'Amérique. Combien je vous dois **(1)** ?
2 Où puis-je **(2)** trouver un téléphone ? Avez-vous de la monnaie ?

Au magasin

3 Il faut que j'achète **(N-2)** des chaussures. J'ai mal aux pieds !
4 — Vous chaussez du combien ? — Ah, je ne connais pas ma pointure **(3)** en français.
5 — Payez à la caisse. — Acceptez - vous des travellers-chèques ?
6 — Avec une pièce d'identité. — Voici mon permis de conduire.

PRONONCIATION

2 pweezh. . .
3 . . .foh ke
4 . . .pwantyoor.

Fill in the blanks

1 - verrai - aidera - – **2** - dont - connaissez - bon nombre . – **3** en - exprès. – **4** Pourriez-vous - ? – **5** - voudrions -.

* * *

Second Wave : Quarante-cinquième Leçon

96th LESSON

In a post-office

1 – I would like a stamp for A. please. How much do I owe you ?
2 Where can I find a telephone ? Do you have [any] change ?

In the shop

3 I must buy some shoes. My feet hurt !
4 – What size do you take (How much do you shoe ?) Ah ! I don't know my size in French.
5 – Pay at the cash-[desk]. Do you accept traveller's cheques ?
6 – With some proof of identity -Here is my driving licence.

NOTES

(1) Remember that *devoir* means not only "must" but "to owe" *Il me doit vingt francs depuis un an :* He has owed me 20 F for a year.
(2) A more elegant form of : *Où est-ce que je peux . . .* In common usage, we only find *puis* in this form.
(3) *La taille :* size of clothes
la pointure : size of shoes
The shop-assisant's rather convoluted question :
Vous chaussez du combien ? is the normal way of asking shoe-size.
The answer would be :
Je chausse du quarante-deux : I take size 42.
Le rez-de-chaussée (in a lift *R. d. C.)* : ground floor.

A l'hôtel

7 — Je voudrais une chambre simple.
— Il ne reste que (4) des doubles.
8 — Je la veux avec douche et W.C. Est-ce que le petit déjeuner est compris ?
9 Voulez-vous me préparer la note ? Je pars demain matin.

Enseignes

10 Entrée ; entrée interdite ; sortie ; sortie de secours ;
11 Stationnement gênant (5). Défense d'afficher. Complet.
12 Lavabos (6). Vestiaire ; Service en sus (7). Pourboire interdit.
13 (Propos (8) entendu dans‿un piège à touristes à Paris :)
14 — Garçon ! Est-ce que le service est compris ? — Oui Monsieur,
15 mais le pourboire ne l'est pas !

PRONONCIATION

11 . . .zhenohn. .komplay
12 . .vesteeyair. . .syooss

EXERCICES

1. Il faut que je trouve un nouveau sac à main ; celui-ci est trop petit. — **2.** Il ne faut pas que vous‿oubliiez de demander la note. — **3.** Est-ce qu'il l'acceptera ? -Je l'espère. — **4.** Où puis-je trouver une banque ? — -Par là. — **5.** Il nous reste deux leçons à étudier. — **6.** Voici mon permis de conduire.

At the hotel

7 – I would like a single room.
– We only have doubles left.
8 – I want it with shower and toilet. Is breakfast included (understood) ?
9 Will you prepare me the bill ? I am leaving tomorrow morning.

Signs

10 Entrance ; no entrance (forbidden) ; exit ; emergency exit.
11 No parking (p. annoying !). Post no bills. Full.
12 Bathroom ; cloakroom ; service extra ; tipping forbidden.
13 (Remark [over] heard in a tourist trap in P.)
14 – Waiter ! Is the service included ? – Yes Sir
15 but the tip isn't !

NOTES (suite)

(4) *Il ne me reste que dix minutes :* I only have 10 minutes left.
Il vous reste combien d'argent ? : How much money do you have left ?
Prenez -ça ; moi, je prendrai le reste : Take that ; I'll take the rest.
Les restes : leftovers.
(5) Another way of saying : *stationnement interdit*
stationner : to park
un parking (sic) : a car-park (To park is also *se garer* from which we get *un garage).*
(6) *un lavabo* is a wash-basin but in some places it is used as an euphemism for "toilet" much in the same way as Americans use "bathroom".
(7) or *service en plus.*
(8) *un propos :* a remark, an opinion
A propos ! : By the way !

EXERCISES

1. I must find a new handbag ; this one is too small. – **2.** You must not forget to ask for the bill. – **3.** Will he accept it ? -I hope so. – **4.** Where can I find a bank ? -That way. – **5.** We have 2 lessons left to study. – **6.** Here is my driving licence.

Fill in the blanks :

1 Il n' . a .... de riz ; il .. .. des frites.

There is no more rice ; there are only chips left.

2 Vous .... cent francs. Je .... par chèque.

You owe us 100 F. -I will pay by cheque.

3 .. .. je téléphone ; avez-vous de .. .. ?

I must telephone ; have you any change ?

4 J' .. .. cinq ; combien .. .. ?

I want five (of them) ; how much do I owe you ?

QUATRE-VINGT-DIX-SEPTIEME (97ème) LEÇON

Un pot-pourri d'expressions idiomatiques

1 — Ça y est ! Elle pleure. Tu as encore mis les pieds dans le plat !
2 — S'il continue à étudier comme ça, il risque (1) de réussir son examen.

PRONONCIATION

1 .sa - yay. . .plah

5 En France, je ...... partout avec des travellers chèques.

In France, I used to pay everywhere with travellers' cheques.

VOUS
CHAUSSEZ
DU COMBIEN ?

Fill in the blanks

1 - y - plus - ne. reste que - — **2** - nous devez - payerai - — **3** Il faut que - la monnaie ? — **4** - 'en voudrais - je vous dois ? — **5** - payais - —

* * *

Second Wave : Quarante-sixième Leçon

97th LESSON

A "pot-pourri" of idiomatic expressions

1 — There ! She's crying ! You've put your foot in it (in the plate) again !

2 — If he continues studying like that, he'll probably get his exam.

NOTES

(1) *risquer :* to risk does not always imply danger.
It means that something will very probably happen :
Ils risquent de passer tout à l'heure : They' ll probably come by later.
Est-ce que vous risquez de la voir ? : Is there a chance you will see her ?
Il risque de pleuvoir : It will probably rain.

3 — Mais‿il ne travaille pas du tout ! Il fait semblant **(3)**.
4 — Je ne peux pas continuer. J'en‿ai ras le bol **(4)** !
5 — Ce type-là, je ne peux pas le voir en peinture – Moi non plus **(5)**.
6 — Au moins, elle dit ce qu'elle pense. Elle ne tourne pas autour du pot.
7 — Jeudi étant férié, je vais faire le pont **(6)**. A lundi !
8 — On n'arrive pas à le joindre. Tu crois qu'il est sorti ?
9 — Vous‿êtes au courant ? **(7)** Ils‿ont pu vendre leur maison.
10 — On a eu son message, mais on ne sait pas ce qu'il veut dire **(8)**.

JE NE PEUX PAS CONTINUER,
J'EN AI RAS LE BOL !

PRONONCIATION

4 . . .ralbol
8 . .zhwandr

3 – But he's not working at all ! He's pretending
4 – I can't continue. I'm fed up !
5 – I can't stomach that bloke. – Neither can I
6 – At least she says what she thinks. She doesn't beat (turn)around the bush (pot).
7 – Thursday being a holiday, I'm going to have a long weekend. [See you] on Monday !
8 – We can't manage to get in touch with (join) him. Do you think he's gone out ?
9 – Did you know ? They were able to sell their house.
10 – We had his message but we don't know what he means.

NOTES (suite)

(2) Remember our "false friends" ?
avoir ou passer un examen : to sit an exam
réussir à un examen : to pass an exam. *(rater :* to fail)

(3) Another "false friend" : to pretend : *faire semblant(de..)*
Il fait semblant de dormir. He is pretending to sleep.
Ne faites pas semblant ! : Don't pretend !
The verb *prétendre* means "to claim""to state",(we find it in this sense in English when we talk of the "pretender" (claimant) to the throne).

(4) *le ras :* the lip, edge of a container.
Il a rempli mon verre à ras (bord) : He filled my glass to the brim. The idiom signifies that the bowl *(bol)* is full to the brim i.e. one cannot accept any more. A familiar term, it is often found in graffiti !
(un pullover ras du cou : a crew-necked jumper)

(5) *Je l'aime beaucoup -Moi aussi* (so do I ; me too)
Il n'en veut pas. -Elle non plus (neither does she)
Ils sont‿allemands -Eux aussi.

(6) *un jour férié* is a public one-day holiday. If this falls on a Thursday or a Tuesday, many people "make the bridge" i.e. take off the Friday or the Monday to form a 4-day weekend. (If one takes off longer, the holiday is called cheekily *un viaduc !)*
Le pont de l'Ascension : the long weekend on Ascension-Day (The last Thursday of May).

(7) *être au courant :* to be in the know ; to know the news. *Se mettre au courant de quelque chose :* to find out about something

(8) *Qu'est-ce que ce mot veut dire ? :* What does this word mean? *Qu'est-ce que tu veux dire par là ?:* What do you mean by that ?
Le sens d'un mot : the meaning of a word.

EXERCICES

1. Arrête de chanter comme ça ! J'en ai ras le bol ! – **2.** Ne tournez pas autour du pot comme ça ; – **3.** Dites-nous ce que vous voulez dire ! – **4.** Je ne sais pas pourquoi, mais il ne peut pas me voir en peinture. – **5.** J'ai pu le joindre hier ; – **6.** Allez, à lundi !

Fill in the blanks :

1 Ils ... . de ne rien savoir.

They pretended to know nothing.

2 Tu .. .. ? Nous n'avons ... .. le trouver.

Did you know ? We weren't able to find him.

3 Vous savez .. .. ' .... ?

Do you know what she means ?

QUATRE-VINGT-DIX-HUITIEME (98ème) LEÇON

REVISION ET NOTES

1. There is one more important tense that we have to study : the conditional (I would. . .) It is simple in both its construction and use.
We form it by adding the endings for the imperfect *(-ais, -ais, -ait, ions, -iez, -aient)* to the stem of the future. Look at the two following examples :

EXERCISES

1. Stop singing like that ! I'm fed up ! — **2.** Don't beat around the bush like that ; — **3.** Tell us what you mean ! — **4.** I don't know why, but he can't stomach me. — **5.** I was able to get in touch with him yesterday ; — **6.** O.K. See you on Monday !

4 Je ..... le pont si jeudi est .....

I will take a long weekend if Thursday is a holiday.

5 J'aime ceci ... . Mais pas ça, - ... ...

I like this. -Me too. But not that. -Neither I do.

Fill in the blanks

1 - ont fait semblant - — **2** -es au courant - pas pu - — **3** - ce qu'elle veut dire. — **4** - ferai - férié - — **5** Moi aussi - Moi non plus.

* * *

Second Wave : Quarante-septième Leçon

98th LESSON

donner	*je donnerai*	*je donnerais ;*	*tu donnerais*
		il donnerait ;	*nous donnerions*
		vous donneriez ;	*ils donneraient*
finir	*je finirai*	*je finirais ;*	*tu finirais ;*
		il finirait ;	*nous finirions ;*
		vous finiriez ;	*ils finiraient ;*

The tense is used in much the same way as in English (let us accept that the auxiliary in English is "would" and that "should" is the conditional form of "must). We usually find the conditional in a construction with "if"...
If you left now you would arrive on time.
but instead of using the past tense after "if", we must use the imperfect : *Si vous partiez* (imp.) *maintenant, vous arriveriez* (cond.) *à l'heure.*
Never use the conditional after *si.* The main confusion that beginners make is due to the similarity between these two tenses. Remember that the conditional endings are added to the **future** stem.
If I had a lot of money, I would buy a car :
Si j'avais (imp) *beaucoup d'argent, j'achèterais* (cond.) *une voiture.*
If I knew his number, I would call him :
Si je connaissais (imp.) *son numéro, je l'appellerais.*
He would tell you if he knew : *Il vous le dirait* (cond.) *s'il le savait* (imp.)

A major use of the conditional - as in English - is to convey politeness : Could you tell me . .? I would like to know, etc. .
For this, we must look at two irregular conditionals :

vouloir *je voudrais* (the remainder of the conjugation follows the normal rules)

pouvoir *je pourrais*

and of course, our auxiliaries *être* and *avoir :*

être — je serais etc. . *avoir — j'aurais* etc. . .

Pourriez-vous me dire . . .? : Could you tell me . . .?
Je voudrais savoir. . .: I would like to know . . .
(We know already that Would you (close the window) is translated by
Voulez-vous (fermer la fenêtre).

There are a few minor differences in usage which we will not worry about for the moment.

(You will probably have realized that, between the first person singular future *-je partirai* and the first person singular conditional *-je partirais* the only difference is a silent "s". You will have to live with this minor inconvenience : if you remember the construction *Si*. . imperfect . . .conditional, life will be much easier !

3. *il faut que j'achète : achète* is a subjunctive.
The subjunctive is not a tense but a mood. Up to now we have seen tenses in the indicative mood - i.e. they indicate real actions and definite events : using the subjunctive mood suggests doubt, hypothesis or condition (if you like, the verb in the subjunctive is joined to another verb on which its existence depends).

Let us straight away make the difference between when we **must** use a subjunctive (after certain conjunctions or certain verbs) and when using subjunctive adds nuance and depth to the sentence. The latter category is a subject of debate - and sometimes error - even among well-educated French people.
In this first book we intend to touch briefly on the former category and leave the latter to the second volume - and your own intuition. First, to form the subjunctive we add the endings *-e -es -e -ions -iez -ent* to - in most cases -the stem of the third person plural present :

donner	*ils donnent*	*je donne ;*	*tu donnes*
		il donne ;	*nous donnions*
		vous donniez ;	*ils donnent*

When you are sure of this, check in the grammatical appendix for the verbs *boire ; devoir ; prendre ; recevoir ; tenir ;* and *venir* where there is a slight difference. We must also learn *être* and *avoir :*

être : je sois ; tu sois ; il soit ; nous soyons ; vous soyez ils soient.
avoir : j'aie ; tu aies ; il ait ; nous ayons ; vous ayez ; ils aient.

(other major irregular verbs are : *aller ; faire ; pouvoir ; savoir ; vouloir)*
There is also an imperfect subjunctive which is so little used that we will not bother with it.

When must the subjunctive be used ?
Look at this sentence in English :
I demand that he be found. "be" is a subjunctive. It depends on :
I demand. . .and is "sub-joined" to it by "that".
In French we often express this by the impersonal form *il faut que . . .*

Any verb following this construction must be put into the subjunctive
(the two verbs are "sub-joined" by the word *que).*

Il faut que vous soyez à l'heure : You must be on time
Il faut que je vous parle : I must talk to you
Il faut que vous finissiez à huit heures : You must finish at 8.00.

Likewise if I impose my desires on someone - I want him to come early - I say : *Je veux que* and a subjunctive :

QUATRE-VINGT-DIX-NEUVIEME (99ème) LEÇON

Au revoir ... et à bientôt

1 Nous voici à la fin de notre livre, mais non pas à la fin du voyage.
2 Il ne faut pas que vous vous‿arrêtiez (1) maintenant.

Je veux qu'il vienne tôt.

He wants me to tell him the secret : *Il veut que je lui dise le secret.*
Do you see how, in both cases, the second idea is dependent on a first verb expressing command or desire ? And that the two ideas are "subjoined" by the relative *que ?*
Well, enough for now. (If you want a list of more conjunctions which must be followed by the subjunctive check in the grammatical appendix).
Since the aim of this first volume is to allow you to understand everyday conversation and to enable you to express yourself, we have deliberately omitted further discussion of the subjunctive to avoid swamping you with information. As long as you can recognize the mood, and have an idea of when it is used, we consider this sufficient for now.

* * *

Second Wave : Quarante-Huitième Leçon

99th LESSON

Goodbye . .and see you soon

1 Here we are at the end of our book, but not at the end of the journey.
2 You must not stop now.

NOTES

(1) Subjunctive after : *il faut que .* We could avoid the subjunctive by not using **you** and making the sentence "impersonal" *Il ne faut pas s'arrêter. Il faut que vous soyez‿à l'heure :* **or** *il faut être à l'heure.*

3 Bien‿entendu, vous ne parlez pas‿encore le français comme un Parisien-né (2)
4 mais vous‿êtes capables de comprendre une conversation
5 et de vous faire comprendre (3) dans les circonstances usuelles de la vie quotidienne.
6 Reprenez le livre tous les jours et feuilletez-le. Choisissez une leçon,
7 réécoutez les‿enregistrements et continuez à faire la deuxième vague.
8 Il y a des points de grammaire, d'expression et de vocabulaire que nous n'avons pas‿encore vus –
9 ainsi nous vous donnons rendez-vous (4) dans notre deuxième tome :

"La Pratique du français",

10 où nous continuerons ensemble notre découverte de cette langue française
11 que vous‿avez apprise (5) **"sans peine"**.

12 "Ce qui n'est pas clair n'est pas français" (Rivarol)

SI J'AVAIS BEAUCOUP D'ARGENT, J'ACHÈTERAIS UNE VOITURE.

PRONONCIATION

6 . .feuyetay le
7 . rayekootay

3 Of course, you don't yet speak F. like a born Parisian
4 but you are capable of understanding a conversation
5 and of making yourself understood in the usual circumstances of daily life.
6 Take the book again every day and flip through it.
7 Listen again to the recordings and continue to do the 2nd wave.
8 There are points of grammar, of expression and of vocabulary that we have not seen yet.
9 so we make an appointment with you in our second volume "La Pratique du français"
10 where we will continue together our discovery of this French language
11 which you have learnt without difficulties.

12 "What is not clear is not French" (Rivarol).

NOTES (suite)

(2) *C'est‿un comédien-né :* He's a born actor.
C'est‿une Parisienne-née : She is a native Parisian.
Il est né en mil neuf cent deux : He was born in 1902.

(3) *Je me fais comprendre :* I make myself understood
Vous me faites rire : You make me laugh.
French also simplifies the English construction : to have + past participle. I am having my watch repaired : *Je fais réparer ma montre.*
Have him come in : *Faites-le entrer.*
If we use a pronoun for the direct object, we place it before *faire : Je la fais réparer :* I am having it repaired.
If we use the noun itself, we place it after the infinitive : *Il fait faire un costume :* He is having a suit made.

(4) *Je vous donne rendez-vous :* Let's see each other
(This phrase is often used to close each programme in a regular television series) :
Nous vous donnons rendez-vous la semaine prochaine : We'll see you next week.
Prendre rendez-vous : to make an appointment
(Note : *un rendez-vous* is unchangeable, even if we use the *tu* form in the sentence : *Je te donne rendez-vous)*

(5) Feminine form because the nearest preceding direct object is "... *la langue française.*

EXERCICES

1. Ecoutez-la ; c'est une vendeuse-née ! – 2. Non, je ne le lis pas ; je le feuillette. – 3. Je voudrais prendre rendez-vous avec le docteur, s'il vous plaît. – 4. Il se fait comprendre partout. – 5. C'est la fin de l'exercice mais non pas de la leçon. – 6. Au revoir et à bientôt.

Fill in the blanks :

1 Il faut ... vous vous .... tout de suite.

You must stop at once.

2 J'ai .... le livre et j'ai ...... une leçon.

I flipped through the book and I chose a lesson.

3 Il .... que c'est très dur.

It must be understood that it is very hard.

EXERCISES

1. Listen to her ; she's a born saleswoman ! — **2.** No I'm not reading it, I'm flipping through it. — **3.** I would like to make an appointment with the doctor, please. — **4.** He makes himself understood everywhere. — **5.** It's the end of the exercise but not of the lesson. — **6.** Goodbye and see you soon.

4 Il .... un nouveau costume

He is having a new suit made.

5 .. ... . ' ... ... ' ... ...

....

What is not clear is not French.

Fill in the blanks

1 - que - arrêtiez — **2** - feuilleté - choisi - — **3** - faut comprendre - — **4** - fait faire - — **5** Ce qui n'est pas clair n'est pas français.

* * *

Second Wave : Quarante-neuvième Leçon

APPENDICE GRAMMATICAL

This brief section is intended purely for reference, to allow you to check a form or a tense.

NOUNS

All French nouns are either masculine or feminine. The word for 'a' or 'the' (the article) changes accordingly.
Masculine : *un livre - le livre*
Feminine : *une voiture - la voiture*
The plural for both genders is *les*
Gender has to be learned parrot fashion. Always learn the gender when you learn the noun ;
Here are a couple of hints to help you work out the gender :
— most nouns which end in a mute *e* are feminine
— all nouns ending in *-ée* are feminine (save for a few exceptions)
— all nouns ending in *-ion* are feminine (save for a few exceptions)

The plural of most nouns is formed by adding an *s* (unpronounced) to the end ;
— those nouns ending in *-eau* (masculine) add an *x*
— there is a series of seven nouns ending in *-ou* (masculine), the most common of which are *chou* (cabbage) ; *genou* (knee) ; *bijou* (jewel) ; they also form the plural by adding an *x*

ADJECTIVES

These words usually come **after** the word they describe and must 'agree' i.e. they must be in the same gender and form.
The usual form given in dictionaries etc. is the masculine form. The feminine form is formed in several different ways :
adjectives ending in :
-eux become *-euse* e.g. *dangereux-dangereuse*
adjectives ending in :
-en ; -on ; -il ; double the final consonant and add 'e' e.g. *bon - bonne ; moyen* (average) - *moyenne ; gentil-gentille.* Most other adjectives simply add *e*
Adjectives usually come after the noun they qualify (i.e. describe) but there are certain common exceptions. Some examples :
bon (good) ; *mauvais* (bad) ; *beau* (handsome) ; *grand* (big) *petit* (small) *autre* (other) ; *long* (long)
This of course applies to the feminine form. These adjectives which are placed before the noun have a second masculine form if they end in a vowel and the word they qualify begins with a vowel. For example : *un bel appartement ;* this avoids any difficulty in pronunciation (called a 'hiatus')

If two (or more) nouns of both genders are the subject of a sentence, we use the masculine plural form for a single adjective qualifying them :
Son fils et sa fille sont grands
Adjectives of nationality do not take a capital letter : *une voiture française ; un livre allemand*

ADVERBS

Most of these are formed by simply adding *-ment* to the feminine form of the adjective.

lent - lente - lentement ; heureux - heureuse - heureusement

some adjectives are also adverbs :

dur ; vite ; haut ;

adverbs are placed directly after the verb.

VERBS

We have distinguished three main groups of verbs as indicated by their endings in the infinitive. They are : *-er* (the most common) ; *-re* and *-ir.*
Here is an example of each, using the tenses and the moods we have seen so far.

-ER verbs. *ACHETER* (to buy)

PRESENT

j'achète	nous achetons
tu achètes	vous achetez
il/elle achète	ils/elles achètent.

This tense corresponds to the three English present forms :

I buy   I am buying   I do buy

Pronunciation : Remember the final *s* and *-ent* are both silent. Also there is a *liaison* between the final *s* of the pronoun and the initial vowel of the verb : [eelzashet]

FUTURE

The endings which form this tense (which are, in fact, the present tense of *avoir)* are added to the infinitive.

j'achèterai	nous achèterons
tu achèteras	vous achèterez
il/elle achèteras	ils/elles achèteront.

This tense corresponds to the English form : I shall/ will buy.

The future tense is also used in French after conjunctions of time (e.g. *dès que ; aussitôt que ; quand*) where English would use a present :
Quand elle me téléphonera, je te le dirai : When she phones me, I will tell you.

IMPERFECT
The endings which form the imperfect tense are added to the stem of the first person plural present :

j'achetais	nous achetions
tu achetais	vous achetiez
il/elle achetait	ils/elles achetaient

This tense is used to describe any continuous action in the past e.g. She was reading a book : *Elle lisait un livre* or an habitual action e.g.
He always drank wine : *Il buvait toujours du vin*
or for the description of a state e.g.
The flat was small : *L'appartement était petit*

The imperfect is also used in conditional sentences where English uses the past tense:
If he left now he would find a taxi. *S'il partait maintenant il trouverait un taxi.*

PAST TENSE
This tense is called in French *le passé composé* because it is a compound tense formed with the auxiliary *avoir* and the past participle of the verb. The past participle of *-er* verbs is formed by removing the *r* from the infinitive and placing an acute accent on the *e* ; e.g. *acheter - acheté.*
(some verbs - mainly those expressing motion - and all reflexive verbs use *être* as the auxiliary)

j'ai acheté	nous avons acheté
tu as acheté	vous avez acheté
il/elle a acheté	Ils/elles ont acheté

The tense translates both English forms : I bought ; and: I have bought. There does exist another past form - *le passé simple* - but since this is never used in speech or correspondence and is found less and less in modern literature we have decided not to introduce it to you just yet.)

The agreement of the past participle :
Let it be said straight away that this rule rarely changes the pronunciation (except for some *-re* verbs) and also confuses a lot of French people ! Since the past participle is an adjective it must agree with any *direct* object which comes *before* the verb *avoir.*

For example, if we say : I bought some books : *J'ai acheté des livres* there is no agreement since the direct object *(les livres)* comes **after** the verb *avoir ;* but if I say : The books which I bought : *Les livres que j'ai achetés* I must make the past participle agree.
If the direct object is a feminine noun : *la voiture que j'ai achetée.*

Remember that this rule takes a lot of practice to master and for the time being is not our main priority.

CONDITIONAL

The conditional tense is formed by adding the endings of the imperfect tense to the stem of the future :

j'achèterais	nous achèterions
tu achèterais	vous achèteriez
il/elle achèterait	ils/elles achèteraient

This tense corresponds fairly closely to the English use of **would** when that auxiliary denotes a condition.

Remember that the polite use of **would** in English : Would you like. . .. .. . is usually expressed by : *Voulez-vous . . .*

SUBJUNCTIVE

In this volume, we have touched briefly on the subjunctive which is not a tense but a 'mood'. Its use presupposes some doubt or uncertainty in the completion of the action described. We can broadly distinguish two cases for its use, the first being where a subjunctive adds a nuance to the sentence and the second an obligatory use after certain constructions. We shall deal with the second case only in this volume.

The subjunctive is generally formed from the stem of the third person plural present :

j'achète	nous achetions
tu achètes	vous achetiez
il/elle achète	ils/elles achètent

donner

je donne	nous donnions
tu donnes	vous donniez
il/elle donne	ils/elles donnent

One of the most common uses of the subjunctive is after the impersonal form : *Il faut que. . .* It is necessary that. . . One must. . .

Il faut que vous donniez votre réponse demain : You must give your answer tomorrow.

It is also used after a construction with *vouloir* when a person imposes his will on someone else : I want you to buy it : *Je veux que vous l'achetiez.*

Other constructions after which the subjunctive must be used are :

avant que : before
jusqu'à ce que : until
bien que ; quoique ; although
pourvu que : provided that
à moins que : unless
afin que ; pour que ; in order that

You will notice that any verb which follows these constructions does not indicate a definite state or a certainty. The meaning of 'subjunctive' is 'joined under' which means that any verb in the subjunctive mood depends on (or is joined to) an initial state.

We have only given here the present subjunctive. In fact, in modern usage, both spoken and literary, it is the only form commonly found.

There are ways of avoiding the subjunctive ; for example, replacing the impersonal *Il faut que vous. . . ;* or *Il faut que je . . .* by the appropriate form of *devoir* e.g. *Il faut que vous donniez votre réponse demain — Vous devez donner votre réponse demain.*
But there is no escaping the fact that the subjunctive is commonly used in modern French and that we must begin to learn it now.

-RE verbs *VENDRE* (to sell)

PRESENT

je vends	nous vendons
tu vends	vous vendez
il/elle vend	ils/elles vendent

As always, the final *-s* and *-ent* are not pronounced.

FUTURE

Before adding the future endings, we drop the *-e* from the infinitive :

je vendrai	nous vendrons
tu vendras	vous vendrez
il/elle vendra	ils/elles vendront

IMPERFECT

je vendais	nous vendions
tu vendais	vous vendiez
il/elle vendait	ils/elles vendaient

PAST TENSE

j'ai vendu	nous avons vendu
tu as vendu	vous avez vendu
il/elle a vendu	ils/elles ont vendu

Any agreement of the past participle does not change the pronunciation, unless the past participle of the verb ends in *-is* (e.g. *prendre - pris* ; *mettre - mis Les pommes que j'ai prises :* The apples I have taken.)

CONDITIONAL

je vendrais	nous vendrions
tu vendrais	vous vendriez
il/elle vendrait	ils/elles vendraient

SUBJUNCTIVE

Il faut que je vende	Il faut que nous vendions
Il faut que tu vendes	il faut que vous vendiez
Il faut qu'il/'elle vende	il faut qu'ils/'elles vendent

-IR verbs. *FINIR* (to finish)

PRESENT

je finis	nous finissons
tu finis	vous finissez
il/elle finit	ils/elles finissent

FUTURE

je finirai	nous finirons
tu finiras	vous finirez
il/elle finira	ils/elles finiront

IMPERFECT

je finissais	nous finissions
tu finissais	vous finissiez
il/elle finissait	ils/elles finissaient

PAST TENSE

j'ai fini	nous avons fini
tu as fini	vous avez fini
il/elle a fini	ils/elles ont fini

CONDITIONAL

je finirais	nous finirions
tu finirais	vous finiriez
il/elle finirait	ils/elles finiraient

SUBJUNCTIVE

il faut que je finisse	il faut que nous finissions
Il faut que tu finisses	il faut que vous finissiez
Il faut qu'il/elle finisse	il faut qu'ils/elles finissent

Notes on pronouns :

In modern French, the *nous* form of verbs (especially in tenses where pronunciation may be awkward e.g. *nous finirions)* tends to be replaced - to the dismay of purists - by the pronoun *on.* Even though this usage is somewhat 'inelegant' it makes life so much easier that we can only recommend it.

tu - the familiar form of 'you' also presents some problems as to when - or if - to use it. Here are a couple of guidelines :

— always use *vous* to people you do not know
— initially, only reply in the *tu* form if someone uses it with you first
— you may safely use *tu* when talking to small children

The tendency with younger people in France today is to use *tu* to most people of the same age and interests. We recommend that you not use it unless you hear it first.

PRONOUN ORDER

Remember our 'football team' which gives us the order in which object pronouns must come :

me				
te	le			
se	la	lui		
			(y)	(en)
nous	les	leur		
vous				

Examples :
Il me le/la donne : He gives it to me.
On les demande au téléphone : Someone wants them on the phone.
J'y vais : I'm going (there)
Je lui en parlerai : I'll talk to him/her about it.

Object pronouns are placed **after** the verb if it is the imperative form :
Donnez-la moi : Give it to me
Dites-lui : Tell him/her.
(moi and *toi* are used instead of *me* and *te)*
This rule does not apply if the command is negative :
Ne lui dites pas : Don't tell him/her.
Ne le lui donnez pas : Don't give it to him/her.

On
We have already seen that this impersonal pronoun commonly replaces the *nous* form in modern speech. Here are two more uses :
— where English would use the passive form : *On dit qu'il est riche :* He is said to be rich.
— or a 'false' subject *En France, on boit beaucoup de vin :* In France, people/we/they/ drink a lot of wine.

THE AUXILIARIES *AVOIR* and *ETRE*

AVOIR (to have) is used as an auxiliary to form the past tense of most verbs and also in expressions where English uses 'to be'. E.g. I am hot : *J'ai chaud* ; she is hungry : *Elle a faim* etc.

PRESENT

j'ai	nous avons
tu as	vous avez
il/elle a	ils/elles ont

FUTURE

j'aurai	nous aurons
tu auras	vous aurez
il/elle aura	ils/elles auront

IMPERFECT

j'avais	nous avions
tu avais	vous aviez
il/elle avait	ils/elles avaient

PAST TENSE

formed with the present form and the past participle *eu*

j'ai eu	nous avons eu
tu as eu	vous avez eu
il/elle a eu	ils/elles ont eu

CONDITIONAL

j'aurais	nous aurions
tu aurais	vous auriez
il/elle aurait	ils/elles auraient

SUBJUNCTIVE

il faut que j'aie	il faut que nous ayons
il faut que tu aies	il faut que vous ayez
il faut qu'il/'elle ait	il faut qu'ils/'elles aient

ETRE (to be) is used as an auxiliary to form the past tense of all reflexive verbs - those whose infinitive is preceded by *se* - and certain verbs of movement *arriver* (to arrive) *partir* (to leave) *monter* (to go up) *descendre* (to go/come down) *aller* (to go) *venir* (to come) *entrer* (to come/go in) *sortir* (to go/come out) *retourner* (to return) *tomber* (to fall) and also : *naître* (to be born) *mourir* (to die) *rester* (to remain).

A note on agreement :
We have seen that verbs conjugated with *avoir* in the past tense must make the agreement between the past participle of the verb and the nearest preceding direct object. The rule for these verbs, conjugated with *être* in the past, is much simpler : the past participle must agree with the subject of the sentence.
Elle est partie : She has left. *Nous sommes descendus :* We came down. *Elles sont entrées :* They came in. *Ils sont nés en France* They were born in France. (If you look at an official form in England, you will see that the space for a woman's maiden name is entitled : *Née ;* notice that we retain the agreement of the past participle.)

PRESENT

je suis	nous sommes
tu es	vous êtes
il/elle est	ils/elles sont

FUTURE

je serai	nous serons
tu seras	vous serez
il/elle sera	ils/elles seront

IMPERFECT

j'étais	nous étions
tu étais	vous étiez
il/elle était	ils/elles étaient

PAST TENSE

j'ai été	nous avons été
tu as été	vous avez été
il/elle a été	ils ont été

CONDITIONAL

je serais	nous serions
tu serais	vous seriez
il/elle serait	ils/elles seraient

SUBJUNCTIVE

il faut que je sois	il faut que nous soyons
il faut que tu sois	il faut que vous soyez
il faut qu'il/elle soit	il faut qu'ils/elles soient

Just from this brief review we can see that French grammar is more rigorous than ours but, having realised this, it can often work in our favour since there is always a rule for a particular construction and - more often than not- the rules are as 'logical' as any living language can make them.

IRREGULAR VERBS

The tenses not indicated are regular. Ex. : *Imperfect,* j'allais, tu allais, etc.

The past tense is formed by using *avoir* , past participle (exept for these verbs mentionned in lesson 70).

I

Aller *(to go)*
Ind. prés. : je vais, tu vas, il va, nous allons, vous allez, ils vont.
Futur : j'irai, tu iras, il ira, n. irons v. irez, ils iront.
Condit. : j'irais, tu irais, il irait, n. irions, v. iriez, ils iraient.
Subj. prés. : que j'aille, que tu ailles, qu'il aille, que n. allions, que v. alliez, qu'ils aillent.

Envoyer *(to send).*
Futur : j'enverrai, tu enverras, il enverra, n. enverrons, v. enverrez, ils enverront

II

Apprendre *(to learn).* – V. *prendre.*
Atteindre *(to reach).* – V. *peindre.*
Battre *(to beat).*
Ind. pres. : je bats, tu bats, il bat, n. battons, v. battez, ils battent.

Boire *(to drink).*
Ind. prés. : je bois, tu bois, il boit, n. buvons, v. buvez, ils boivent.
Imparf. : je buvais, tu buvais, il buvait, n. buvions, v. buviez, ils buvaient.
Futur : je boirai, tu boiras, il boira, n. boirons, v. boirez, ils boiront.
Condit. : je boirais, tu boirais, il boirait, n. boirions, v. boiriez, ils boiraient.
Subj. prés. : Que je boive, que tu boives, qu'il boive, que n. buvions, que vous buviez, qu'ils boivent.
Impératif : bois, buvons, buvez.
Part. passé : bu – *Part. prés. :* buvant.

Comprendre *(to understand).* — V. *prendre.*

Conduire *(to conduct, to drive, to lead).*
Ind. prés. : je conduis, tu conduis, il conduit, n. conduisons, v. conduisez, ils conduisent.
Imparf. : je conduisais, tu conduisais, il conduisait, n. conduisions, v. conduisiez, ils conduisaient.
Futur : je conduirai, tu conduiras, etc.
Condit. : je conduirais, tu conduirais, etc.
Subj. prés. : que je conduise, que tu conduises, etc.
Part: passé : conduit. — *Part. prés. :* conduisant.

Connaître *(to know ; be acquainted with).*
Ind. prés. : je connais, tu connais, il connaît, n. connaissons, v. connaissez, ils connaissent.
Imparf. : je connaissais, tu connaissais, il connaissait, n. connaissions, v. connaissiez, ils connaissaient.
Subj. prés. : que je connaisse, que tu connaisses, qu'il connaisse, que n. connaissions, que v. connaissiez, qu'ils connaissent.
Part. passé : connu — *Part. prés. :* connaissant.

Construire *(to construct, to build).* — V. *conduire.*

Coudre *(to sew).*
Ind. prés. : je couds, tu couds, il coud, n. cousons, v. cousez, ils cousent.
Imparf. : je cousais, tu cousais, etc.
Subj. prés. : que je couse, que tu couses, etc.
Part. passé : cousu. — *Part. prés. :* cousant.

Craindre *(to fear).*
Ind. prés. : je crains, tu crains, il craint, n. craignons, v. craignez, ils craignent.
Imparf. : je craignais, tu craignais, etc.
Subj. prés. : que je craigne, que tu craignes, etc.
Part. passé : craint. — *Part. prés.* craignant.

Croire *(to believe).*
Ind. prés. : je crois, tu crois, il croit, n. croyons, v. croyez, ils croient.
Imparf. : je croyais, tu croyais, il croyait, n. croyions, v. croyiez, ils croyaient.
Futur : je croirai, tu croiras, il croira, etc.
Condit. : je croirais, tu croirais, etc.
Subj. prés. : que je croie, que tu croies, qu'il croie, que n. croyions, que v. croyiez, qu'ils croient.
Impératif : crois, croyons, croyez.
Part. passé : cru — *Part. prés. :* croyant.

Croître *(to grow).* [intransitive]
Ind. prés. : je croîs, tu croîs, il croît, n. croissons, v. croissez, ils croissent.
Impart. : je croissais, tu croissais, etc.
Subj. prés. : que je croisse, etc
Part. passé : crû. — *Part. prés. :* croissant.

Détruire *(to destroy).* — V. *conduire.*

Dire *(to say, to tell).*
Ind. prés. : je dis, tu dis, il dit, n. disons, v. dites, ils disent.
Imparf. : je disais, tu disais, il disait, n. disions, v. disiez, ils disaient.
Futur : je dirai, tu diras, il dira, n. dirons, v. direz, ils diront.
Condit. : je dirais, tu dirais, il dirait, n. dirions, v. diriez, ils diraient.
Subj. prés. : que je dise, que tu dises, qu'il dise, que n. disions, que v. disiez, qu'ils disent.
Impératif : dis, disons, dites.
Part. passé. : dit. — *Part. présent :* disant.

Ecrire *(to write).*
Ind. prés. : j'écris, tu écris, il écrit, n. écrivons, v. écrivez, ils écrivent.
Imparf. : j'écrivais, tu écrivais, il écrivait, n. écrivions, v. écriviez, ils écrivaient.
Futur : j'écrirai, tu écriras, il écrira, n. écrirons, v. écrirez, ils écriront.
Condit. : j'écrirais, tu écrirais, il écrirait, n. écririons, v. écririez, ils écriraient.
Subj. prés. : que j'écrive, que tu écrives, qu'il écrive, que n. écrivions, que v. écriviez, qu'ils écrivent.
Impératif : écris, écrivons, écrivez.
Part. passé : écrit. — *Part. prés. :* écrivant.

Eteindre *(to extinguish).* — V *peindre.*

Faire *(to do, to make).*
Ind. prés. : je fais, tu fais, il fait, n. faisons, v. faites, ils font.
Imparf. : je faisais, tu faisais, il faisait, n. faisions, v. faisiez, ils faisaient.
Futur : je ferai, tu feras, il fera, n. ferons, v. ferez, ils feront.
Condit. : je ferais, tu ferais, il ferait, n. ferions, v. feriez, ils *feraient.*
Subj. prés. : que je fasse, que tu fasses, qu'il fasse, que n. fassions, que v. fassiez, qu'ils fassent.
Impératif : fais, faisons, faites.
Part. passé : fait — *Part. prés. :* faisant.

Frire *(to fry) (used only in these forms).*
Ind. prés. : je fris, tu fris, il frit.
Futur : je frirai, tu friras, il frira, n. frirons, v. frirez, ils friront.
Part. passé : frit. *(In the other tenses,* faire frire *is ised instead of* frire).

Instruire *(to instruct).* V. *conduire.*

Joindre *(to join).*
Ind. prés. : je joins, tu joins, il joint, n. joignons, v. joignez, ils joignent.
Imparf. : je joignais, etc. –
Futur : je joindrai, tu joindras, etc.
Condit. : je joindrais, tu joindrais, etc.
Subj. prés. : que je joigne, etc.
Part. passé : joint. – *Part. prés. :* joignant.

Lire *(to read):*
Ind. prés. : je lis, tu lis, il lit, n. lisons, v. lisez, ils lisent.
Imparf. : je lisais, tu lisais, il lisait, n. lisions, v. lisiez, ils lisaient
Futur : je lirai, tu liras, il lira, n. lirons, v. lirez, ils liront.
Condit. : je lirais, tu lirais, il lirait, n. lirions, v. liriez, ils liraient
Subj. prés. : que je lise, que tu lises, qu'il lise, que n. lisions, que v. lisiez, qu'ils lisent.
Impératif : lis, lisons, lisez.
Part. passé : lu – *Part. prés. :* lisant.

Mettre *(to put).*
Ind. prés. : je mets, tu mets, il met, n. mettons, v. mettez, ils mettent.
Imparf. : je mettais, tu mettais, il mettait, n. mettions, v. mettiez, ils mettaient.
Futur : je mettrai, tu mettras, etc.
Condit. : je mettrais, tu mettrais, etc.
Subj. prés. : que je mette, que tu mettes, qu'il mette, que n. mettions, que vous mettiez, qu'ils mettent.
Impératif : mets, mettons, mettez.
Part. passé : mis. – *Part. prés. :* mettant.

Naître *(to be born).*
Ind. prés. : je nais, tu nais, il naît, n. naissons, v. naissez, ils naissent.
Imparf. : je naissais, tu naissais, etc.
Subj. prés. : que je naisse, que tu naisses, etc.
Part. passé : né. – *Part prés. :* naissant.

Paraître *(to appear, to seem).* – V. *connaître.*

Peindre *(to paint).*
Ind. prés. : je peins, tu peins, il peint, n. peignons, v. peignez, ils peignent.
Imparf. : je peignais, tu peignais, il peignait, n. peignions, v. peigniez, ils peignaient.
Subj. prés. : que je peigne, que tu peignes, etc.
Part. passé : peint. —*Part. prés. :* peignant.

Permettre *(to allow).* — V. *mettre.*

Plaindre *(to pity).* — Se plaindre *(to complain).* — V. *craindre.*

Plaire *(to please).*
Ind. prés. : je plais, tu plais, il plaît, n. plaisons, v. plaisez, ils plaisent.
Imparf. : je plaisais, tu plaisais, il plaisait, n. plaisions, v. plaisiez, ils plaisaient.
Subj. prés. : que je plaise, que tu plaises, qu'il plaise, que n. plaisions, que v. plaisiez, qu'ils plaisent.
Part. passé : plu. —*Part. prés. :* plaisant.

Prendre *(to take).*
Ind. prés. : je prends,tu prends, il prend, n. prenons, v. prenez, ils prennent.
Imparf. : je prenais, tu prenais, il prenait, n. prenions, v. preniez, ils prenaient.
Subj. prés. : que je prenne, que tu prennes, qu'il prenne, que n. prenions, que v. preniez, qu'ils prennent.
Impératif : prends, prenons, prenez.
Part. passé : pris. —*Part. prés. :* prenant.

Produire *(to produce).* — V. *conduire.*

Promettre *(to promise).* — V. *mettre.*

Remettre *(to put back or to hand over).* — V. *mettre.*

Rire *(to laugh).*
Ind. prés. : je ris, tu ris, il rit, n. rions, v. riez, ils rient.
Imparf. : je riais, tu riais, il riait, n. riions, v. riiez, ils riaient.
Futur : je rirai, tu riras, etc.
Condit. : je rirais, tu rirais, etc.
Subj. prés. : que je rie, que tu ries, qu'il rie, que n. riions, que vous riiez, qu'ils rient.
Impératif : ris, rions, riez.
Part. passé : ri. —*Part. prés. :* riant.

Suivre *(to follow).*
Ind. prés. : je suis, tu suis, il suit, n. suivons, v. suivez, ils suivent.
Imparf. : je suivais, tu suivais, il suivait, n. suivions, v. suiviez ils suivaient
Sub. prés. : que je suive, que tu suives, qu'il suive, que n. suivions, que v. suiviez, qu'ils suivent.
Impératif : suis, suivons, suivez.
Part. passé : suivi. — *Part. prés. :* suivant.

Surprendre *(to surprise).* — V. *prendre.*

Se taire *(to keep silent to shut up).* — V. *plaire.*

Vivre *(to live).*
Ind. prés. : je vis, tu vis, il vit, n. vivons, v. vivez, ils vivent.
Imparf. : je vivais, tu vivais, il vivait, n. vivions, v. viviez, ils vivaient
Subj. prés. : que je vive, que tu vives, qu'il vive, que n. vivions, que vous viviez, qu'ils vivent.
Impératif : vis,vivons, vivez.
Part. passé : vécu. — *Part. prés. :* vivant.

III

Acquérir *(to acquire)*
Ind. Prés. : j'acquiers, tu acquiers, il acquiert, n. acquérons, v. acquérez, ils acquièrent.
Imparf. : j'acquérais, tu acquérais, il acquérait, n. acquérions, etc.
Futur : j'acquerrai, tu acquerras, il acquerra, n. acquerrons, etc.
Condit. : j'acquerrais, tu acquerrais, il acquerrait, n. acquerrions, etc.
Subj. Prés. : que j'acquière, que tu acquières, qu'il acquière, que n. acquiérions, etc.
Part. Passé : acquis. — *Part. Prés. :* acquérant.

Bouillir *(to boil).*
Ind. Prés. : je bous, tu bous, il bout, n. bouillons, v. bouillez, ils bouillent.
Imparf. : je bouillais, etc.
Subj. Prés. : que je bouille, que tu bouilles, etc.
Part. Prés. : bouillant.

Conquérir *(to conquer).* — V. *acquérir*

Courir *(to run).*
Ind. Prés. : je cours, tu cours, il court, n. courons, v. courez, ils courent.
Imparf. : je courais etc.
Futur : je courrai, tu courras, il courra, n. courrons, etc.
Condit. : je courrais, tu courrais, il courrait, n. courrions, etc.
Part. Passé : couru.
Subj. Prés. : que je coure, etc. *Part Prés. :* courant.

Couvrir *(to cover).* — V. *ouvrir.*

Cueillir *(to gather, to pluck).*
Ind. Prés. : je cueille, etc.
Imparf. : je cueillais, etc.
Futur : je cueillerai, etc. — *Condit. :* je cueillerais, etc.
Subj. Prés. : que je cueille, etc. — *Part. Prés. :* cueillant.

Découvrir *(to discover).* — V. *couvrir.*

Dormir *(to sleep).*
Ind. Prés. : je dors, tu dors, il dort, n. dormons, v. dormez, ils dorment.
Imparf. : je dormais, etc.
Subj. Prés. : que je dorme, etc.
Part. prés. : dormant.

Fuir *(to flee, to seak)*
Ind. Prés. : je fuis, tu fuis, il fuit, n. fuyons, v. fuyez, ils fuient.
Imparf. : je fuyais, etc.
Subj. Prés. : que je fuie, que tu fuies, qu'il fuie, que n. fuyions, que v. fuyiez, qu'ils fuient.
Part. Passé : fui. — Part. Prés. : fuyant.

Mentir *(to lie : tell a lie).*
Ind. Prés. : je mens, tu mens, il ment, n. mentons, v. mentez, ils mentent.
Imparf. : je mentais, etc.
Subj. Prés. : que je mente, que tu mentes, qu'il mente, que n. mentions, que v. mentiez, qu'ils mentent.

Mourir *(to die).*
Ind. Prés. : je meurs, tu meurs, il meurt, n. mourons, v. mourez, ils meurent.
Imparf. : je mourais, etc.
Futur : je mourrai, tu mourras, etc.
Condit. : je mourrais, tu mourrais, etc.
Subj. Prés. : que je meure, que tu meures, qu'il meure, que n. mourions, que v. mouriez, qu'il s meurent.
Part. passé : mort. — *Part. Prés. :* mourant.

Offrir *(to offer).*
Ind. Prés. : j'offre, etc.
Imparf. : j'offrais, etc. —*Subj. Prés. :* que j'offre etc.
Part. Passé : offert — *Part. Prés. :* offrant.

Ouvrir *(to open).* — V. *offrir.*

Partir *(to leave, go away.* — V. *mentir.*

Repentir (se) *(to repent).* — V. *mentir.*

Secourir *(to succour).* — V. *courir.*

Sentir *(to feel or to smell).* — V. *mentir.*

Servir *(to serve).*
Ind. Prés. : je sers, tu sers, il sert, n. servons, v. servez, ils servent.
Imparf. : je servais, tu servais, etc.
Impératif. : sers, servons, servez.
Part. passé : servi. —*Part. prés. :* servant.

Souffrir *(to suffer).* — V. *offrir.*

Tenir *(to hold).*
Ind. Prés. : je tiens, tu tiens, il tient, n. tenons, v. tenez, ils tiennent.
Imparf. : je tenais, etc.
Futur : je tiendrai, tu tiendras, il tiendra, etc.
Condit. : je tiendrais, tu tiendrais, il tiendrait, etc.
Subj. Prés. : que je tienne, que tu tiennes, qu'il tienne, que n. tenions, que v. teniez, qu'ils tiennent.
Impératif : tiens, tenons, tenez.
Part. Passé : tenu. —*Part. Prés. :* tenant.

Venir *(to come).* — V. *tenir.*

Asseoir (s') *(to sit down).*
Ind. Prés. : je m'assieds, tu t'assieds, il s'assied, n. n. asseyons, v. v. asseyez, ils s'asseyent.
Imparf. : je m'asseyais, etc.
Futur : je m'assiérai etc.
Condit. : je m'assiérais, etc.
Subj. Prés. : que je m'asseye, etc.
Impératif : assieds-toi, asseyons-nous, asseyez-vous.
Partic. Passé : assis. —*Part. Prés. :* s'asseyant.

Devoir *(to owe,* or *must).*
Ind. Prés. : je dois, tu dois, il doit, n. devons, v. devez, ils doivent.
Imparf. : je devais, tu devais, il devait, n. devions, etc.
Subj. Prés. : que je doive, que tu doives, qu'il doive, que n. devions, que v. deviez, qu'ils doivent.
Part. Passé : dû. —*Part. Prés. :* devant.

Falloir *(to be necessary, must) (impersonal).*
Ind. Prés. : il faut. —*Imparf. :* il fallait.
Futur : il faudra. —*Condit. :* il faudrait.
Subj. Prés. : qu'il faille. —*Part. Passé :* il a fallu.

Pleuvoir *(to rain) (semi-impersonal).*
Ind. Prés. : il pleut, ils pleuvent.
Imparf. : il pleuvait, ils pleuvaient.
Futur : il pleuvra, ils pleuvront. —*Condit. :* il pleuvrait, ils pleuvraient.
Subj. prés. : qu'il pleuve, qu'ils pleuvent.
Part. passé : plu. —*Part. Prés. :* pleuvant

Pouvoir *(to be able to, can* or *may).*
Ind. Prés. : je peux, tu peux, il peut, n. pouvons, v. pouvez, ils peuvent.
Futur : je pourrai, tu pourras, il pourra, n. pourrons, v. pourrez, ils pourront.
Condit. : je pourrais, tu pourrais, il pourrait, n. pourrions,. v. pourriez, ils pourraient.
Subj. Prés. : que je puisse, que tu puisses, qu'il puisse, que n. puissions, que v. puissiez, qu'ils puissent.
Part. Passé : pu. —*Part. Prés. :* pouvant.

Savoir *(to know).*
Ind. Prés. : je sais, tu sais, il sait, n. savons, v. savez, ils savent.
Futur : je saurai, tu sauras, il saura, n. saurons, v. saurez, ils sauront.
Condit. : je saurais, tu saurais, il saurait, n. saurions, v. sauriez, ils sauraient.
Subj. prés. : que je sache, que tu saches, qu'il sache, que n. sachions, que v. sachiez, qu'il sachent.
Impératif : sache, sachons, sachez.
Part. passé : su. —*Part. prés. :* sachant.

Valoir *(to be worth).*
Ind. prés. : je vaux, tu vaux, il vaut, n.valons, v. valez, ils valent.
Imparf. : je valais, tu valais, il valait, n. valions, v. valiez, ils valaient.
Futur : je vaudrai, tu vaudras, il vaudra, n. vaudrons, etc.

Condit. : je vaudrais, tu vaudrais, il vaudrait, n. vaudrions, etc.
Subj. prés. : que je vaille, que tu vailles, qu'il vaille, que n. valions, que v. valiez, qu'ils vaillent.
Part. passé : valu. — *Part. prés. :* valant.

Voir *(to see).*
Ind. prés. : je vois, tu vois, il voit, n. voyons, v. voyez, ils voient.
Imparf. : je voyais, tu voyais, il voyait, n. voyons, v. voyez, ils voyaient.
Futur : je verrai, tu verras, il verra, n. verrons, v. verrez, ils verront.
Condit. : je verrais, tu verrais, il verrait, n. verrions, v. verriez, ils verraient.
Subj. prés. : que je voie, que tu voies, qu'il voie, que n. voyions, que v. voyiez, qu'ils voient.
Impératif : vois, voyons, voyez.
Part. passé : vu. — *Part. prés. :* voyant.

Vouloir *(to want, to will).*
Ind. prés. : je veux, tu veux, il veut, n. voulons, v. voulez, ils veulent.
Imparf. : je voulais, tu voulais, il voulait, n. voulions, v. vouliez, ils voulaient.
Futur : je voudrai, tu voudras, il voudra, n. voudrons, v. voudrez, ils voudront.
Condit. : je voudrais, tu voudrais, il voudrait, n. voudrions, v. voudriez, ils voudraient.
Subj. prés. : que je veuille, que tu veuilles, qu'il veuille, que n. voulions, que v. vouliez, qu'ils veuillent.
Impératif : veuille, veuillons, veuillez.
Part. passé : voulu. — *Part. prés. :* voulant.